Asia East by South

A series published under the auspices of
the Southeast Asia Program, Cornell University

Government and Society in Malaysia
by Harold Crouch

Cambodian Culture since 1975: Homeland and Exile
edited by May M. Ebihara, Carol A. Mortland, and Judy Ledgerwood

Southeast Asia in the Early Modern Era: Trade, Power, and Belief
edited by Anthony Reid

The Dark Side of Paradise: Political Violence in Bali
by Geoffrey Robinson

*Opium to Java: Revenue Farming and Chinese Enterprise in
Colonial Indonesia, 1860–1910*
by James R. Rush

An Age in Motion: Popular Radicalism in Java, 1912–1926
by Takashi Shiraishi

Opium and Empire: Chinese Society in Colonial Singapore, 1800–1910
by Carl A. Trocki

D1508060

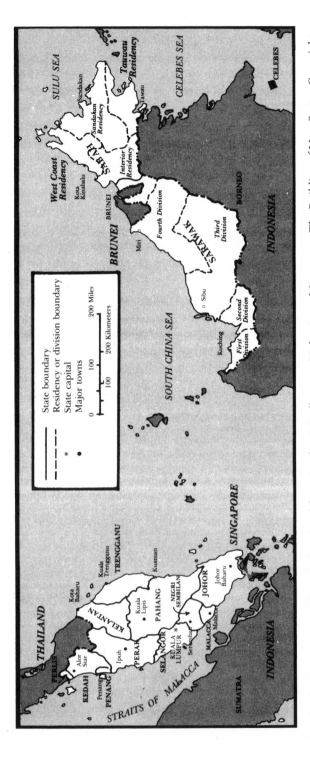

Malaysia, Singapore, and Brunei. Reprinted from Stanley S. Bedlington, *Malaysia and Singapore: The Building of New States*. Copyright © 1978 by Cornell University. Used by permission of the publisher, Cornell University Press.

GOVERNMENT AND SOCIETY IN MALAYSIA

HAROLD CROUCH

AG 10 '99

JQ
712
.C76
1996

Cornell University Press

ITHACA AND LONDON

SOCIAL SCIENCES

CARNEGIE LIBRARY OF PITTSBURGH

Copyright © 1996 by Cornell University

All rights reserved. Except for brief quotations in a review, this book, or parts thereof, must not be reproduced in any form without permission in writing from the publisher. For information, address Cornell University Press, Sage House, 512 East State Street, Ithaca, New York 14850.

First published 1996 by Cornell University Press.

Printed in the United States of America

⊗ The paper in this book meets the minimum requirements
of the American National Standard for Information Sciences—
Permanence of Paper for Printed Library Materials. ANSI Z39.48-1984.

Library of Congress Cataloging-in-Publication Data

Crouch, Harold A., 1940–
    Government and society in Malaysia / Harold Crouch.
        p.   cm.
    Includes bibliographical references and index.
    ISBN 0-8014-3218-9 (alk. paper). — ISBN 0-8014-8310-7 (alk. paper)
    1. Malaysia—Politics and government. 2. Malaysia—Social conditions. I. Title.
JQ712.C76   1996
306.2'09595—dc20   95-45155

Contents

Preface

DURING THE LAST DECADE or so political scientists have given much attention to the process of democratization. Earlier they had been challenged by the need to explain why democracies failed and were replaced by authoritarian rule. The challenge today is to explain why democracies have emerged or re-emerged in regions as diverse as Southern Europe, Eastern Europe, Latin America, Africa, and Asia. But not all countries are part of this process. In some, the sharp dichotomy between "democracy" and "authoritarianism" does not seem to apply. Instead, the political system seems to be an amalgam of both democratic and authoritarian features, which together form a cohesive, coherent political structure that is neither democratic nor authoritarian. Although such systems are by no means unchanging, the changes do not seem to add up to a clear movement toward either democracy or authoritarianism. One such case is Malaysia.

The Malaysian case is also relevant to another worldwide political phenomenon—the prevalence of ethnic politics. Malaysian society is ethnically divided, and its politics have always revolved around ethnic issues. In the late 1960s the nation seemed on the brink of collapse, and the prognoses of many observers were extremely pessimistic. Yet despite the continuing centrality of ethnic divisions, the Malaysian polity has not only held together but achieved a degree of coherence that has provided the foundation for a remarkably stable political order. On the basis of that stability the Malaysian economy was growing at one of the fastest rates in the world during the first half of the 1990s.

My close association with Malaysia began in 1974 when I accompanied my wife back to her homeland. After teaching briefly at the University of Malaya, I joined the Universiti Kebangsaan Malaysia (UKM or National University of Malaysia) in 1976 as the first lecturer in its newly established

Department of Political Science. It was from that vantage point that I observed political developments in Malaysia for the next fifteen years. My research on Malaysian politics, therefore, did not follow a preconceived plan but gradually developed along with its subject. My understanding of Malaysian politics increased as much through osmosis as through conscious research. Countless casual conversations were as important as formal interviews.

My debt is large, therefore, to my colleagues and students at UKM who provided me with many insights into the way they understood politics. I am particularly indebted to students in my courses on Western political philosophy whose reactions to the questions posed by the great Western thinkers illuminated distinctive Malaysian approaches to the same issues. I also benefited greatly from the friendship of colleagues at the University of Malaya in Kuala Lumpur and the Universiti Sains Malaysia (USM) in Penang.

I also had the opportunity to interview many politicians. It is only through face-to-face discussion that an observer can get a feel for the political process. In my experience the politicians I met were frank and forthright, although occasionally what they said had to be taken with the proverbial grain of salt. Although I have not usually mentioned them as sources by name, I here acknowledge that this book could not have been written without their cooperation. I also enjoyed the company of many other political observers, particularly journalists.

I thank the publishers and editors listed below for granting permission to draw on material published earlier in the following articles:

"The Politics of Islam in the ASEAN Countries," in Ralph H. C. Hayburn, ed., *New Zealand and the ASEAN Countries: The Papers of the Twenty-third Foreign Policy School*. Dunedin: University Extension, University of Otago, 1988.

"The Politics of Islam in the ASEAN Countries," in Alison Broinowski, ed., *ASEAN into the 1990s*. London: Macmillan, 1990.

"The Military in Malaysia," in Viberto Selochan, ed., *The Military, the State, and Development in Asia and the Pacific*. Boulder, Colo.: Westview Press, 1991.

"Authoritarian Trends, the UMNO Split and the Limits of State Power," in Joel S. Kahn and Francis Loh Kok Wah, eds., *Fragmented Vision: Culture and Politics in Contemporary Malaysia*. Sydney: Allen and Unwin, 1992.

"Malaysia: Neither Authoritarian nor Democratic," in Kevin Hewison, Richard Robison, and Garry Rodan, eds., *Southeast Asia in the 1990s: Authoritarianism, Democracy and Capitalism*. Sydney: Allen and Unwin, 1993.

"Industrialization and Political Change," in Harold Brookfield, ed.,

Transformation with Industrialization in Peninsular Malaysia. Kuala Lumpur: Oxford University Press, 1994.

Friends and colleagues read and commented on versions of this manuscript at various stages. Among those who read one or another version of the full manuscript were George Kahin, Jomo K. S., and Ben Kerkvliet. Lee Poh Ping, Lee Kam Hing, and Peter Searle provided suggestions for improving individual chapters. The anonymous readers for Cornell University Press also provided valuable criticism.

HAROLD CROUCH

Canberra

Glossary/Abbreviations

ABIM	Angkatan Belia Islam Malaysia (Malaysian Islamic Youth Movement)
APU	Angkatan Perpaduan Ummah (Muslim Unity Movement)
ASN	Amanah Saham Nasional (National Trust Fund)
AWSJ	*Asian Wall Street Journal*
Berjasa	Barisan Jamaah Islamiah Se-Malaysia (Malaysian Islamic Council Front)
Berjaya	Bersatu Rakyat Jelata Sabah (United Common People of Sabah)
Bhd./Berhad	Ltd./Limited
BN	Barisan Nasional (National Front)
bumiputera, bumiputra	indigenous person (lit. son of the soil)
CPM	Communist Party of Malaya
CUEPACS	Congress of Unions of Employees in the Public and Civil Services
dakwah	Islamic revival (lit. call)
DAP	Democratic Action Party
Dato'	alternative spelling of Datuk
Datuk	Malaysian title (below Tan Sri)
Datuk Paduka	Malaysian title (equivalent to Datuk)
Datuk Seri	Malaysian title (equivalent to Datuk)
FEER	*Far Eastern Economic Review*
FELDA	Federal Land Development Authority
FOA	Farmers' Organization Authority
Gagasan Rakyat	People's Concept
GDP	gross domestic product
Gerakan	Gerakan Rakyat Malaysia (Malaysian People's Movement)

xi

Hamim	Hizbullah Muslimin Malaysia (Malaysian Muslim Association)
Hicom	Heavy Industries Corporation of Malaysia
hudud	Koranic criminal punishment
Iban	Indigenous community in Sarawak
ISA	Internal Security Act
jawi	Arabic script
Kadazan	Indigenous community in Sabah
kampung	village
Kemas	Kemajuan Masyarakat (Community Development Program)
konfrontasi	Indonesia's confrontation campaign against the formation of Malaysia
LNG	liquified natural gas
MARA	Majlis Amanah Rakyat (People's Trust Council)
MCA	Malaysian Chinese Association
MCS	Malayan Civil Service
Menteri Besar	chief minister
Merdeka Day	Independence Day
Merdeka University	Freedom University
MIC	Malaysian Indian Congress
MNP	Malay Nationalist Party
MPH	Multipurpose Holdings
MTR3MP (MTR4MP etc.)	midterm review of the Third Malaysia Plan (and Fourth Malaysia Plan, etc.)
MTUC	Malaysian Trade Union Congress
NEP	New Economic Policy
NOC	National Operations Council
NST	*New Straits Times*
NUPW	National Union of Plantation Workers
padi	rice
PAP	People's Action Party
Parti Bumiputera	Bumiputera Party
PAS	Parti Islam Se-Malaysia (see PMIP)
PBB	Parti Pesaka Bumiputera Bersatu (United Bumiputera Pesaka Party)
PBDS	Parti Bansa Dayak Sarawak (Sarawak Dayak Party)
PBS	Parti Bersatu Sabah (United Sabah Party)
Pekemas	Parti Keadilan Masyarakat Malaysia (Malaysian Social Justice Party)
penggawa	local official
penghulu	local official
Peremba	property development subsidiary of UDA
Pernas	Perbadanan Nasional (National Corporation)
Petronas	Petroleam Nasional Berhad (National Oil Corporation)
PFF	Police Field Force

PMIP	Pan-Malaysian Islamic Party
PNB	Permodalan Nasional Berhad (National Equity Corporation)
PPP	People's Progressive Party
PRM	Parti Rakyat Malaysia (Malaysian People's Party)
PSRM	Partai Sosialis Rakyat Malaya (Malayan People's Socialist Party)
PTD	Perkhidmatan Tadbir dan Diplomatik (Administrative and Diplomatic Service)
SCA	Sabah Chinese Association
SEDC	State Economic Development Corporation
Semangat '46	Spirit of '46
SNAP	Sarawak National Party
syariah	Islamic law
Tan Sri	Malaysian title (below Tun)
Tengku	prince
towkay	Chinese businessman or trader
Tun	highest nonhereditary Malaysian title
Tunku	prince
UDA	Urban Development Authority
UDP	United Democratic Party
UEM	United Engineers (M) Berhad
UM	*Utusan Malaysia*
UMNO	United Malays National Organisation
UMNO Baru	New UMNO
Ungku	prince
USNO	United Sabah National Organisation
wakil rakyat	member of parliament
Yang di-Pertuan Agong	king
2MP	Second Malaysia Plan
3MP	Third Malaysia Plan
4MP	Fourth Malaysia Plan
5MP	Fifth Malaysia Plan
6MP	Sixth Malaysia Plan

PART ONE

INTRODUCTION

I *Ambiguous Regimes*

POLITICAL SCIENTISTS commonly conceptualize forms of government in terms of their approximation to democracy on one hand and authoritarianism on the other. In essence, a democratic government is one with a high degree of responsiveness to the political expectations of its citizens whereas an authoritarian regime is one in which the ruling elite is able, through strategies of manipulation, control, and repression, to maintain itself in power without accommodating popular demands.

Governments in democracies are responsive to pressures from below because their right to rule is derived from popular support manifested in competitive elections held in a free political atmosphere.[1] Democracies are therefore characterized by the presence of institutions that force governments to take serious account of the demands and interests of their citizens. Regular elections are held in which all citizens are free to participate, rival political parties compete for electoral support, many types of interest groups attempt to influence government policies, an independent press freely reports on and critically discusses political issues, and an independent judiciary ensures that the government itself adheres to the constitution and the law.

Authoritarian governments maintain themselves in power by other means. Such governments take many forms—ranging from military regimes to single-party dictatorships, personalist autocracies, and absolute monarchies.[2] Although elections are often held by authoritarian regimes, such elections are conducted so that the ruling party or group cannot lose; and thus they provide little scope for the expression of popular prefer-

---

[1] My understanding of democracy follows Schumpeter 1943:269–73 and Dahl 1971:1–4.
[2] For a discussion of types of authoritarian regime, see Linz 1975.

3

ences. Opposition parties are either banned or intimidated, independent interest groups are unable to develop, the press is controlled by the government, and the judiciary does not constitute a check on government power. The most outspoken critics of authoritarian regimes are usually imprisoned as "threats to national security."

Many governments fall somewhere between the democratic and authoritarian models.[3] Such regimes might be described as "mixed" or "ambiguous" and placed somewhere along a continuum between authoritarianism and democracy.[4] Some writers have described them as "limited," "guided," "tutelary," "quasi," or "semi" democracies; others prefer terms like "soft," "constitutional," "liberalized," or "pluralist" authoritarianism. In Southeast Asia the political systems of Singapore, Thailand, and Malaysia could all, despite their significant differences, be placed in the ambiguous or mixed category.[5]

But is it analytically satisfactory to place such regimes in an in-between category as if their position were just a matter of exhibiting more or less democracy or authoritarianism? The mix of democratic and authoritarian characteristics varies from case to case. In one a democratically elected government is shadowed by an interventionist military; in another an elected government itself maintains controls on opposition activity; and in yet another the government is elected but the electoral system is heavily biased. Whatever the particular mix of authoritarian and democratic characteristics, governments of this sort continue to be sigtnificantly responsive to some pressures from society while repressing others.

The difficulties in properly characterizing regimes become particularly acute when we attempt to analyze political change.[6] Political transition can be seen in terms of a regime's becoming more authoritarian or more democratic. In the case of dramatic political change—the collapse of a regime and its replacement by something else—it is usually easy enough to identify the direction of the transition, but in mixed regimes the trends sometimes seem to be in both directions at the same time. Opposition parties, for example, might be playing an increasingly active role, but at the

[3] In the early 1970s Dahl guessed that "perhaps the preponderant number of national regimes in the world today would fall into the mid-area." Dahl 1971:8.

[4] Huntington suggests that, despite the existence of "ambiguous, borderline and mixed cases . . . the classification of regimes in terms of their degree of procedural democracy remains a relatively simple task." Huntington 1991: 8–9. On the other hand, Diamond, Linz, and Lipset acknowledge that "The boundary between democratic and nondemocratic is sometimes a blurred and imperfect one, and beyond it lies a much broader range of variation in political systems." Diamond, Linz, and Lipset 1989:xvii.

[5] For characterizations of Malaysia as a quasi-democracy see Zakaria 1989; as a semi-democracy see Case 1993.

[6] Regime transition, particularly from authoritarianism toward democracy, has attracted much attention from political scientists in recent years. Among the most influential studies are O'Donnell and Schmitter 1986; Diamond, Linz, and Lipset 1989; and Huntington 1991.

same time more opponents of the government are being detained without trial. Elections can become more competitive while government control of the media becomes tighter. Members of the middle class can enjoy new freedoms while the working class experiences more severe repression. In any political system it is only to be expected that there will be contradictory subtendencies that are eventually resolved in the process of long-term change, but in some countries apparent contradictions seem to remain unresolved indefinitely. In these cases it is necessary to build the contradictions into our concepts.

In this book I argue that the democratic and authoritarian characteristics found in many Third World regimes do not necessarily contradict each other but can often be mutually supporting. An increase in a regime's democratic characteristics does not always mean a reduction in its authoritarian characteristics. A regime can become more responsive and more repressive at the same time. A quarter of a century ago, Juan Linz theorized about the nature of authoritarianism, arguing that it could not be adequately understood simply as a kind of midpoint along a continuum between democracy and totalitarianism but had its own peculiar characteristics that distinguished it from both democracy and totalitarianism.[7] In the case of semi-democratic, semi-authoritarian regimes, too, there is a need to understand them as integrated and coherent political systems with their own particular characteristics. It is necessary to study more precisely the interrelationship between their democratic and authoritarian traits so that such regimes can be conceputalized as regime types in their own right and not just as a bit of this and a bit of that.

In this book we will examine the politics of a country where significant democratic and authoritarian characteristics are inextricably mixed. The constitutional framework of the Malaysian political system is essentially democratic. Elections have been held regularly, the government is responsible to an elected parliament, and the judiciary is constitutionally independent. But the democratic framework is accompanied by a wide range of authoritarian controls that greatly limit the scope for effective political opposition and make it very difficult to envisage the defeat of the ruling party at the polls. Taking the period from independence in 1957, especially since the serious racial rioting of 1969, authoritarian controls became incrementally more prevalent. At the same time, however, the structure of the party system and the electoral mechanism ensured that the government continued to respond in important ways to pressure from below. Moreover, changes in the social structure seem to have stimulated political competition and increased government responsiveness to at least some popular demands. The system, therefore, became more repressive and more re-

---

[7] Linz 1970. The article was originally published in 1964.

sponsive at the same time. Of course, such contradictions are normal when a system approaches a critical turning point and are resolved after that point has been reached; but in the Malaysian case these trends have been present for several decades and have not undermined the essential coherence and stability of the political system.

In their survey of democracy in developing countries Diamond, Linz, and Lipset mention Malaysia—together with Turkey, Sri Lanka, Colombia, and Zimbabwe—among the countries where evaluation of democratic status "is replete with nuance and ambiguity." Among the points along the authoritarian-democratic continuum they identify semi-democracies and hegemonic party systems and place Malaysia in the semi-democratic category where "the effective power of elected officials is so limited, or political party competition so restricted, or the freedom and fairness of elections so compromised that electoral outcomes, while competitive, still deviate significantly from popular preferences." Moreover, they note that in semi-democracies "civil and political liberties are so limited that some political orientations and interests are unable to organize and express themselves." While the Malaysian case seems to fit the description of semi-democracy, it could as easily be placed in the category of hegemonic party systems, further toward the authoritarian end of the continuum. According to Diamond et al. the hegemonic party system—under which they place Mexico—is one "in which opposition parties are legal but denied—through pervasive electoral malpractices and frequent state coercion—any real chance to compete for power."[8]

Similarly, the Malaysian case seems to fit comfortably into both categories proposed by O'Donnell and Schmitter when they distinguish between liberalized authoritarianism (*dictablandas,* or soft dictatorship) and limited democracy (*democraduras,* or hard democracy). Under liberalized authoritarianism, "Authoritarian rulers may tolerate or even promote liberalization . . . without altering the structure of authority, that is, without becoming accountable to the citizenry for their actions or subjecting their claim to rule to fair and competitive elections." On the other hand, under limited democracy, rulers "may well continue old, or even create new, restrictions on the freedoms of particular individuals or groups who are deemed insufficiently prepared or sufficiently dangerous to enjoy full citizenship status."[9]

If it is hard to place Malaysia in a clear-cut category between democracy and authoritarianism, it is even more difficult to perceive the direction in which its political system is moving. In his analysis of the third wave of democratization since the 1970s, Samuel Huntington suggests that transi-

[8] Diamond, Linz, and Lipset 1989:xvii.
[9] O'Donnell and Schmitter 1986:9.

tion toward democracy normally goes all, or at least most of, the way: "The experience of the third wave strongly suggests that liberalized authoritarianism is not a stable equilibrium; the halfway house does not stand."[10] But the Malaysian political system has been balancing between repression and responsiveness since Malaya, as it was known then, obtained its independence in 1957. That balance, however, has not remained unchanged. At times the government has been inclined to resort to authoritarian measures, while at other times it has adopted a relatively liberal attitude. Nevertheless, these oscillations have taken place within a limited range and do not fundamentally change the nature of the political system. In essence, the regime continues to exhibit simultaneously a repressive and a responsive character.

The mutually supporting roles of the democratic and authoritarian aspects of the Malaysian political system were neatly encapsulated in a small incident that took place shortly before the 1990 election.[11] To ease traffic congestion the government had contracted to build a number of toll roads leading into Kuala Lumpur. The toll-collection points were on the outskirts of the city except for one that was located at Cheras in a heavily populated area. As a result, many residents faced the prospect of paying tolls twice every time they went shopping, collected their children from school, or visited friends and relatives on the other side of the toll-collection point. It so happened that Cheras was a largely Chinese area that had supported the opposition Democratic Action Party (DAP) in the previous election. When toll collection commenced on 1 September 1990, large crowds of demonstrators gathered at the collection point, including some who threw stones at police. The government quickly accused the DAP of instigating violence and arrested the local member of Parliament and four of his supporters under the Internal Security Act (ISA). But a few days later, responding to popular protests and the prospect that voters might support the opposition in the coming election, the government suspended collection of the toll; and eventually the toll payment was halved. In this incident the use of the ISA to detain an opposition politician leading a campaign on a popular issue in the weeks before an election was an unambiguous resort to authoritarian repression. At the same time the competitive nature of the forthcoming election forced the government to respond in a democratic way to popular sentiments.

[10] Huntington 1991:137. But in the last chapter of his book Huntington seems to envisage a kind of halfway or perhaps three-quarters' way house when he refers to "democracy without turnover" in East Asia. "The East Asian dominant party systems that may be emerging seem to involve competition for power but not alternation in power, and participation in elections for all, but participation in office only for those in the 'mainstream' party." Huntington 1991:306.

[11] See Gurunathan 1990.

After an introductory chapter on the evolution of the Malaysian political system before 1970, I move, in Part 2, to an analysis of its main features during the period of rapid economic growth and communal restructuring under the New Economic Policy during the 1970s and 80s. My purpose is to examine in detail the simultaneous development of both authoritarian and democratic features in the Malaysian political system, revealing that the political system cannot be described as either democratic or authoritarian without major qualification. Nor can it be said that the system was unambiguously in transition, although changes were taking place.

Malaysian politics revolve around issues linked to race. The government has always been dominated by the Malay component of the ruling coalition, but the Malay party needs the support of its Chinese, Indian, and East Malaysian partners. As I show in Chapter 3, the multicommunal Malaysian government has lacked the unity of purpose that characterizes fully authoritarian regimes. Electoral politics, the theme of Chapter 4, constitute another check on government power, forcing the ruling coalition to appeal for votes to a politically and ethnically divided electorate. Although the government has been forced by elections to respond to popular aspirations, it has also arranged the electoral process virtually to ensure government victory. Moreover, the government, as outlined in Chapter 5, has acquired a range of authoritarian powers that enable it to detain political opponents, control the press, and prevent the emergence of mass organizations opposed to the governing coalition. During the 1970s and 80s, as I describe in Chapter 6, the government expanded its authoritarian powers incrementally to deal with perceived political threats. Following the split in the dominant Malay party, however, the political system became more competitive, forcing the government to be more responsive to popular expectations, as described in Chapter 7. Finally, Chapter 8 focuses on the role of and rivalries within the Malay establishment in the bureaucracy, armed forces, and judiciary as well as the position of the Malay sultans.

To what extent does the nature of the political system reflect the nature of and pressures from society? In Part 3 I examine Malaysia's communal and class structures together with its changing strategies to promote economic growth and industrialization. Although I do not argue that the nature of the Malaysian political system has been somehow determined by the nature of its society, I suggest that the communal structure, the evolving class structure, and Malaysia's stage of economic development are all roughly congruent with its political system. While communal, social, and economic factors have all contributed to shaping the Malaysian political system, they have often been ambiguous in their impact because all have generated pressures in both democratic and authoritarian directions.

Communal conflict has been explained by scholars in a variety of ways.[12] Some believe that the very presence of several ethnic communities within a single state with their contrasting values, cultures, and ways of life, will lead almost inevitably to political conflict. According to this view ethnic identity is based on more or less permanent primordial attachments that bind group members together and distinguish them from other ethnic groups.[13] Ethnic conflict has also been linked to the process of modernization, which, it has been argued, is more likely to exacerbate than ameliorate ethnic suspicions and tensions. When members of previously isolated ethnic groups come into contact as a result of urbanization, education, and involvement in the modern economy, their sense of ethnic identity is likely to be strengthened and rivalry between them is likely to become more intense.[14] One consequence of modernization is that some groups are likely to advance more rapidly than others. According to another perspective, therefore, ethnic conflict often has its roots in economic or class competition. What appears to be ethnic conflict can, in fact, be a disguised form of class conflict where members of particular groups are concentrated in certain economic classes.[15] Another approach emphasizes the quest for group status, especially among ethnic groups that others consider backward. According to this view, ethnic conflict involves struggle not simply for material gain but for the symbols of status, particularly those that enhance "group worth" and self-esteem by identifying the group with the state.[16] Whatever its origins, ethnic conflict can also be aggravated by the political struggle for power. When rival elites, even if they share a common socioeconomic status, belong to different ethnic communities, they often find it convenient to turn to ethnic issues in order to mobilize popular support. As a result, ethnic passions are heightened; and previously tolerant or indifferent groups may become convinced that other ethnic groups threaten their well-being or existence.[17] These explanations are not mutually inconsistent but may all be relevant in different degrees in particular concrete circumstances. Together they virtually guarantee that ethnic ten-

---

[12] In the Malaysian context, community and ethnicity are defined in terms of race. In this study, therefore, I use terms such as race, community, and ethnic group interchangeably. It is now common for anthropologists to argue that ethnic identity is not based on objective characteristics but socially constructed. Thus, "to take it as axiomatic that Malaysian society is somehow made up of discrete and highly different groups, whether these are defined in racial or cultural terms, instead of a group of human beings who in all essential characteristics are the same is, therefore, more problematic than first appears." Kahn 1992:163. Nevertheless, it can hardly be denied that most Malaysians define themselves in these terms.

[13] See Gertz 1963.

[14] See Melson and Wolpe 1970; Connor 1972.

[15] Referring to black Africa, Wallerstein claims that "behind the ethnic 'reality' lies a class conflict, not very far from the surface." Wallerstein 1979:179. See Brown 1994:ch. 6 for a class interpretation of ethnic politics in Malaysia.

[16] Horowitz 1985:part 1.

[17] See Brass 1985.

sions and conflict will be a major challenge in all ethnically divided societies.

Contradictory hypotheses have been suggested about the consequences of communal conflict on the political system. It is often believed that communally divided countries are inherently unstable because they are subject to periodic outbursts of intercommunal conflict. In such societies all political issues have communal connotations so that what appear as minor policies in other societies become major issues of contention when they affect the interests of communal groups. In these circumstances it is likely that dominant ethnic groups will feel compelled to defend their position by authoritarian means.[18] But one can also argue that, if communal tensions are kept from boiling over into rioting and civil war, the society's division into ethnic communities organized to protect communal interests can provide a solid foundation for the checks and balances of democracy. When ethnic minorities are large, their interests cannot be easily ignored. The legitimacy of political organizations representing minorities can be recognized and their leaders brought into a bargaining process along consociational or semi-consociational lines.[19] There is no guarantee that the resulting system will be fully democratic, but the communal structure represents a built-in obstacle to the establishment of authoritarian rule exclusively in the hands of the ethnic majority. In Chapter 9 I discuss some of the main ethnic issues in Malaysia, showing the nature of the communal compromise between Malay and non-Malay communities.

The nature of the class structure also affects the political system. Economic growth and industrialization inevitably bring about significant changes. According to the typical pattern of development, agrarian societies became increasingly urban and industrial. In many societies established agrarian and aristocratic-bureaucratic elites were challenged by expanding business and middle classes, while the working class grew and the proportion of the population engaged in rural occupations contracted. One might expect that the increased complexity of the class structure would lead to an intensification of class conflict as each class struggles to defend or advance its position, leading to a "praetorian" situation in which no single class is dominant. In such circumstances, it is common for the military to intervene or for authoritarian regimes to be established in other ways.[20] On the other hand, especially as economic growth continues and the business, middle, and working classes expand, the changing class structure can support demands for liberalization and democratization.[21]

---

[18] Rabushka and Shepsle 1972.
[19] Lijphart 1977; Horowitz 1985:part 3.
[20] Huntington 1968:ch. 4.
[21] Moore 1969.

The business, middle, and working classes increasingly demand that the government be more responsive and that wider rights to participate be permitted. Typically these classes call for fair elections, the right to organize opposition parties and interest groups, freedom of the press, and an independent judiciary.

The evolution of the class structure in ex-colonial Third World countries, however, did not follow the Western pattern. In the ex-colonies, the state, inherited from the colonial era, is often powerful while foreign capital's domination of the economy inhibits the development of a domestic bourgeoisie, which often continues to be weak and heavily dependent on the state. The main potential check on state power, therefore, is not found in the business class but in the educated, professional, white-collar middle class, which has expanded as a consequence of economic growth.[22] In the Malaysian case it is also necessary to consider ethnicity because the political impact of the class structure has been blurred by communal divisions. In Chapter 10 I focus on the evolution of the class structure as a consequence of economic development, while Chapter 11 explores why the Malaysian bourgeoisie has not played the democratizing role that we see in the classic European model of development.

The impact of economic growth on the political system has also been ambiguous and much debated by theorists. As Seymour Lipset has argued, wealthier countries are more likely to be democratic than poor countries, which are more likely to have authoritarian governments.[23] But Lipset recognized that rapid growth itself could be politically destabilizing and create conditions leading to the emergence of authoritarianism. Basing his ideas on Latin America's experience, Guillermo O'Donnell suggested that the transition to higher levels of industrialization—from early import substitution to heavy industrialization—did not create conditions conductive to democratization. On the contrary it led to what he called "bureaucratic authoritarianism."[24] Similarly, in East Asia the transition from import-substitution strategies to export-oriented industrialization in the Newly Industrializing Countries has been associated with authoritarian rather than democratic government.[25] Thus, it is plausible to argue that rapid economic growth and industrialization, at least in the early stages, are likely to create social and political tensions that are often overcome by the establishment of authoritarian regimes. In Malaysia, however, as I explain in Chapter 12, the tensions arising from the industrialization process were ameliorated by a number of special factors related to economic and social

---

[22] Rueschemeyer, Stephens, and Stephens 1992:272.
[23] Lipset 1960:ch. 2.
[24] O'Donnell 1973, 1978.
[25] Deyo 1987.

development, with the result that the government felt less need to impose severe authoritarian controls.

In the Conclusion I argue that these diverse socioeconomic influences were congruent with the development of a repressive-responsive regime that can be called neither democratic nor authoritarian but contains elements of both. We shall see that the regime has exhibited democratic tendencies in some respects and authoritarian tendencies in others. The result, however, has been a political system that combines both in a mutually supporting way. In the foreseeable future it seems unlikely to move significantly toward either democracy or authoritarianism.

2   Politics and Society
Before 1970

W HEN MALAYA BECAME independent in 1957, its constitution was modeled on British democracy. The government was responsible to a national Parliament elected at least once every five years, and politics were relatively open as shown by the variety of parties that were contesting elections. Nevertheless, significant limitations were imposed on political freedoms. During the colonial period a state of emergency had been declared to deal with increasing Communist and nationalist opposition, and provision for the use of emergency powers was written into the new constitution. When the twelve-year emergency was lifted in 1960, new legislation in the form of the Internal Security Act (ISA) gave authorities wide powers of preventive detention, which were later used against leftists, Communists, communalists, and other opponents of the government.

By the time Malaya obtained independence, the Communist rebellion had been broken, although mopping-up operations continued.[1] The Communists' main support had come from Chinese in the trade unions and among squatters illegally occupying agricultural land. The party's potential to re-emerge as a vehicle for the expression of Chinese lower-class frustrations was a major justification for the introduction of the ISA. The communal nature of Malaysian society, however, provided deeper, more long-term justification for restricting democratic liberties.

A classic case of the plural society, Malaysia's racial divisions tended to coincide with and be reinforced by linguistic, cultural, religious, and, most important, economic divisions. All political issues were inextricably interwoven with communal considerations—economic policy, regional development, language, education, immigration, recruitment to the civil service

[1] See Short 1975; Khong 1984; Stubbs 1989.

13

and armed forces, and many more. Virtually all government policies were seen as benefiting one or another of the main communities, while anything that benefited one community tended to be seen as depriving the others. Despite the government's attempt to work out an acceptable balance between the communities, communal sentiments remained strong; and frustrations often rose to the surface.

Thus, the political system was an amalgam of democratic and authoritarian characteristics. While the provision of political representation for each community within a democratic framework was one means of keeping communal tensions in check, the government believed it was necessary to exercise authoritarian powers to repress the Communist movement and prevent communal conflict from running out of hand.

Politics in a Plural Society

In 1957 the population of the Malay peninsula was almost evenly divided between indigenous inhabitants and the immigrant communities. Slightly less than 50 percent of the people were Malays or aborigines, 37 percent were Chinese, and 12 percent were Indians. There was a small category of others, most of whom were Pakistanis or Ceylonese.[2] The formation of Malaysia in 1963 resulted in a large increase in the Chinese population when Singapore joined the federation; but this was balanced by the entry of Sabah and Sarawak, which had mainly indigenous populations that were expected to align with the peninsular Malays in national politics. The expulsion of Singapore from the federation in 1965, however, tilted the balance in favor of the indigenous or *bumiputera* (sons of the soil) communities. According to the 1970 census, the bumiputeras made up 55.5 percent (Malays 46.8 percent and other indigenous communities 8.7 percent), while non-bumiputeras amounted to 44.5 percent (Chinese 34.1 percent, Indians 9.0 percent, and others 1.4 percent).[3] In the peninsula alone those classified as Malay had risen to 52.7 percent.[4]

The Malays are not only the largest community but also the most homogeneous. All Malays are Muslim and speak Malay, which, despite differences among spoken dialects, is a common language in its standard written form. On the other hand, the Chinese and Indians are internally divided along religious, linguistic, and cultural lines. Among the Chinese a small proportion is Christian, while the traditional Chinese religions (Buddhism, Confucianism, and Taoism) are divided into too many strands and combi-

[2] Ratnam 1965:1.
[3] Milne and Mauzy 1978:3.
[4] 4MP:74.

nations to become symbols of communal identity. The Indians are mainly Hindu but divided into castes, although some are Muslim or Christian. The Chinese and Indians are also heterogeneous culturally and linguistically. The largest Chinese group, the Hokkien, make up about one-third of the community, followed by the Cantonese, Hakka, Teochiu, and other smaller groups, each with its own spoken language and customs. The Indians are mainly Tamil, but there are also smaller Malayalee, Telugu, and Sikh communities. In both East Malaysian states there are substantial Chinese minorities; and the bumiputeras are divided between Muslims and non-Muslims and consist of many groups, each with its own language, customs, and sense of identity.

The Malay and non-Malay communities were affected differently by the modern economy. The Malays had always been an overwhelmingly rural community largely engaged in agriculture and fishing. Only one in five city or town dwellers in 1957 was a Malay, and most of those were employed by the government.[5] On the other hand, although many non-Malays also pursued agricultural activities, the Chinese and Indians were mainly employed in the modern economy and reflected its range of class divisions. While Indian workers were largely employed on plantations or by the government, Chinese were engaged in mining, industry, and commerce. The Chinese, in particular, were dominant in small- and medium-scale trade and as proprietors of tin mines; and both Chinese and Indians were found among the white-collar employees of foreign enterprises and in the professions. The working class was overwhelmingly non-Malay. Many non-Malays were also employed in the government's technical services, but the higher levels of the bureaucracy were largely a Malay preserve, a result of the British policy of regarding the Malays as the legitimate rulers of the country.[6] Thus, Malays were predominant in the bureaucracy (especially at higher levels) and agriculture, while non-Malays predominated in commerce, the professions, and the working class. East Malaysia followed a similar pattern, although the number of bumiputera bureaucrats was very small and the overwhelming majority still pursued traditional rural occupations.

The Malay community was far less mobilized socially and politically than the non-Malays. A large majority remained attached to their rural way of life. In a world dominated by a ritualistic version of Islam and long-established custom, Malay peasants were poor but not desperately so by the standards of neighboring countries. Educated in vernacular schools, few rural Malays had the opportunity to transfer to the English-medium schools that offered social mobility via secondary school, university, and

[5] Ratnam 1965:2.
[6] Roff 1967:ch. 4.

beyond. Politically, the Malays tended to be deferential toward their community leaders who were drawn largely from a small English-educated elite, many of them aristocratic and employed mainly in the civil service. The muted character of class divisions in the rural areas and the weakness of intracommunal cultural cleavages strengthened the position of the Malay political leadership. Moreover, in the west-coast states and the south, where the Malay community was faced with and sometimes outnumbered by large non-Malay communities, the Malays united behind their leaders to avoid being overwhelmed by outsiders. On the east coast and in the north, however, where the non-Malays were small minorities, the threat from that quarter was not so immediate; thus, the Malays were more divided politically.

The Chinese and the Indians, on the other hand, were relatively mobilized. Immigrants and descendants of immigrants, they had moved out of their own traditional milieus and sought to establish themselves in a new environment. Initially, most had planned to work temporarily overseas in order to return home with accumulated wealth. Eventually, however, many settled in Malaya. By 1957 nearly 75 percent of the Chinese and 65 percent of the Indians were locally born, proportions that were bound to increase as immigration virtually stopped.[7] The geographically mobile immigrants were also socially mobile. Concentrated in the modern sectors of the economy, they had more opportunities to advance themselves than had the rural Malays. Those living in urban centers had greater access to schools, especially English-language schools, which enabled them to obtain higher education and entry to the professions. Social mobility tended to make the non-Malays more aware politically and resulted in their being spread across a wide range of occupations with a corresponding rise in class consciousness that added further lines of cleavage in communities already internally divided along cultural and religious lines. The non-Malay communities were thus both mobilized and fragmented, conditions that were reflected in their politics. In contrast to the relatively united Malays (at least in the west-coast states), the Chinese were always divided in their political loyalties. A large proportion identified with opposition parties ranging from the Communists to a succession of leftist and reformist parties. While often noncommunal in stated ideology, these parties in fact relied heavily on non-Malays for political support.

Malaysian politics were dominated by the elite of the Malay community.[8] From the beginning the British regarded the Malays as the legitimate owners of the land, while the non-Malays were seen as temporary guests.

[7] Ratnam 1965:9–10.
[8] For general studies of the politics of this period see von Vorys 1975; Means 1976; Milne and Mauzy 1978; Bedlington 1978.

Early in the century, the British set out to create an English-educated administrative class recruited from the Malay aristocracy; and members of
this class filled the highest echelons of the bureaucracy after independence.[9] English-educated Malays were also recruited to the officer corps of
the police and armed forces; and, although non-Malays were also recruited
to both, the top positions were generally held by Malays. Controlling the
bureaucracy, police, and armed forces, the Malay elite also developed a
political wing—the United Malays National Organisation (UMNO).

Most of the first generation of UMNO leaders were members of the
English-educated administrative elite that served the colonial government.
The party was established in 1946 in response to a British plan to create a
Malayan Union out of the nine Malay states and two crown colonies in
the peninsula. Under the proposed union the Malays would lose their special status as the indigenous community, and non-Malays would acquire
the same citizenship rights as Malays. This led to a massive reaction from
the Malay community, including those in the British-nurtured elite who
were shocked by their mentor's betrayal. This deviation from the traditional British policy proved temporary, however, and in 1948 a federation
was established under which the states retained some autonomy and Malays their special position. In the immediate postwar period UMNO had
been challenged by the Malay Nationalist Party (MNP), a radical, Indone-
sian-influenced body with a base of support among Malay-educated
schoolteachers. But the MNP was banned after the proclamation of the
state of emergency in 1948, leaving UMNO as the only major Malay political organisation. Essentially conservative and pro-British, UMNO nevertheless pressed for independence and became the dominant party in the
pre-independence government elected in the first nationwide election in
1955, which steered the nation to independence in 1957.

Although UMNO had been established to fight exclusively for Malay
interests, its leaders soon realized that the special circumstances of Malayan society made it imperative for them to come to some understanding
with moderate non-Malay leaders. The British had made it clear that they
did not intend to grant independence to an exclusively Malay government
that would have little chance of guaranteeing stability in the future. In
particular, the British believed that a Malay government would be unable
to deal with the Communist rebellion and its mainly Chinese base of support. Nevertheless, the exigencies of electoral politics provided the immediate incentive for UMNO to come to an arrangement with a non-Malay
party.[10] In the Kuala Lumpur municipal elections of 1952, UMNO joined
with a conservative Chinese body, the Malayan Chinese Association

[9] Khasnor 1984.
[10] Horowitz 1985:401–3.

(MCA), in an alliance against a Malay-led multiracial party. This alliance met with great success and later admitted the Malayan Indian Congress (MIC) to its ranks. Known as the Alliance, it won every national election between 1955 and 1969. The secret of its success lay in its ability to win votes from all three communities, while the appeal of opposition parties was usually limited to only one community in each case.

Although it was formally committed to bringing Malays into the modern sector of the economy, UMNO seemed more concerned about maintaining the relatively harmonious racial status quo which it might have upset by taking vigorous measures on behalf of the Malays. The party's moderation on racial issues, however, made it vulnerable electorally to campaigns waged by the Pan-Malayan Islamic Party (PMIP, now referred to in Malay as Parti Islam Se-Malaysia [PAS]). PAS's platform was religious and communal, exploiting UMNO's willingness to ally itself with non-Malay infidels and its reluctance to take drastic steps to improve the position of Malays at the expense of non-Malays. PAS relied on religious officials and teachers to rally mass support, which was particularly forthcoming in the northern and northeastern states where the poorer peasantry had benefited least from UMNO-sponsored developmental programs.

In the pre-independence national election of 1955, PAS won only one seat out of fifty-two; but in 1959 it made spectacular progress by winning control of the state governments in Kelantan and Terengganu, the two states where Malays made up more than 90 percent of the population. Although PAS was maneuvered out of power in Terengganu in 1961, it retained its hold on Kelantan and was also able to establish strong bases in Kedah and Perlis where Malays made up more than 70 and 80 percent of the population respectively. But UMNO's call for Malay unity to preserve the community's position had a strong appeal on the west coast and in the south where the Malays were faced with large non-Malay communities.

On the non-Malay side, UMNO's partners, especially the MCA and to a lesser extent the MIC, experienced a steady erosion of credibility as representatives of the Chinese and Indian communities. Headed at the national level by English-educated leaders who developed good rapport with their UMNO colleagues, both parties represented primarily the conservative, well-to-do parts of their communities and relied on established community leaders for support at the local level. The MCA, at the grassroots level, was dominated by *towkays*—local businessmen, often not conversant with English, who were also patrons of Chinese-medium schools and cultural associations as well as leaders of local Chinese chambers of commerce. The MIC, on the other hand, depended on local leaders with influence over plantation workers such as Tamil schoolteachers, clerical workers in plantations, and Indian shopkeepers. Both the MCA and the

MIC attempted to promote the interests of their communities by raising issues such as vernacular education, citizenship, recruitment to the civil service, and so on; but their alliance with and dependence on UMNO forced them to rely on private representations rather than mass campaigns. Although they succeeded to some extent in protecting non-Malay interests threatened by popular Malay demands, they could do little to advance non-Malay causes. This failure to achieve clear-cut progress made the MCA and MIC leaders vulnerable to the charge of selling out to the Malays. Increasingly, both parties came to be seen as patronage machines that gave members of the non-Malay middle class, especially businesspeople, access to the Malay-dominated government and bureaucracy but offered fewer benefits to supporters at lower levels in the hierarchy. The result was a growing sense of frustration among members of non-Malay communities, especially the Chinese.

The non-Malay opposition was not concentrated in a single party in the way that the Malay opposition tended to converge in PAS. The Labour Party, a Socialist party with roots in the trade unions, was the initial focus of non-Malay opposition, although it made little headway in the state of Perak where its potential base of support had been pre-empted by the People's Progressive Party (PPP). The Labour Party was the target of Communist infiltration, which contributed to internal conflict and the departure of many moderate leaders in 1967 and 1968. With many of its radical activists arrested under the ISA, the party decided to boycott the 1969 election; but most of its supporters ignored the boycott call and switched their votes to other opposition parties. The main beneficiary was the Democratic Action Party (DAP), which had its origins in the Singapore People's Action Party (PAP). In Penang a new party, Gerakan (Gerakan Rakyat Malaysia—Malaysian People's Movement), not only took over the Labour Party vote but added to it, defeating the Alliance and winning control of the state government.

The mosaic of communal parties had been further complicated in 1963 by the formation of Malaysia with the addition of Singapore and the two East Malaysian states, Sabah and Sarawak, to the federation. The entry of Singapore injected a new element to Chinese politics that threatened to polarize the Malay-led Alliance and the Singapore-based PAP; but this phase was brief, ending with Singapore's expulsion from the federation in August 1965. In Sabah and Sarawak elections were contested by parties based on the Malay and Chinese minorities as well as the various indigenous communities.

The political system was thus dominated by a relatively homogeneous Malay elite. The leading figures of UMNO, the bureaucracy, the judiciary, the armed forces, and the police had similar values, orientations, educational backgrounds, and life-styles. Many had their origins in the old

Malay upper-class families, while others from less elevated backgrounds had been recruited into the elite after receiving an English-language education, adjusting their outlook and life-styles to suit their new status. But the Malay elite did not rule alone. The leaders of the non-Malay communities were brought into the government through the Alliance: some senior posts in the bureaucracy were allocated to non-Malays, and some non-Malays attained high rank in the armed forces and police. Moreover, many government policies, especially economic ones, benefited non-Malays—in particular the Chinese upper class.[11]

The political system had some of the characteristics of consociationalism.[12] According to the consociational model, political stability in plural societies can be achieved through elite-level integration even though the communities that their leaders represent remain divided. Under the Alliance system, UMNO, MCA, and MIC leaders met together to reach compromises on communal issues rather than carry out public campaigns that might aggravate intercommunal tensions. The smooth functioning of a consociational system, however, requires not only a willingness on the part of the elites to reach compromises on communal issues but also ability to retain the support and confidence of their respective communities. During the twelve years between independence in 1957 and the election of 1969, Chinese support for the Alliance had steadily declined as the MCA became increasingly ineffective in fighting for non-Malay interests. On the Malay side, UMNO succeeded in establishing itself as the premier party of that community. But in 1969 it, too, suffered a substantial loss of support. By 1969, therefore, the consociational foundations of the system had become very shaky. The reasons for the undermining of Alliance-style consociationalism lay in the social and economic developments of the postindependence period.

The Plural Economy and the 13 May Riot

The 1960s were a time of rising social tensions that threatened to escalate into communal conflict. The elite-level pre-independence negotiations in 1956 and 1957 had reached an understanding that the Malays would retain their political preeminence. At the same time the non-Malays' economic position would not be disturbed, and they would be permitted to maintain their cultures and traditions. It was understood that in the long

[11] Funston argues that the benefits received by non-Malay interests were in fact so great that the system could not be accurately described as 'Malay-dominated'. Funston 1980:ch. 1.

[12] For the concept of consociationalism see Lijphart 1977; for further discussion, see Chapter 8.

run measures would be taken to raise the economic level of the Malays and establish a national identity with Malay as the national language. While the basic principles of the understanding had been broadly accepted in 1957, their detailed implementation aggravated communal tensions in the 1960s as the Malay and non-Malay masses reacted to policies decided on their behalf in elite-level compromises.

Political developments in Malaysia had taken place against the background of steady economic growth, per capita income increasing by 25 percent between 1957 and 1970.[13] But rising prosperity was not evenly spread among the population. The available data suggest that during this period the income of the top 10 percent of income recipients increased by an average of 51 percent while the average income of the lowest 40 percent actually declined by 13 percent.[14]

This inequality was reflected in communal disparities. Malays outnumbered non-Malays in the traditional rural sector by about three to one, and non-Malays outnumbered Malays in the modern sector (both rural and urban) by about five to two.[15] Even when Malays worked in the modern sector, they tended to have low-level, semiskilled, or unskilled jobs. The concentration of Malays in low-productivity occupations resulted in a substantial imbalance in wealth between communities. The mean household income for Malays in 1970 was $172 per month compared to $304 for Indians and $394 for Chinese.[16] Of the 792,000 households in West Malaysia officially considered as poor in 1970 (almost half the total), 89 percent were located in the predominantly Malay rural areas. Of those classified as poor, 74 percent were Malay; and 65 percent of all Malays were regarded as poor compared to 26 percent of Chinese and 39 percent of Indians.[17] The low representation of Malays in modern economic activities was evident in all sectors except government employment where the ratio was five to three in favor of Malays.[18]

The economic backwardness of the Malay community was starkly illustrated by statistics on the ownership of share capital in limited companies in West Malaysia. While 63.3 percent of capital was held by foreigners and 34.3 percent by non-Malay Malaysians, only 1.6 percent was held by Malay individuals or trust funds and another 0.8 percent by government agencies considered to be holding shares on behalf of Malays.[19] Many companies appointed a nominal Malay aristocrat, politician, or retired

[13] Jomo 1986:249.
[14] Snodgrass 1980:81.
[15] 2MP:38.
[16] 3MP:179.
[17] 3MP:72–74.
[18] 2MP:38.
[19] 3MP: 184.

civil servant to their boards of directors or even as chairperson; but control of the modern sector of the economy was clearly not in Malay hands.

Although the imbalance between the races in their economic functions had been, despite occasional protests, reluctantly tolerated during the colonial period, the atmosphere changed after independence. Increasingly, Malays expected UMNO to use its political power not just to defend but to advance Malay economic interests. In the 1960s the government began to take significant steps to improve the economic position of the Malay community. But by 1969 these measures had barely made a dent in the problem of Malay economic backwardness and poverty; indeed, they probably served more to raise expectations than living standards.

It was not only Malays who felt that they had not received adequate benefits from the economic growth of the 1960s. Although non-Malays were predominant in the professions, white-collar occupations, business, and trade, the majority followed more humble occupations. Substantial proportions of both the Chinese and Indian communities remained poor and had little reason to believe that their conditions would improve materially under a government that saw the problem of poverty in essentially Malay terms. Non-Malays were also aggrieved by the government's education policy, which closed or converted to English most Chinese-medium and all Tamil-medium secondary schools.

On several occasions during the 1960s, intercommunal tensions approached flashpoint. The entry of Singapore into the new federation of Malaysia in 1963 had an extremely unsettling impact on an already delicate communal balance. Intended to curb Chinese radicalism in Singapore, the merger meant that the Chinese now formed the largest single ethnic community (with about 42 percent), although they were balanced by the inclusion of non-Malay bumiputeras from Sabah and Sarawak. The young, dynamic leaders of the Singapore PAP initially restrained themselves from direct participation in peninsular politics. Inevitably, however, they attracted the sympathy of many Chinese in the peninsula who believed that the staid conservative leadership of the MCA had become too much a part of the established order to protect Chinese interests effectively. The PAP's campaign for a "Malaysian Malaysia" was welcomed enthusiastically by many non-Malays, but Malays considered it a challenge to the 1957 understanding that recognized Malay preeminence in politics. As the gap between the PAP's and the Alliance's perceptions of Malaysia's future became unbridgable and open conflict likely, the Malaysian prime minister decided in August 1965 to expel Singapore from the federation, a move that restored Malay political dominance to a point where it was virtually unassailable.

The period of Singapore's membership in Malaysia had involved a non-Malay challenge to the principles of 1957 and a Malay backlash. In this atmosphere a new issue emerged like a time bomb set ten years earlier. The 1957 constitution had provided for the continued use of both English and Malay for official purposes for a period of ten years. In the atmosphere of heightened tension surrounding Singapore's expulsion, there was strong Malay pressure for the full implementation of Malay as the national language when the ten years expired on 31 August 1967. The campaign found widespread support among Malays, including many leading figures in UMNO, but was strongly opposed by the MCA and MIC as well as the non-Malay opposition parties. With passions aroused on both sides, the prime minister, Tunku Abdul Rahman, worked out a compromise that established Malay as the sole national language but permitted "the continued use of the English language for official purposes as may be deemed fit."[20] To the relief of non-Malays, the National Language Act was passed in 1967. The new law was regarded as a sellout by many Malays; in UMNO itself, a dissident faction no longer had faith in the leadership of the Tunku whom they saw as unwilling to act vigorously in the Malay cause.

Rising racial tensions led to several outbreaks of rioting.[21] In 1964, when Singapore was still in Malaysia, twenty-two people were killed in one riot in Singapore and eight in another. In November 1967 twenty-three people were killed in communal rioting in Penang. Finally, the biggest riot of all broke out in Kuala Lumpur in the wake of the 1969 national election.[22] The election was held in an atmosphere in which non-Malays feared further encroachment on what they considered their established rights and Malays were demanding a more vigorous assertion of Malay interests. It resulted in a substantial swing of Malay votes to PAS in traditional UMNO areas and a big increase in the number of seats won by non-Malay opposition parties. Although the Alliance won at the national level, it was defeated at the state level in Penang. Its fate was uncertain in Perak and Selangor, while its share in the peninsular vote declined to 48.5 percent, compared to 58.4 percent in 1964 and 51.8 percent in 1959. The non-Malay opposition parties' success was due in part to increased votes but, no less important, to an electoral arrangement between the DAP, PPP, and Gerakan while the Labour Party boycotted the election. As a result, non-Malay opposition candidates won twenty-four parliamentary seats, and the MCA's representation fell from twenty-seven to thirteen. Malay reaction to exuberant postelection celebrations among supporters of the

[20] Vasil 1972:15.

[21] Memories of the racial conflagration at the end of World War II were still strong in the 1960s. As Cheah has written, "when compared to the numbers of people killed and the areas affected during the post-Japanese surrender interregnum of 1945, the May 1969 race riots pale into insignificance." Cheah 1983:xiv.

[22] See von Vorys 1975:ch. 13.

non-Malay opposition ignited the conflagration of 13 May. Between that day and the end of July, it was officially reported that 172 people had been killed in Selangor (the state in which Kuala Lumpur was then situated), eleven in Perak, seven in Melaka, four in Negeri Sembilan and one in Terengganu. Of a total of 196 killed, only 25 were Malays while 143 were Chinese.[23] Unofficial accounts suggest that the number of Chinese killed was much higher.

The riot of 13 May 1969 was a turning point in Malaysian political history. A proclamation of emergency was immediately issued, the parliamentary system suspended, and power placed in the hands of the newly created National Operations Council (NOC) headed by the deputy prime minister, Tun Abdul Razak. The new council was composed of members drawn from the Malay elite—political, bureaucratic, and military—together with leaders of the MCA and MIC. The Malay leaders realized that they were in danger of losing their base of support in the Malay community itself. The election had shown a strong swing among Malays away from the government, not so much in the east-coast strongholds of PAS but in the west-coast states that UMNO regarded as its own territory. The rioting in Kuala Lumpur had suddenly revealed pent-up frustrations, the existence of which had hitherto only been suspected. The Malay elite came to the conclusion that the moderate, gradual approach to racial questions exemplified by the policies of Tunku Abdul Rahman was no longer sufficient to retain mass support among the Malays. Instead, a new program had to be launched in which Malay political power would be used to bring Malays into the mainstream of the modern economy and thus enable them to enjoy more of the fruits of development.

The New Economic Policy and the Curtailing of Political Pluralism

In the aftermath of the racial rioting, the Malay elite, through the NOC, concluded that the gradualist policies of the past were no longer adequate and that the long-run solution to the government's need to maintain political stability and UMNO's need to prevent further erosion of its political base lay in a far-reaching program to raise the socioeconomic position of the Malay community. In 1971 the government launched what it called its New Economic Policy (NEP), which had two major goals or prongs.[24] The first prong was "to reduce and eventually eradicate poverty, by raising

[23] National Operations Council 1969:88.
[24] The thinking and discussion that led to the NEP's formulation are outlined in Faarland, Parkinson, and Saniman 1990:ch. 2.

income levels and increasing employment opportunities for all Malaysians, irrespective of race." The second aimed at "accelerating the process of restructuring Malaysian society to correct economic imbalance, so as to reduce and eventually eliminate the identification of race with economic function."[25] It was assumed that the disparity between the economic and social positions of the Malays on the one hand and the non-Malays, especially the Chinese, on the other had been the root cause of racial tensions and was the major threat to political stability in the future.[26] By reducing and eventually removing this disparity, political stability might be strengthened and the outbreak of further racial conflict avoided.

An Outline Perspective Plan for 1971–90 envisaged that the incidence of poverty could be reduced from almost 50 percent in 1970 to less than 20 percent in 1990. The largest reduction would take place in the rural areas where it was hoped that the rate would decline from 59 percent to 23 percent.[27] As the rural areas were overwhelmingly Malay in composition, the benefits provided under the poverty reduction program would naturally flow largely to the Malay community, although it was envisaged that poor non-Malays would also gain.

The prong concerned with restructuring society explicitly promised benefits exclusively for Malay and other indigenous communities. There were two major targets. First, "employment in the various sectors of the economy and employment at all occupational levels should reflect the racial composition of the country by 1990." Second, "ownership of productive wealth should be restructured so that by 1990 the Malays and other indigenous people own and operate at least 30% of the total."[28] The restructuring of employment implied a massive rise in the number and proportion of Malays employed in the modern sector of the economy. Although this also meant that steps would have to be taken to increase the size of the Malay working class in urban areas, the main goal was to expand the educated Malay middle class, a goal that also required a revamping of educational policy. Related to the expansion of the middle class was the plan to create a Malay entrepreneurial and shareholding class. In later years progress toward the 30 percent target became one of the main criteria of the NEP's success. Although the initial target was intended only as an indicator of Malay participation in the modern economy, in practice progress was largely measured in terms of Malay shareholdings in public companies.

---

[25] 2MP:1.

[26] According to the future prime minister, Mahathir Mohamad, "racial equality can only be said to exist when each race not only stands equal before the law, but also when each race is represented in every strata of society, in every field of work, in proportion more or less to their percentage of the population." Mahathir 1970:79.

[27] 3MP:75.

[28] 3MP:76.

The implementation of the NEP involved measures that strongly discriminated in favor of Malays and against non-Malays. The government expanded existing agencies and established new ones intended to help Malays go into business; gave special preference to bumiputeras in the distribution of licenses, concessions, contracts, and credit; and put heavy pressure on non-Malay and foreign enterprises to accept Malay partners. At the same time all enterprises were under pressure to restructure their work forces in line with the goals of the NEP. In the field of education, a massive expansion of secondary and tertiary institutions took place, scholarships being generously provided to Malay students while severe quotas limited non-Malay entry to universities to guarantee high Malay participation. The government also adopted a new language policy that favored Malays.

The new approach involved an assault on the dominant position of foreign, particularly British, capital. The common perception that the modern economy was dominated by the Chinese masked the even more dominant role of foreigners. In 1970 foreigners were estimated to own 63.3 percent of share capital in West Malaysia.[29] The pain of restructuring felt by non-Malays could therefore be ameliorated by reducing the foreign share. The goal of raising bumiputera ownership of the corporate sector to 30 percent would be achieved not by reducing the non-Malay share (which, on the contrary, was expected to rise from 34.3 to 40 percent) but by restricting the foreign share, which was targeted to fall to 30 percent by 1990. The government was careful to point out that, despite the decline in the foreign share, new foreign investment was still wanted. In absolute terms rapid economic growth would allow, and indeed require, foreign participation to increase. The implementation of NEP was premised on the assumption of rapid economic growth. It was anticipated that an expanding economy would provide sufficient resources to finance the growth of Malay participation in the modern economy while non-Malay participation would also continue to grow, although at a slower rate.

In the immediate aftermath of the 1969 rioting the Malaysian political system turned in a markedly authoritarian direction with the declaration of emergency, the suspension of Parliament, and the transfer of power to the NOC. Authoritarian powers, it was believed, were necessary to deal with the tensions that had manifested themselves in the rioting. Some twenty months later, however, the country returned to what was called normalcy. In fact, however, the political system was less open and liberal than before May 1969. The turn toward authoritarianism had not been merely a response to the immediate crisis of 1969. The government's long-term goal of eliminating the identification of economic function with race

[29] 3MP:86.

by restructuring society inevitably meant a sharpening of communal tensions. On the one hand, the new policy clearly favored Malays at the expense of non-Malays; on the other, it gave rise to expectations among Malays that would be difficult to satisfy fully. At the same time the policy involved an effort to reduce the domination of foreign capital in an economy that depended on foreign investment for its dynamism. The maintenance of communal harmony in these circumstances required the continuation of steady economic growth so that the relative and absolute advance of the Malays would only be to the relative and not absolute disadvantage of the others. But even with economic growth, it was expected that the tensions inherent in the restructuring policy could only be contained by a government confident of its authority and protected against appeals from its opponents to the communally divided masses.

PART TWO

THE POLITICAL SYSTEM

THE MALAYSIAN POLITICAL SYSTEM could not be described as either demo-cratic or authoritarian without substantial qualification. Since indepen-dence in 1957, the forms of democratic government were maintained, but the government also gradually acquired increased authoritarian powers that made it almost impossible for the ruling coalition to be forced out of office.[1] Nevertheless, the government continued to be confronted with a meaningful opposition expressed through political parties, social organiza-tions, and the peripheral press; significant competition took place between parties within the ruling coalition; and the courts continued to be more or less independent.

The political system was dominated by the Malay elite whose members, in the name of the Malay masses, occupied the key institutions: UMNO, the bureaucracy, the military and police, and the judiciary. Despite occa-sional conflicts and rivalries among its members, the Malay elite cohered around a set of common values and interests. For them, Malaysia was a Malay country whose destiny had to be determined by the Malays. But the Malay elite did not completely monopolize power, recognizing that it would be easier to govern in Malaysia's multicommunal society if leaders of non-Malay communities were also represented. Non-Malays were ap-pointed, therefore, to positions in the cabinet, bureaucracy, military, and judiciary. But they always constituted a minority, and their appointments depended on their acceptance of the idea of Malay dominance and their own subordination.

---

[1] Prime Minister Tun Razak told the Commonwealth Parliamentary Conference in 1971, "The view we take is that democratic government is the best and most acceptable form of government. So long as the form is preserved, the substance can be changed to suit conditions of a particular country." Quoted in Ong 1987:40.

The Malay-dominated government turned to authoritarian and semi-authoritarian means to maintain its grip on power. Although free, competitive elections were held, the electoral system was gerrymandered to ensure a substantial government majority in Parliament, while the government machinery was routinely used to persuade voters to support the ruling front. Free and open discussion was hampered by the Sedition Act, which removed so-called sensitive issues from the realm of public debate. In addition, the opposition's views were often ignored or distorted in the mainstream press (largely owned by the government parties) as well as radio and television, which were effectively government monopolies. Various regulations restricted the scope of organizations such as trade unions, peasant associations, student movements, and other social groups that may have been inclined to support the opposition. In reserve were the Internal Security Act, which permitted the government to detain indefinitely its recalcitrant critics, and the emergency provisions that allowed the government to rule without recourse to Parliament and elections if considered necessary.

But the government did not rule by authoritarian means alone. The ruling coalition developed a political strategy superior to the opposition's in the context of a multicommunal society. While the opposition was divided into competing parties based on ethnic identity, the government parties had formed first the Alliance and then the Barisan Nasional (National Front, or BN) through which votes were channeled to government candidates from all the major communities. Although the government won most of its votes from the Malay community, it provided enough for non-Malays to ensure that it obtained significant support from that quarter as well. With the advantage of incumbency, the BN further consolidated its dominance by distributing patronage to its supporters—the lion's share going to UMNO but not to the exclusion of non-Malay BN parties.

The electoral system meant that the ruling coalition's victory in elections was virtually assured, but competitive elections forced the government parties to be somewhat responsive to the political aspirations of their respective ethnic communities. UMNO presented itself as a party championing the cause of the Malays, while the non-Malay parties represented themselves as defenders of the interests of Chinese, Indian, and various East Malaysian ethnic communities.

Until the mid-1980s the BN formula worked well, but its durability was based on two premises: first, that UMNO as the party of the Malay elite would remain united and, second, that the opposition parties would remain divided along communal lines. But in the late 1980s UMNO split in two, and in the 1990 election a multicommunal semi-alliance was formed in which all the major opposition parties participated. Although the BN scored a convincing victory in this election, it faced its most serious challenge and became aware of its vulnerability. Developments in the late 1980s showed that despite the authoritarian controls imposed by the government, the system still allowed the opposition to mount a serious challenge to the government. But in the 1990s UMNO regained much of its support in the Malay community, and the opposition semi-alliance fell apart, allowing the BN to restore its overwhelming supremacy in the 1995 election.

The Malaysian political system, therefore, continued to display authoritarian and democratic characteristics in a mutually supporting way. There was no indication that the system would shift decisively in a democratic direction, nor were there signs that it was likely to turn to full authoritarianism. The system forced the government to take account of demands from society in order to win votes in elections. At the same time it was able to buttress its authority by resorting to authoritarian manipulation, control, and repression. The stability of the system thus rested on an evolving combination of repression and responsiveness.

3 *The Government*

IN CONTRAST to most Third World countries Malaysia has experienced politics characterized by extraordinary continuity since its independence in 1957. That continuity has been based on the essential stability of the government, despite constant political tensions and occasional upheavals. The government has taken the form of a semipermanent coalition of representatives from the main communal groups. Unlike the shifting coalitions between rival parties that are common in other countries, the ruling coalition in Malaysia constitutes a distinct entity with its own constitution and rules. At its core is the alliance between the dominant Malay party, UMNO, and parties representing the non-Malay communities, of which the Chinese MCA is the most important.

From Alliance to Barisan Nasional

The original alliance between UMNO and the MCA was not the product of farsighted statesmanship. It arose, as I mentioned in Chapter 2, from the exigencies of electoral competition in local government elections introduced by the British in 1952. Joined in 1955 by the Indian MIC, the Alliance claimed that it represented all three major races in Malaya and then Malaysia.

The Alliance formula worked well for its constituent parties during the first dozen years after independence. The top party leaders not only cooperated closely in government but became warm personal friends. Although there was no shortage of political conflicts involving the interests of the racial communities, the Alliance arrangements facilitated their settlement through compromise within the cabinet. Certainly UMNO's dominance was not doubted; but its leaders, headed by Prime Minister Tunku Abdul Rahman, were usually sensitive to the interests represented of their MCA and MIC partners.

The problem for the Alliance lay not so much in the relations between the leaders of UMNO, MCA, and MIC but in the extent to which they represented the interests of the wider communities in whose name they ruled. The electoral advances of the Chinese opposition at a time of growing frustration among lower-class urban Malays precipitated the racial riots that followed the 1969 election and led to the imposition of emergency rule until 1971. The long-serving deputy prime minister, Tun Abdul Razak bin Datuk Hussein, who succeeded Tunku Abdul Rahman as prime minister in 1970, believed that steps had to be taken to reduce the level of open political competition, which inevitably led to heightened emotions when political leaders sought votes on the basis of appeals to one race or another. He therefore decided to expand the original coalition to include former opposition parties.

Although a product of conscious deliberation, the scheme was implemented gradually in response to evolving circumstances. In December 1970, a broad state-level coalition was formed in Sarawak, followed in 1972 by a coalition with the Chinese-based Gerakan in Penang and the small People's Progressive Party (PPP) in Perak. Then the main Malay opposition party, PAS, joined the coalition on 1 January 1973. This network of separate coalitions, together with the ruling Sabah Alliance in Sabah, was consolidated in the BN, which was officially registered as a confederation of parties in June 1974, two months before the August 1974 national election.[1]

The formation of the BN served two main purposes. First, by bringing former opposition parties into the government, BN leaders hoped that conflicts could be settled behind closed doors in ways that did not inflame passions, as had occurred so often during the 1960s. The constituent parties would be guaranteed appropriate representation in cabinet, Parliament, and state assemblies and would therefore not need to espouse communal causes so openly or vigorously. Second, the formation of the BN allowed UMNO to consolidate further its control over the government. By bringing the main Malay opposition party into the government, the new coalition protected UMNO from encroachments from the Malay opposition. At the same time the influence of the MCA was undermined by the entry of a second peninsular Chinese party into the government. The failure to bring in the other major Chinese opposition party, the Democratic Action Party (DAP), however, left both Chinese parties in the BN electorally vulnerable. In addition, the BN arrangement allowed the old

[1] For a full account, see Mauzy 1983.

Alliance parties to gain representation in the Kelantan and Penang state governments, which had been controlled by PAS and Gerakan respectively, as well as the PPP-controlled Ipoh Municipal Council.

As anticipated, the BN (which had fourteen members in 1995) proved electorally successful. It not only won every national election after its formation but was able to retain the two-thirds parliamentary minority that enabled it to alter the constitution at will. Further, the BN was able to hold power continuously at the state level in almost all states. The exceptions were Sabah, where an opposition party won in 1985 but was quickly co-opted into the BN in 1986 before leaving again in 1990, and Kelantan, where an opposition coalition ruled after 1990.

UMNO consolidated its domination of the BN. It always had the largest share of the BN's seats in Parliament. Since 1978 UMNO occupied between 64 and 74 percent of the BN's peninsular seats and between 53 and 56 percent of its total number of seats. UMNO also controlled all BN state governments in the peninsular states—except in Penang, where Gerakan headed the government, and Kelantan, where PAS was dominant until its expulsion from the BN in 1977.

In essence the BN was a coalition between a central core party, UMNO, and less influential parties that allied themselves with it. It was certainly not a coalition between equals. Despite the formal equality of party representation in the front's organizational structure, there was no question of non-UMNO parties ganging up against the dominant party. Parties joined the BN on UMNO's terms; and when they could not accept those terms, they were forced out, as the expulsion of PAS showed. In the Alliance, the MCA and MIC, sole representatives of their communities, had substantial bargaining power vis-à-vis UMNO; but their influence was greatly diluted in the broader BN. In particular, the recruitment of the multiethnic but Chinese-based Gerakan undermined the influence of the MCA, which was no longer the sole voice of the Chinese community in the government. While the Alliance could have been characterized as a partnership (although an unequal one), the BN was in effect a facade for UMNO rule. Nevertheless, it provided machinery for consultation and representation.

The Constituent Parties

According to a common view, the BN's constituent parties can be distinguished from the opposition parties by their moderation on communal issues.[2] Thus, some people argue that UMNO and the MCA, as parties that are moderate in outlook, are prepared to make compromises on com-

[2] See, for example, von Vorys 1975; Means 1976; Milne and Mauzy 1978.

munal issues that are necessary for an enduring coalition. On the other hand, the "chauvinist" DAP and the "fanatical" PAS are, by nature, unable to work together effectively. In reality, however, the communal aspirations of the BN parties are often not so different from those of the opposition. Resolutions passed on ethnic issues at the assemblies of UMNO and the MCA, especially their youth wings, are often no less extreme than the positions taken by the opposition parties. But there is a fundamental structural difference between the government and opposition parties: the government parties are part of the governing coalition, while the opposition parties are not. Thus, whatever their communal aspirations, the government parties have no choice but to compromise if they want to maintain the coalition. But the opposition parties, except when they can work out semi-alliance arrangements as they did in the 1990 election, are usually under no such constraint.

UMNO and the MCA, together with the other BN parties, are often portrayed as defenders of upper-class interests in their respective communities. In contrast, PAS and the DAP are seen as articulating the frustrations of the lower classes, which, although often couched in communal terms, do not necessarily originate in communalism.[3] Of course, the BN parties undeniably represent elite interests; but it is quite another thing to say that they serve *only* elite interests. In competitive elections, however circumscribed they may be, success depends in part on meeting the expectations of large numbers of voters. To retain popular support and acceptance, government parties must provide benefits that extend beyond the small bureaucratic, business, and professional elites of each community. While the BN parties undoubtedly exploit communal issues to win votes, they also must look to the material needs of their supporters. Thus, in a competitive political system, parties cannot be reduced to vehicles that essentially serve elite interests without representing other significant interests in the community.

A third approach sees the BN parties as patronage machines distributing benefits to supporters at all levels of society to ensure a winning margin of votes. These parties are distinguished from the opposition parties because, as members of the government, they have access to government patronage denied to the opposition. The parties continue to serve the interests of elite groups, but party patronage machines allow elites to maintain their dominant positions by providing material satisfactions to other sections of society in the expectation that those sections will continue to provide electoral support.

The BN's overwhelming domination means that election results have

[3] For examples of the class approach see Brennan 1985; Hua Wu Yin 1983; Jomo 1986; Brown 1994.

been largely foregone conclusions. At the same time, however, sharp struggles have taken place from time to time within each of the main BN parties. To some extent, factional rivalries might be seen as reflecting ideological debate or contrasting strategies to attain party goals. But most intraparty contests have been concerned primarily with personalities and power—including, of course, the patronage associated with power. Factional battles, except perhaps the one that brought about the 1970 downfall of Tunku Abdul Rahman in UMNO, have generally not resulted in major directional changes but have simply rearranged patronage networks within the party while having minimum impact on society at large.

UMNO

UMNO was founded in 1946 as a communal party concerned exclusively with the protection of Malay interests.[4] It organized a mass campaign that forced the British to abandon their plan to establish the Malayan Union, a move that outraged Malays saw as allowing the country to fall under Chinese domination. But UMNO was by no means a radical nationalist party. Many of its leaders were employed as civil servants; and, in fact, the party worked closely with the British, who were seen as a bulwark against Chinese domination. Only in the 1950s did UMNO begin to campaign for independence from British rule.

In the negotiations leading to the 1957 constitution UMNO insisted on provisions that symbolized the Malay nature of the state: the office of Yang di-Pertuan Agong (king), Islam as "the religion of the Federation," Malay as the national language, and the guaranteed preponderance of Malays in the elite class of the civil service. In the 1970s, following the shock of 1969, UMNO emphasized its Malay nature even more strongly through the NEP and its language policy. UMNO's rank-and-file members strongly supported policies that brought benefits to Malays and generally opposed concessions to non-Malays. Nevertheless, UMNO leaders continued to be conscious of the need to consider the interests and sentiments of their non-Malay partners in order to preserve the coalition. Whatever their personal inclinations, they realized that non-Malay support was essential for the continuation of UMNO rule through the BN.

UMNO's policies reflected the interests of its leaders, who were largely drawn from the Malay upper and middle classes. Most of its early leaders were civil servants, often from aristocratic or semi-aristocratic family backgrounds. In later years, aristocratic leaders were less prominent than

---

[4] See Funston 1980:ch. 4. Chandra Muzaffar (1979) argues that UMNO replaced the sultans as "protector" of the Malays. Just as the Malays had given their loyalty to the sultans in the past, they were now loyal to UMNO, which protected them against the non-Malays.

a new class of educated Malays, often from fairly humble backgrounds, who were produced by post-independence education policies. Grassroots leaders were often local officials, teachers in Malay schools, and rural landowners. In the late 1970s, as a result of the NEP, Malay businesspeople became more prominent as business opportunities were channeled to party supporters. Nevertheless, leaders with civil-service backgrounds remained important. Thus, UMNO represented mainly conservative groups that had little interest in far-reaching social reform for the peasants, smallholders, and fishermen who made up a large part of the Malay population. Still, electoral politics ensured that UMNO could not ignore the Malay masses; and many policies were designed to attract their support, such as land-settlement schemes and opportunities for rural Malay children to experience social mobility through education.

While UMNO always portrayed itself as the party of the Malay community as a whole, much of its appeal lay in its patronage-dispensing function.[5] In the 1960s it was able to give supporters access to land, government employment, and commercial facilities, among which timber licenses were of great importance at the state level.[6] At that time few Malays were involved in the modern sector of the economy, and government involvement in business was limited. In the 1970s, however, the introduction of the NEP was accompanied by a huge expansion of the state role in the economy, both in terms of controls over the private sector and active participation in business. As a result, the scope for patronage distribution increased enormously. Simultaneously, the NEP brought more Malays into the modern sector and thus led to a rise in the demand for government services and favors. In control of the government at all levels, UMNO was well positioned to provide material benefits to its supporters whose loyalty to the party was thereby strengthened.

One of the NEP's goals was the creation of a Malay business class. Malay businesspeople, virtually all of whom had UMNO connections, were given preference in obtaining licenses, credit, and government contracts. As part of the strategy to increase Malay participation in the modern economy, the government forced established Chinese and foreign enterprises to restructure in such a way that at least 30 percent of their shares would be owned by Malays—either government agencies acting "on behalf of" the Malay community or private Malay businesspeople. Enterprises that failed to restructure found it increasingly difficult to renew

[5] The following discussion draws in part on Crouch 1992:27–28.

[6] In 1970 Mahathir, who had recently been expelled from UMNO, wrote, "The party was held together not because the members had generally identical ideas on politics, but through a system of patronage and disguised coercion based on Government rather than party authority." Mahathir 1970:9. On the role of land allocation in two states in the 1960s, see Guyot 1971. At that time state governments devoted about 80 percent of their time to land matters.

necessary licenses or obtain contracts with the expanding state sector. The normal way for large companies to restructure was through the issue of new shares that were made available for Malay purchase at below-par prices. In the 1970s the actual allocation was in the hands of the Ministry of Trade and Industry, which kept a list of potential Malay shareholders who were given the option to buy shares before they came on the market. By the 1980s, however, while part of the issue was still reserved for companies on the ministry's list, it was common for at least some shares to be distributed by open ballot. The ministry also played a big role in finding local partners for foreign investors and in the appointment of local agents and distributors for imports. A later source of patronage was the $500 million Bumiputera Rehabilitation Fund established in 1988 to help Malay businesspeople who faced bankruptcy following the recession of the mid-1980s.

The central role of the Ministry of Trade and Industry in patronage distribution was described vividly in a letter written in 1984 by the deputy prime minister, Datuk Musa Hitam. In the letter, which was addressed to the prime minister and marked "top secret-personal" but later leaked, Musa protested against the move of his rival, Tengku Razaleigh, from the Ministry of Finance to the Ministry of Trade and Industry. Musa listed some of the ways in which Razaleigh could use the ministry to strengthen his political position through the dispensing of patronage. Among them were:

1) He shall use it to the full by giving out the following perks to his followers and would-be followers—Import permits (cars, materials etc.), licences for businesses (MTI looks after Registrar of Companies); licences and control/supervision of manufacturing ventures.

2) He shall have a very strong hold on the take-overs, purchases, distributions, approvals over companies wanting to divest or transfer shares either ordinarily or to comply to the NEP.

3) He shall choose, recommend, suggest Malaysian (Malay, more important) partners to foreign investors wishing to invest in Malaysia.

4) He shall control the licencing and supervision of the distributive trade.

5) He shall choose, recommend, suggest names of individuals for distribution of shares.

6) He shall not only continue to have the support of the monied group but widen it greatly to the general business (Malay especially) community.

7) PATRONAGE would be aplenty to those of his choice. And MON DIEU! he shall have the greatest opportunity ever to prepare himself for his political future, even better than Finance![7]

[7] The letter is reproduced in Muhammad Azree and Sudirman Hj Ahmad 1987. I am very grateful to Peter Searle for drawing my attention to it.

A new field for patronage distribution opened with the privatization policy launched in 1983. Shares in public enterprises were allocated partly by ballot to the public and partly by preferential distribution to staff and government agencies holding shares on behalf of Malays. Allocated shares were often extremely undervalued, with the result that those fortunate enough to obtain them were able to reap enormous rewards by reselling them on the stock exchange. For example, the value of shares in the newly privatized Telekom (floated in 1990) doubled within eight months. The electricity utility, renamed Tenaga Nasional when floated in April 1992, issued shares at $4.50, which rose to $8.75 on the first day of trading.[8]

Patronage distribution was also important at the middle levels. UMNO members of Parliament or state assembles *(wakil rakyat)* were normally offered special commercial opportunities. In addition to receiving salaries as members, they were usually appointed to the boards of directors of four or five state corporations or their subsidiaries, thus gaining several thousand extra ringgit per month in directors' fees. In addition, UMNO politicians normally had their own enterprises, which received special preference in the government's allocation of opportunities. It was common, for example, for politicians to be involved with timber companies or own construction companies. Shamsul Amri Baharuddin notes that in the district he studied in Selangor, "a common practice is for the *wakil rakyat* to set up their own *syarikat* [companies] to 'compete' for the more lucrative contracts—those above M$25,000. . . . Predictably, it is not uncommon for those *wakil rakyat* and their political supporters to become simply the 'sleeping partners' of the Chinese or Malay contractors who actually run the business."[9] UMNO politicians also had special access in obtaining land grants from the government. In Malaysia state governments have authority to convert state land to private ownership on application from interested individuals or companies. Thus, many UMNO politicians were able to obtain land for housing projects on behalf of companies with which they were associated, usually in league with Chinese housing developers who might otherwise have faced difficulties in getting access to land. Alternatively, the politician might obtain the state land at a low price, subdivide it (a process that also requires government permission), and resell it at a much higher price.[10] As a World Bank report noted, "obtaining land alienation licenses and constructing office or residential property became an easy route to instant wealth."[11] Naturally, politicians could not monopo-

---

[8] A World Bank report noted that "the public offerings have been heavily oversubscribed, suggesting that the government underpriced its shares, perhaps losing as much as US$150 million in the sale of four big companies." World Bank 1993:31.

[9] Shamsul 1986b:222–23.

[10] A politician could expect to make several million ringgit in such a deal over a few years. Interview with a former UMNO state assemblyman.

[11] World Bank 1989:9.

lize such opportunities for themselves but had to ensure that their party supporters were also rewarded.

The extensive licensing provisions for most types of economic activity provided another area for patronage distribution. The overall NEP goal of bringing Malays into business legitimated the preferential provision of licenses, loans, and other amenities for Malays in general. Thus, there was plenty of scope to select Malays who had UMNO loyalties. Evidence of support for UMNO was helpful for applicants for taxi licenses, for example, or a permit to run a lorry or set up a rice mill. Loans from government bodies, such as the Majlis Amanah Rakyat (MARA) were also more easily available to those with political backing. For example, in the 1970s the brother of a prominent UMNO leader received a loan of $120,000 from MARA, more than twice the normal limit for MARA loans.[12] One problem in making loans to politicians and other VIPs, said Datuk Sanusi Junid, the minister for national and rural development, under whom MARA was placed, was the "general feeling that MARA loans do not have to be repaid."[13] The government's program of building low-cost houses for the poor provided another avenue for patronage distribution. In Johor, for example, it was the practice to reserve 20 percent of low-cost houses for those described as "pillars of the Government"—that is, "staunch members of UMNO, MCA and MIC."[14]

At the village level, government patronage was used blatantly to win support for UMNO. Relatively well-off farmers affiliated with UMNO almost always controlled local Village Development and Security Committees (Jawatankuasa Kemajuan dan Keselamatan Kampung, or JKKK) and the government-sponsored Farmers' Associations through which government aid was channeled in principle to the village as a whole or the very poor but in reality to UMNO supporters.[15] Moreover, villagers' applications for title to land were considered by committees dominated by UMNO stalwarts, usually including the local state assembly member. Often authority to distribute assistance such as fertilizer, seedlings, or livestock was delegated "to local *ketua kampung* (village heads) who are, more often than not, the chairmen of UMNO branches in their respective

---

[12] Gale 1981b:55, 81.

[13] *NST* 4 April 1983. (Here and elsewhere *NST* indicates *New Straits Times*.)

[14] *NST* 24 December 1980, 12 June 1984. One consequence of this and similar practices in other states was the discovery that about 15 percent of low-cost houses throughout the country were awarded to ineligible people whose incomes exceeded the limit for such housing. *UM* 30 March 1983. (Here and elsewhere *UM* indicates *Utusan Malaysia*.) In Pahang a survey showed that six hundred out of two thousand low-cost houses were in fact being rented out. *NST* 22 September 1984.

[15] For a fascinating description of how this is done, see the Kedah study in Scott 1985:220–31. It was often necessary to be an UMNO member even to apply for government amenities. Rogers quotes a Malay rubber tapper in Johor who said, "When we ask for any kind of [government] form, they ask if we are UMNO members." Rogers 1992:105.

villages."[16] Shamsul writes that "my detailed findings show that most of the peasants who receive these aids are either immediate relatives of the village heads, or loyal UMNO supporters."[17] Through what James Scott calls "petty but systematic loan fraud" the better-off UMNO-affiliated farmers ensured that much of the Farmers' Association credit went to themselves.[18] Moreover, he points out that "increasing rates of delinquency in repayment . . . indicate that many large farmers have managed to turn the loans into outright subsidies. The accumulated bad debts had gone unprosecuted because the debtors, drawn largely from the ranks of the local, ruling party stalwarts, are well-nigh untouchable."[19]

Politics also played a big role in the selection of new settlers in the giant FELDA land-settlement project that theoretically is open to all the rural poor. While most of those accepted into FELDA schemes were indeed poor, a 1976 survey showed that only slightly more than half were in the poorest income category before joining the scheme. In fact, a small minority was relatively well-off, suggesting that political pull may have been a major factor in their selection.[20] Once accepted into a FELDA scheme, settlers were expected to support UMNO. In 1983 the minister for land and regional development, Datuk Rais Yatim, lamented that "only" 65–70 percent of FELDA settlers were UMNO members.[21] In 1984 he said that 365 settlers had been expelled for "opposing and speaking badly of the government."[22] In Pahang, the Menteri Besar, Datuk Mohamed Najib Tun Razak, declared that in future only genuine UMNO members would be accepted in FELDA projects in his state.[23]

In his study of a rice-growing village in Kedah, Scott does show that the very poor also benefited from being supporters of UMNO—for example, in the distribution of work opportunities in labor-intensive public works programs and assistance for school uniforms and exercise books.[24] Even social welfare aid to the destitute was provided on the recommendation of UMNO-dominated village committees. While the benefits flowing to the poor were small compared to those going to the better-off peasants, they were, of course, very significant for the poor themselves.

At the village level, then, it seems that access to patronage is the key to political loyalty. After spending more than a year in his Kedah village,

[16] Shamsul 1986b:220. In Johor, Rogers found that "at least 80 percent" of village headmen were also chairmen of UMNO branches. Rogers 1992:114.
[17] Shamsul 1986b:220.
[18] Scott 1985:128.
[19] Scott 1985:84. See also 128–29.
[20] Tan 1982:90.
[21] *UM* 25 April 1983.
[22] *UM* 29 April 1984.
[23] *UM* 3 March 1985.
[24] Scott 1985:129–31.

Scott noted that "not more than six or seven villagers, most of them members of the JKK [Village Development Committee], even bother to refer to *any* public-spirited reasons for siding with UMNO."[25]

The distribution of patronage is both a means of consolidating support within a political party and a source of dissension; it is inevitable that some party activists will feel inadequately rewarded.[26] Factional rivalries in UMNO at the local and state levels have been concerned almost exclusively with the struggle for access to the power and patronage associated with control of government bodies rather than with ideological or policy differences. In the past UMNO was a rural-based organization that usually gave almost automatic support to its leaders, but the economic opportunities provided by the NEP brought about increased competitiveness in the party. In the 1950s and 60s it was common for local meetings to be held in the friendly atmosphere of a member's house while wives provided light refreshments. Many local office holders were Malay schoolteachers, who in the 1970s usually made up about 40 percent of the delegates to the annual assembly at the national level. By the late 1970s and 80s the composition of the party was undergoing substantial change as schoolteachers and other local leaders were increasingly pushed aside by a new generation of businesspeople and university-educated professionals produced by the NEP. The new leaders usually resided in Kuala Lumpur or the state capitals but regularly returned to their home kampungs to consolidate political support. Party meetings were no longer held in members' homes but often in big hotels with expenses met by aspirants for party positions.[27]

NEP-produced business opportunities inevitably increased the stakes in the struggle for party power. Victory in a local party election meant a chance to become a member of Parliament or a state assembly with all the attendant commercial opportunities. Huge sums were spent on local UMNO elections; and the prime minister himself expressed concern about candidates' offering supporters all-expenses-paid trips to Tokyo, Medan, or, for those so inclined, Mecca. Datuk Seri Mahathir Mohamad mentioned the case of one leader who was said to have spent $600,000 in his campaign to head a local division in 1985.[28] The deputy prime minister, Musa Hitam, was forced to admit that "if an analysis of this question is made today, it will reveal that many had joined the party to acquire more wealth."[29] Future party Secretary-General Sanusi Junid got to the essence of the problem when he said, "These people are 'investing' money to reap

[25] Ibid.:281.
[26] This and the next paragraph are based on Crouch 1992:32–33.
[27] See *NST* 11 April 1984 (Zainah Anwar, "Battle for Grassroots Support").
[28] *NST* 20 May 1985. The salary of a senior civil servant at that time was $60,000–70,000 per year.
[29] *NST* 30 November 1980.

material gains when they are in power."[30] By 1994 money politics had become so rife that UMNO amended its constitution to empower its Supreme Council to draw up a code of ethics that "prohibits abuse of power and money with the intention of securing votes or support."[31] Nevertheless, most observers remained skeptical.

As long as the national leadership of the party was more or less united, local factional conflict was essentially a matter of proper management for the national leaders. But when the national leadership itself was divided, rivalries at the national level meshed with ongoing local struggles. Often a local faction would ally itself with a national leader to strengthen its own position in the local struggle. Thus, if one local faction, for one reason or another, supported one national leader, the other local faction would line up behind the other national leader. Although factional conflict at the national level increased in the 1980s when Musa and Razaleigh fought bitterly for the deputy presidency of the party, UMNO's basic unity was not threatened until the 1986 split between Prime Minister Mahathir and his deputy, Musa, and the subsequent formation of Semangat '46 (Spirit of '46), the party of UMNO dissidents under the leadership of Razaleigh. Control over patronage resources later proved vital in allowing Mahathir's faction to consolidate its position and win back former dissidents.

The capacity of UMNO to ride through serious internal upheavals was due in large part to its essentially nonideological patronage-dispensing nature. Insofar as UMNO could be said to have an ideology, it was expressed in terms of Malay privileges and domination and therefore won almost universal approval from the entire Malay community. This is not to say that broader issues were never at stake. In 1970 Tunku Abdul Rahman was replaced partly because he was seen as insufficiently vigorous in pursuing Malay causes, while it has been argued that the rivalry between Mahathir and Razaleigh stemmed in part from contrasting economic strategies.[32] But behind such difference always lay struggles over positions in government and the opportunities for patronage distribution that went with them. As a result, defeated groups usually made their peace with winners to regain access to the life blood of patronage.

The Peninsular Non-Malay Parties

The non-Malay parties in the BN have, with one partial exception, been no less communally oriented than UMNO. The original parties of the old Alliance, the MCA and the MIC, never pretended to be anything but par-

[30] *NST* 21 May 1985.
[31] *NST* 20 June 1994.
[32] See Khoo Kay Jin 1992.

ties representing the Chinese and Indian communities. The partial exception, the Gerakan, was formed originally as a noncommunal party and continued to espouse a noncommunal ideology. In reality, as we shall see, its dependence on Chinese votes turned it into a party concerned primarily with non-Malay issues.

Like UMNO, the non-Malay parties were largely concerned with serving elite interests in the Chinese and Indian communities; but they also operated as patronage machines providing benefits to nonelite classes to mobilize electoral support. A major part of the appeal of the MCA, the MIC, and Gerakan has been their ability to provide their supporters with business and other opportunities, assistance in their dealings with government agencies, and sometimes protection of threatened non-Malay interests.

Nevertheless, while UMNO has largely succeeded in fulfilling the communal aspirations of much of the Malay community, the non-Malay parties have been involved in a rearguard action to preserve the non-Malay position, which they perceive as being under constant threat. As a result, the BN's non-Malay parties are regularly criticized from within their respective communities; and it has been relatively easy for dissident groups in each party to claim that leaders have failed to achieve community goals. A widespread sense of political frustration and powerlessness has contributed to factionalism within these parties. Further, although party leaders, like those of UMNO, have used their control over patronage to stave off factional challenges, their resources have been much less than those at the disposal of UMNO. As a result, patronage distribution has been less effective in limiting intraparty upheaval.

MCA. The MCA was formed as a Chinese welfare association in 1949 and was at first led by members of the English-educated Chinese business elite. Soon, however, it became a political party and joined UMNO to form the Alliance and then the BN.[33] Although led by members of the English-educated elite, the MCA was generally perceived as the party of the towkays—Chinese businessmen ranging from mining, plantation, and commercial magnates to Chinese-educated local businessmen and shopkeepers. At the local level, the MCA was dominated by the leaders of local Chinese communities. Judith Strauch's study of a small town in Perak revealed that "the party organization in the small towns meant little more than just another committee membership for the established local leaders who already manned school, temple and native-place association committees."[34] In the 1970s and 80s, however, the party's image as a towkay

[33] For the early years of the MCA, see Heng 1988.
[34] Strauch 1981:24.

party was gradually modified as well-educated professionals moved into important posts. Members of Chinese educational and cultural associations also saw the MCA as a channel for bringing their demands to the attention of the government, although many preferred to work through the opposition parties.

The MCA portrays itself as the voice of the Chinese community in the government. Unlike the DAP and other opposition parties, its leaders believe that Chinese interests can best be preserved in closed-door negotiations with UMNO leaders.[35] Therefore, the MCA usually avoids a confrontational stance and has gone along with the general policies of the government, which favor Malays. At the same time it tries to ensure that Chinese interests are taken into account in practice. For example, the MCA supported the NEP in principle but in practice sought to keep open opportunities for Chinese business. Similarly, it publicly endorsed the government's education policy but insisted on the retention of Chinese-medium primary schools and adequate quotas for non-Malay students in universities. This approach has led to a credibility gap in the party's efforts to establish itself as the champion of Chinese interests. As UMNO's junior partner in the government, it cannot dissociate itself from policies that are unpopular in the Chinese community. Even when it is successful in obtaining concessions from UMNO in behind-the-scenes negotiations, it is hesitant to proclaim its achievements too loudly for fear of provoking a negative Malay backlash. At best, as one party activist concluded, "The MCA may be able to prevent changes of policies which are likely to adversely affect its constituents, but rarely can it initiate changes to improve the welfare of the community it represents."[36] The party has always been vulnerable to the charge of selling out Chinese interests, and it is hardly surprising that it has never been able to attain the preeminence in the Chinese community that UMNO enjoys among the Malays.

During the 1960s the MCA was the sole representative of the Chinese community in the government; and its leaders held key posts in the cabinet, especially those concerned with economic policy such as minister of finance or commerce and industry. Top leaders enjoyed close personal ties with Prime Minister Tunku Abdul Rahman. But following the party's severe losses in the 1969 election and the formation of the BN, the MCA became only one of several parties in the ruling coalition, all of which were clearly subordinate to UMNO. Worse still, it was no longer the sole representative of the peninsular Chinese in the government. Reflecting the party's declining influence in the 1970s, MCA leaders lost key economic

---

[35] In an interview, one former senior leader of the MCA said, "I think the same as Lim Kit Siang [the DAP leader] but what I say is different."

[36] H'ng Hung Yong, quoted in Jesudason 1989:78.

policy-making and patronage-dispensing portfolios—minister of trade and industry in 1969 and minister of finance in 1974. After the launching of the NEP, these posts were allotted to UMNO, while the MCA was relegated to relatively minor ministries such as Labor, Transport, Housing, and Health.

Unlike UMNO, where factionalism did not normally threaten the national leadership and overall party coherence, the MCA was almost torn apart on several occasions during the 1970s and 80s.[37] While the leadership group was always forced by circumstances to emphasize the need to work closely with UMNO, the rebels usually demanded that leaders take a firmer stand in fighting for Chinese interests. But apparent differences over strategy and tactics often disguised straightforward struggles between "ins" and "outs" for power and the patronage opportunities that go with it.[38]

The MCA's first major internal crisis occurred in 1959 when its new president, Dr. Lim Chong Eu, unsuccessfully demanded that the party stand up to UMNO over the allocation of seats on the Alliance ticket.[39] In 1973 a group of "Young Turks" was expelled from the party when they demanded that the MCA take a more assertive line in dealing with UMNO and sought to revitalize the party's organization to attract support from the Chinese lower class.[40] In the late 1970s the party was again bitterly divided when its new leader, Datuk Lee San Choon, was challenged by Datuk Michael Chen, who was narrowly defeated.[41] Following Lee's resignation from the party presidency in 1983, another debilitating leadership struggle broke out.[42] After two years of upheaval and the intervention of UMNO, which was worried about the BN's electoral prospects if the MCA remained in disarray, a party election was held in November 1985 that resulted in an overwhelming victory for Tan Koon Swan who had succeeded in presenting himself as the herald of a new era for the MCA. Tan was a self-made businessman who had established the MCA-sponsored corporation Multi-Purpose Holdings (MPH), which succeeded in

[37] Pye suggested that Chinese fractiousness is due in part to Confucian political culture. He claims that "Confucian political culture does not contain any guidelines for minority leadership in a community dominated by a non-Confucian culture." Thus, "large numbers of Chinese in Malaysia feel that a truly national politics is unattainable for them and that any Chinese who acts as a leader must be an impostor if he is subservient to the Malay majority leadership." Pye 1985:251.

[38] In interviews, MCA leaders regularly denied that different factions stood for different policies. Usually they described factional struggles as being concerned with the simple question of who is the best leader.

[39] Vasil 1971:23–33.

[40] See Loh 1982; Lee Kam Hing 1977; Strauch 1981:ch. 7.

[41] See Lee Kam Hing 1980.

[42] For detailed accounts of this crisis, see Ho 1984; Lao 1984; Means 1991:176–79.

mobilizing capital from small Chinese investors and became one of Malaysia's biggest corporations.[43]

But Tan Koon Swan did not last long as MCA leader. The MPH empire had been built mainly on borrowed funds and was therefore very vulnerable to the recession that hit Malaysia in 1985. Meanwhile, Tan was involved in another recession-hit company, the Singapore-based Pan-Electric Industries (Pan-El), which faced bankruptcy in late 1985. Tan was arrested in Singapore on fifteen counts of criminal breach of trust, cheating, and fraud and eventually sentenced to two years of imprisonment. On his return to Malaysia after his release from jail in Singapore, Tan was charged with misusing MPH funds to bail out Pan-El, resulting in another jail sentence. Meanwhile, the leadership of the MCA passed to one of Tan's lieutenants, Datuk Ling Liong Sik, whose tenure as party president was relatively uneventful following an early unsuccessful challenge.

Despite the MCA's declining capacity to defend Chinese interests during the 1970s and 80s and the way in which it dissipated its energies in almost constant faction fighting, the party nevertheless continued to win substantial, although by no means majority, support from the Chinese community. First, the party continued to espouse causes, such as in the field of education, that were important not only for businesspeople and the middle class but for all levels of the Chinese community.[44] Second, whatever the weaknesses of the MCA, many Chinese recognized that it did have an established position in the government and access to UMNO leaders. The argument that it was more effective to operate quietly on the inside rather than vociferously on the outside made some sense. If the Chinese were to turn against the MCA, the result might simply be a reduction of Chinese influence in the government; there was no guarantee that another party would rise to take its place. Third, the memory of 1969 remained vivid. A massive swing to the opposition might only lead to a sharp rise in racial tensions with consequences that could not be favorable for the Chinese.

Patronage was also important. Although many Chinese businesspeople at the highest levels preferred to establish direct contact with the relevant UMNO ministers, medium and small businesspeople represented in the various Chinese chambers of commerce continued to use MCA connections for business purposes. The launching of MPH, which was designed to mobilize the savings of small Chinese investors, and the establishment of Kojadi, an educational cooperative intended to finance the education of members' children, also helped to tie Chinese citizens to the MCA, at least until the financial crises of 1985. At the local level the MCA was able to help supporters get various benefits such as government-subsidized hous-

[43] See Gale 1985 and Chapter 11.
[44] Loh 1984.

ing, the conversion of land held under temporary licenses to long-term leases, tin-washing licenses, government scholarships, loans for students, and so on. As Lee and Ong put it, "unhappy as the Chinese may be with the MCA [about] issues such as education, the dissatisfaction is of less importance than are the water supply, electricity and land."[45] Chinese voters also looked to the MCA for personal protection against unfavorable administrative decisions such as the transfer of a schoolteacher, the withdrawal of a license for a petrol kiosk, or the interpretation of building regulations.

Gerakan. Gerakan was founded as a multiracial party in 1968. Its core group came from the United Democratic Party (UDP), which had been formed by MCA rebel Lim Chong Eu in 1961; but support also came from moderate former members of the Labour Party such as Tan Chee Khoon, trade unionists including V. David, and intellectuals such as Wang Gung Wu and Syed Hussein Alatas. Gerakan benefited from the Labour Party's boycott of the 1969 election, which enabled it to win control of the Penang state government for the opposition. But the party's electoral success harmed its multicommunal image because clearly its main base of support was in the Chinese community; and in 1971 the main non-Chinese leaders, including Syed Hussein Alatas and V. David, left the party.

Gerakan never abandoned its multicommunal ideology and, unlike the MCA, remained open to non-Chinese members. In practice, however, the party became increasingly identified with the Chinese community. It had initially appealed to the better-educated, English-speaking Chinese; but it soon realized that future expansion depended on winning the support of the "Chinese" Chinese. This meant competing with the MCA's unabashed emphasis on its Chinese character.

The increasing Chinese-ness of Gerakan made it a natural home for MCA dissidents, whose entry into the party reinforced its Chinese character. The departure of its own dissidents in 1971, including former Labour Party leaders, left Gerakan clearly under the control of the ex-UDP group that had left the MCA after the 1959 crisis. They were soon joined by a second wave of dissidents who were expelled from the MCA following their challenge to its leadership in 1973. The next wave came in 1981 when Michael Chen and his supporters transferred their loyalties to the party. The identification of Gerakan with the Chinese community became even stronger in 1982 when it recruited several prominent activists in the Chinese education movement, including Koh Tsu Koon, who eventually succeeded Lim Chong Eu as chief minister of Penang in 1990. In practice,

[45] Lee and Ong 1987:138.

there was little to distinguish Gerakan from the MCA, as shown by the ease and frequency with which individual dissidents switched from one party to the other. Nevertheless, Gerakan continued to have a sprinkling of non-Chinese leaders.

MIC. The MIC, the other substantial non-Malay peninsular party, was formed in 1946 and joined the original Alliance before the 1955 election. Unlike the Chinese community, which makes up the majority of voters in some constituencies and large minorities in others, the Indians were a majority nowhere. Therefore, the bargaining position of the MIC is not strong, although it has always been represented in the national cabinet.

In the 1950s and 60s the MIC was able to mobilize the Indian plantation labor force to vote for the government. But as the proportion of Indians working on plantations declined, it had to find ways of winning the votes of urban Indians as well. Party President Tun Sambanthan, whose support came largely from plantation labor, was challenged and eventually replaced in 1973 by his deputy, V. Manickavasagam, whose base lay more with urban workers. Sharp factional rivalries continued under Manickavasagam and came to a head in 1977 in a bitter contest for the deputy presidency between Samy Vellu, a wheeler-dealer populist from Perak, and S. Subramaniam, the young, university-educated, secretary-general of the party. Samy Vellu won and later succeeded to the party leadership when Manickavasagam died in 1979. But the rivalry between the Samy Vellu and Subramaniam factions continued with unabated ferocity and still preoccupied the party at the beginning of the 1990s. There appeared to be no ideological differences between the two factions.

Despite its internal rivalries the MIC continued to garner a large majority, perhaps 70–80 percent, of Indian votes in elections.[46] As a small minority, the Indians, unlike the Chinese, seemed to be less confident about standing on their own feet and apparently felt the need for leaders who had close ties with the government. Indian plantation workers, in particular, were easily mobilized to support the MIC because they needed patrons to protect them in times of need and were vulnerable to retribution if they sided with the opposition. Unlike the Chinese, whose contacts with relatives in China had been cut or become tenuous during the period of China's isolation, Indians often maintained close ties with their ancestral villages. Many men married women from India, leading to all sorts of difficulties in regard to immigration and citizenship for which they needed the MIC's assistance.

[46] In 1990 the MIC claimed that 72 percent of Indian voters were actually members of the party. It aimed to raise the percentage to 85 percent. *NST* 20 May 1990.

The East Malaysian Parties

From the perspective of the Malay elite in Kuala Lumpur, the main reason for bringing the Borneo states into the Malaysian federation in 1963 was to strengthen the indigenous side of the ethnic balance, which would have been upset if Singapore had joined the federation alone. Therefore, the East Malaysian states were given more seats in the national Parliament than was justified by the size of their populations. The expulsion of Singapore from the new federation in 1965 left the East Malaysian states even more overrepresented. This overrepresentation was preserved because UMNO leaders in Kuala Lumpur assumed that the indigenous parties in East Malaysia would naturally align with UMNO in national politics. But indigenous politics in East Malaysia had its own dynamic and by no means conformed fully to the peninsular pattern.[47]

The ethnic makeup of the East Malaysian states was quite different from the peninsula's. As in the peninsula, the Chinese constituted a substantial minority—32 percent in Sarawak and 23 percent in Sabah at the time of merger with Malaysia in 1963—but the bumiputera population in both states was much more diverse. A substantial part of the indigenous population was non-Muslim. In Sarawak, the non-Muslim Iban (Sea Dayaks) were the largest indigenous group, making up 31 percent of the total population, while the Bidayuh (Land Dayaks) made up about 8 percent. In Sabah the mainly non-Muslim Kadazan or Dusun made up 32 percent and the Muruts another 5 percent. Indigenous Muslims also formed a large community. In Sarawak the Muslim Malay and Melanau groups together constituted 23 percent, while in Sabah Muslim bumiputeras made up about 30 percent. In addition, nearly 10 percent of the population of Sabah consisted of Indonesian or Filipino immigrants who were also almost all Muslim.[48] By 1980, heavy proselytization by the Tun Mustapha government and increased migration from the southern Philippines brought the Muslim population of Sabah up to 51.3 percent, although a substantial proportion were not citizens.[49] Thus, in each state there were substantial Chinese, non-Muslim bumiputera, and Muslim bumiputera communities. In contrast to the peninsula, however, the balance between ethnic groups did not facilitate the emergence of a natural majority in either state.

In Sabah, the Sabah Alliance, based on the peninsular model, was

---

[47] Among the early studies of East Malaysian politics are Milne and Ratnam 1974; Roff 1974; Leigh 1974.

[48] Bedlington 1978:131. See also Roff 1974:19–31.

[49] NST 28 April 1985. (Supriya Singh, "Drawing the Line between Indigenous and Non-indigenous"). Heavy pressure was applied on Kadazans and Muruts to "convert" to Islam. Financial incentives were also given. See Hussin 1990:91; Ross-Larson 1976:107–9; Roff 1974:111–12.

formed. By the late 1960s it was completely dominated by Tun Mustapha Datu Harun's United Sabah National Organisation (USNO) with its base in the Muslim community. The Alliance also included the Sabah Chinese Association (SCA), and an earlier Kadazan party had dissolved itself and been absorbed by USNO. USNO leader Tun Mustapha, initially with the backing of Kuala Lumpur, ruled in blatantly authoritarian style; but by 1975 the federal government was unhappy with his support for the Muslim rebellion in the southern Philippines, his reluctance to cooperate with Kuala Lumpur, and perhaps his extravagant misuse of resources. Prime Minister Tun Razak therefore encouraged the formation of a new party of USNO dissidents. Berjaya (Bersatu Rakyat Jelata Sabah, or the United Common People of Sabah) was led by a leading Kadazan politician, Tun Fuad Stephens (previously Donald Stephens before his conversion to Islam). After Mustapha was deprived by the federal government of most of his authoritarian powers, Berjaya defeated USNO in an election held in 1976.[50] Although it had strong Kadazan support, Berjaya was a multiethnic party with important Muslim and Chinese leaders; and its electoral victory was partly due to its capacity to attract crucial Chinese votes. Following the death of Tun Fuad in an airplane crash not long after the election, his place as chief minister was taken by Datuk Harris Salleh, a Muslim. Berjaya was accepted as a member of the BN in 1975 at a time when USNO's status in the front was ambiguous, thus allowing Berjaya to escape the veto that all BN members had over new members. In 1976 an arrangement was worked out whereby both parties were recognized as members of the BN. Both were represented in the national government, but at the state level Berjaya formed the government and USNO was the opposition.

During the next decade the Berjaya government stayed in power through a combination of authoritarian measures and patronage distribution, but by the mid-1980s its reputation for corruption and mismanagement of resources rivaled Tun Mustapha's. As in 1975, a new Kadazanbased party, Parti Bersatu Sabah (PBS, or United Sabah Party), emerged under the leadership of ruling-party dissidents. This time, however, they were not supported by the federal government. Prime Minister Mahathir even declared during the 1985 state election campaign that the BN "would sink or swim with Berjaya."[51] Despite the national BN's support for Berjaya, PBS won by attracting not only Kadazan but also Chinese votes. Like Berjaya, PBS was a multicommunal party, although its main base of support lay in the Kadazan community and many of its leaders were Christian. USNO, in the meantime, consolidated its position as the main Muslim

[50] Ross-Larson 1976:chs. 8–10; Means 1991:40–45.
[51] Chung 1987:55.

party.[52] Following a second electoral success in 1986, PBS was accepted into the BN to sit alongside USNO at the national level (although Berjaya withdrew in protest), while it resisted pressure from Kuala Lumpur to form a coalition government with USNO at the state level.[53]

Relations between PBS and the central government remained cool, and in 1990 PBS suddenly withdrew from the BN and joined Tengku Razaleigh's opposition coalition several days before the election. Feeling betrayed, Mahathir's government attempted to undermine the PBS state government by depriving it of development funds, charging Chief Minister Joseph Pairin Kitingan with corruption and arresting several of his close associates, including his brother Jeffrey, under the ISA.[54] In 1991 UMNO, cooperating with USNO, set up a branch in Sabah; but UMNO's challenge to PBS was undermined in 1992 when USNO aligned itself with PBS. Finally, although the PBS-led government won a narrow victory in a state election held in February 1994, the UMNO-led opposition quickly enticed several members of PBS—including Jeffrey Kitingan, who had recently been released from detention but still faced corruption charges—to cross to the UMNO side. This move resulted in the fall of the PBS government and the establishment of an UMNO-led coalition government.[55]

In Sarawak, too, an attempt was made to form a Sarawak Alliance in the early 1960s; but this was complicated at first by rivalries within ethnic groups. The Sarawak Alliance initially included two Muslim-Malay parties, two non-Muslim indigenous parties, and a Chinese party, while another predominantly Chinese party remained outside and a Chinese-based Communist insurgency continued in the jungles. Following the federal government's use of emergency provisions to dismiss the chief minister in 1966, his Iban-based party, the Sarawak National Party (SNAP), left the Alliance while the two Muslim-Malay parties merged to form the Parti Bumiputera (Bumiputera Party). With Kuala Lumpur's backing, the Parti Bumiputera became the dominant force in the Sarawak Alliance—in a position similar to USNO's in Sabah at the same time, although without Tun Mustapha's dictatorial powers.

In Sabah, Tun Mustapha brooked no opposition and normally prevented even the nomination of opposition candidates in elections. But the balance between parties in Sarawak was fluid. Following racial rioting in Kuala Lumpur in the wake of the 1969 election, voting had been suspended in Sabah and Sarawak. When the elections were eventually held in

---

[52] For a discussion of the growing sense of Kadazan ethnic identity, see Loh 1992.

[53] See Means 1991:153–65.

[54] See Kahin 1992.

[55] In June 1994 Jeffrey Kitingan was appointed a deputy minister in the central government. Ten days earlier the high court had acquitted him of corruption charges, which were withdrawn, without explanation, by the prosecution. *NST* 15, 19, 25 June 1994.

1970, the federal government needed convincing victories in Sabah and Sarawak to ensure that it retained the two-thirds majority in parliament that allowed it to amend the constitution at will. While Mustapha could be relied upon to return a full slate of Sabah Alliance candidates, in Sarawak the leftist, Chinese-based opposition party, Sarawak United People's Party (SUPP), had strong influence. The federal government therefore successfully applied pressure on both Parti Bumiputera and SUPP to form a coalition, which presaged a series of coalitions with opposition parties on the peninsula and the eventual formation of the BN. In 1973 Pesaka, the smaller, non-Muslim indigenous party in the Sarawak Alliance, merged with the Muslims in Parti Bumiputera to form Parti Pesaka Bumiputera Bersatu (PBB, or United Bumiputera Pesaka Party); and in 1976 the Iban-based SNAP returned to the fold.[56]

The composition of the BN in Sarawak remained stable until 1983 when a split occurred in SNAP. Although SNAP drew most of its support from Ibans, it was open to non-Ibans, including Chinese who provided the party with most of its funds. When a prominent Chinese, Datuk James Wong, was elected president of the party, however, many younger Ibans were dissatisfied and eventually set up a rival party, Parti Bansa Dayak Sarawak (PBDS, or Sarawak Dayak Party) under the leadership of Datuk Leo Moggie, a member of the federal cabinet hitherto representing SNAP. PBDS adopted a policy of "Dayakism," demanding a better deal for non-Muslim bumiputeras. When PBDS performed well in the 1983 Sarawak state election, it was accepted into the BN. Later, following conflict within the state coalition, it withdrew at the state level, although it remained in the BN at the national level.[57]

Thus, politics in East Malaysia, were by no means a simple reflection of national politics in Kuala Lumpur. As in Kuala Lumpur, most political parties drew their main support from particular ethnic communities; but the boundaries were not as sharply drawn as in the peninsula. The Muslim-dominated USNO in Sabah was able to absorb an earlier Kadazan party in the 1960s, and in Sarawak the Muslim-dominated PBB was formed in 1973 as a result of a merger between a strong Muslim party and a smaller non-Muslim bumiputera party. In Sabah both Berjaya and PBS were multicommunal parties with Muslim, Kadazan and Chinese leaders, although their main support came from the Kadazans. In Sarawak the Chinese-dominated SUPP had Iban members, and the predominantly Iban SNAP had Chinese members—and in the 1980s even a Chinese president.

As in the peninsula, the parties were dominated by the elites of the ethnic communities; but the low level of political sophistication and mobiliza-

---

[56] On SNAP and Iban politics generally, see Searle 1983.
[57] See Means 1991:165–72. It rejoined the state BN in 1994.

tion of the indigenous communities meant that elites were under less pressure to ensure the material well-being of ordinary voters.[58] In East Malaysia, patronage politics was concentrated on the elite and revolved to a large extent around timber concessions, which were used to consolidate political support from the elite of all ethnic communities.[59] In Sabah the British had attempted to build up the indigenous elite toward the end of the colonial era by awarding big timber concessions to several political leaders, including Mustapha and Stephens. In the 1970s and 80s timber concessions continued to be the most important reward for political support, no matter which party was in power.[60] Similarly, in Sarawak many political leaders from each of the ethnic communities received timber concessions, which tied them to the government that awarded them.[61] One consequence of timber politics was the tendency for members of defeated parties to cross to the government side following elections.

In general, the main bumiputera parties, both Muslim and non-Muslim, fulfilled their expected function of bolstering the BN's majority in the national parliament until 1990, when PBS aligned itself with the opposition. But sharp rivalries continued between them at the state level. In both states it was common for a plethora of "independent" candidates to contest each election, many in fact being proxies for BN parties that hoped to defeat official BN candidates representing a rival party. Rivalries between BN parties were so sharp that in both states there were parties that were BN components at the national level but functioned as opposition parties at the state level.

Malaysia's ruling coalition has remained remarkably cohesive since independence. The BN, like the Alliance before it, was in fact more than a mere coalition of parties working together. In a sense it constituted a party in its own right. It had its own constitution, and in elections it behaved like a single party by putting forward a common team of candidates contesting under a common banner. Once elected, BN members were expected to support common policies and submit to party discipline. But the BN was not really a party because it was made up of distinct parties that maintained their separate identities, were based in different communities, and pursued interests that were often in conflict with each other.[62]

[58] See Milne 1973.

[59] Milne and Ratnam 1974:315–19.

[60] See, for example, Hunter 1976, especially ch. 4, "The Rape of Sabah's Timber Resources," and ch. 5, "How Easy It Is to Obtain Timberland from Tun Mustapha."

[61] In 1987, rivalry between Yang di-Pertua Negeri (governor) and former chief minister Tun Datuk Patinggi Abdul Rahman Yaakub and his nephew, the current chief minister, Datuk Patinggi Amar Taib Mahmud, rose to a point where each camp used newspapers under its control to publicize lists of timber concessions held by members of the other camp. Both lists are reproduced in Ritchie 1987:95–102.

[62] In Horowitz's terms, the BN was a multi-ethnic alliance, not a multi-ethnic coalition or a multi-ethnic party. Horowitz 1985:396–98.

The BN possessed an effective electoral machine that virtually guaranteed large majorities for the government in the national and most state parliaments. As a result, it might appear that the government would feel little need to respond to popular pressures from society. While the BN itself enjoyed an overwhelming majority, however, its constituent parties still had strong incentives to win more seats to bolster their bargaining positions vis-à-vis other BN parties. Individual BN parties could not afford to ignore popular pressures and therefore felt compelled to respond to demands emanating from their respective communities.

The responsiveness of the BN parties to societal pressures was further enhanced by intraparty rivalries. Intraparty factionalism normally centered on personal rivalries and the distribution of patronage rather than party goals and policies. But to win grassroots votes, contestants for party positions had to respond to grassroots aspirations and expectations. UMNO contenders had to present themselves as not only dedicated to the Malay cause but also attentive to local demands. In non-Malay parties, challengers usually won support by accusing incumbents of failing to protect non-Malay interests at all levels. Intraparty competition, therefore, forced contestants for party positions to be somewhat responsive to the demands and expectations of their grassroots supporters.

While UMNO's domination of the BN ensured that Malay interests would always be emphasized by the government, non-Malay interests could not be totally ignored. The BN was not a tightly knit organization bound by common goals and perceptions. Despite its dominant position, UMNO was not always able to run roughshod over the interests represented by the other parties but had to consult and negotiate with them. At the root of UMNO's willingness to consider its partners' demands was its awareness of the BN's need for non-Malay votes in elections.

The BN parties, however, were by no means fully responsive to pressures from society. As we shall see in Chapters 4 and 5, it often resorted to authoritarian measures to consolidate its power by restricting political competition. Nevertheless, its own internal divisions virtually ruled out the possibility of establishing a fully authoritarian regime. The BN was cohesive enough to defeat opposition parties in elections but not enough to repress opposition altogether.

4 Opposition Parties
and Elections

THE MALAYSIAN ELECTORAL SYSTEM greatly favored the government at the expense of the opposition, and the ruling coalition won all national and almost all state elections since independence. The BN's continuing success was partly due to its ability to attract a majority of votes, including a substantial share of the votes from each major community. In the 1970s and 80s it normally won about three-fifths of the votes cast, although its share fell in the 1990 election. The opposition parties, despite limited co-operation in 1990, were generally unable to form an effective counteralliance, partly because they tended to rely on ethnic appeals to one community or another. In addition, the electoral system was heavily weighted in favor of the government, with the result that the number of seats won by opposition parties did not reflect their popular support. Further, as we shall see in Chapter 5, various limitations were placed on the scope that opposition parties had to mobilize popular support.

Despite the bias of the electoral system Malaysian elections were contested vigorously by opposition parties. There was virtually no chance that the government would be defeated; nevertheless, individual members of the ruling coalition often faced stiff fights to retain their seats. Moreover, the government targeted two-thirds of the seats for itself (the proportion required to change the constitution) and thus was under more pressure to attract support than would have been necessary if it had been satisfied merely to win with a comfortable majority. At the state level, the BN usually won almost all the seats in some states; but in others the opposition posed a real threat. Elections, therefore, were meaningful contests even if the outcome for the BN was never seriously in doubt.

The Electoral System

Malaysian elections have not been characterized by widespread fraudulent practices such as ballot-box stuffing or blatant physical pressure on voters, and there has been no serious legal barrier to parties wishing to contest—with the exception of the Communist Party (CPM) and the Labour Party, which the government believed had been infiltrated by Communists. But the electoral system was significantly biased in favor of Malay parties and the government coalition.

Malay political preeminence was based on the changing ethnic balance of the population. In 1957 the Malay and non-Malay populations of Malaya (that is, the peninsula) were more or less evenly divided; the Malays, together with the small aboriginal population, made up slightly less than 50 percent. But by 1985 the Malay proportion had grown to 56.5 percent.[1] The 1963 entry of Sabah and Sarawak into the federation, combined with Singapore's exit in 1965, further strengthened the indigenous communities politically. The bumiputera population of the country as a whole expanded to 60 percent by 1985.[2] The ethnic balance moved further in the Malay direction during the 1970s and 80s when as many as one million Indonesian and Muslim-Filipino workers came to Malaysia, many of them illegally and often not recorded in census statistics.[3]

Initially, the slight population disadvantage of the Malays was more than balanced by their advantage in terms of citizenship. In the 1950s virtually all Malays were citizens, while a substantial proportion of non-Malays were not. In fact, Malays made up 84.2 percent of the electorate in 1955.[4] After independence, however, the proportion of non-Malay voters increased steadily as the older generation of noncitizens gradually died and the Malaya-born generation of citizens came of age and became eligible to vote. Malay predominance in the peninsular electorate declined sharply, the proportion falling to 54.4 percent in 1964, although it rose again to 57.9 percent in 1974 before gradually declining to 55.2 percent in 1990—equal to the proportion of Malays at the time of the most recent census in 1980. In the case of the Chinese, the proportion of the electorate was less than the proportion in the population by 2.5 percent in 1959 but exceeded it by 0.6 percent in 1964. It continued to rise until, by 1990, Chinese made up 35.7 percent of the voters, 1.8 percent more than their proportion of the population. In the case of Indians and "others," the proportion of

[1] Ratnam 1965:1; 5MP:129.
[2] 5MP:129.
[3] Hugo 1993:45.
[4] Ratnam 1965:187.

voters was 5 percent less than the proportion of the population in 1964 but only 1.7 percent less in 1990.[5] The overwhelming majority of non-Malays had been citizens and voters since the 1960s.

There was occasional evidence of manipulation of electoral enrollment to the advantage of the Malays. Between the 1969 and 1974 elections, for example, the Malay proportion of the electorate increased from 55.7 to 57.9 percent while the Chinese proportion fell from 36.3 to 34.5 percent. This sudden change may have been due to an improperly implemented revision of the electoral registers, which removed about 400,000 names, many of whom were eligible to vote. Apparently, more non-Malay than Malay names were removed. Whether this happened as a result of a deliberate directive or was due to overenthusiasm on the part of middle-level Malay officials was never clarified because the government refused to reveal the contents of a report by an investigating committee.[6] Even the pro-government *New Straits Times* was prompted to comment editorially that "without doubt the Election Commission slipped up on its job of voter registration."[7]

Malay predominance in the electorate, however, did not depend on numbers alone. Of more importance was the delineation of constituency boundaries. The 1957 constitution had accepted the principle that there should be some weight in favour of the rural areas because of size and difficulties of communication compared to urban constituencies. But it had limited the disparity to no more than 15 percent from the size of the average constituency. A constitutional amendment in 1962, however, allowed rural constituencies to have as little as half the voters in urban constituencies; and in 1973 the restriction on the extent of disparity between constituencies was abolished altogether.[8] Thus, in 1982 the largest peninsular constituency, Petaling in Selangor with 114,704 voters, had more than four times as many voters as Kuala Krai in Kelantan, where there were only 24,445 voters. The gap was reduced after a new delineation of boundaries in 1986. Nevertheless, the largest constituency in 1990, Selayang in Selangor with 100,488 voters, was still much larger than the smallest, Gua Musang in Kelantan with only 31,064.[9] The political significance of the disparity between rural and urban constituencies lay, of course, in the fact that the rural areas were predominantly Malay and the urban areas predominantly non-Malay. In the 1964 election, Malays formed absolute majorities in only 57 percent of peninsular constituencies (59 out of

---

[5] Sothi 1993:112–13.
[6] Sothi 1980:265–68.
[7] *NST* 5 September 1974.
[8] Sothi 1980:271–75.
[9] These figures refer to the peninsula. Many constituencies were even smaller in East Malaysia, the smallest in 1990 being Hulu Rejang in Sarawak with only 14,004 voters.

104). By 1978 this figure had risen to 69 percent (79 out of 114) and, after the 1986 revision, to 70 percent (92 out of 132). It remained at 70 percent (101 of 144) in 1995.[10]

Since 1963 the bias of the electoral system against non-bumiputeras in the peninsula was reinforced by the inclusion of the two East Malaysian states. Under the terms of the agreement on the formation of Malaysia, Sabah was allocated sixteen seats and Sarawak twenty-four in the national Parliament. With only 15.6 percent of the population, the East Malaysian states had 26 percent of the seats in Parliament.[11] In 1986 the new federal territory of Labuan was represented by one seat, and four more seats were awarded to Sabah. Sarawak's allocation was increased by three in 1990, giving East Malaysia a total of forty-eight parliamentary seats or 27 percent. As expected, the bumiputera majorities in both states generally (although not always) aligned themselves politically with the peninsular Malays.

Thus, the electoral system contained built-in advantages for the Malay community. There was no realistic possibility of a non-bumiputera party's or coalition's "going it alone" and winning an election. The only way for Chinese and Indian politicians to participate in government was by allying themselves with Malays, inevitably as junior partners. In practice, only two types of government could emerge from elections: an all-Malay government or a Malay-dominated coalition.

The electoral system ensured Malay domination, but it did not guarantee victory for the current governing coalition. While conducting elections, however, the government had a variety of subtle and not-so-subtle ways to make it easier for its own candidates to succeed. When examined separately, the many regulations and practices were not always manifestly unfair; but taken together they constituted a substantial barrier for opposition parties. Especially after 1969, elections were held in circumstances very unfavorable for the opposition.

The 1974 election was held in an atmosphere very different from that of 1969. The rioting was still fresh in the minds of non-Malays; and PAS, the major Malay opposition party in 1969, had since joined the governing BN. The dispirited character of the opposition was shown by the fact that the BN won 47 of the 154 parliamentary seats uncontested. By 1978, however, PAS had been expelled from the BN while non-Malay resentment against the NEP had boosted the prospects of the DAP. This time the government could not expect to win forty-seven seats uncontested. Unlike earlier elections, when it was common for officials to help candidates

---

[10] Ratnam and Milne 1967:368; Ismail Kassim 1979:3; Sankaran and Mohd Hamdan 1988:46; *NST* 27 April 1995.
[11] Sothi 1980:275.

complete their nomination papers by correcting technical errors, all nomination forms in 1978 were subjected to rigorous examination, leading to the disqualification of fifty-one parliamentary and seventy-two state candidates. Among the errors leading to disqualification were mistakes in the identity-card numbers of proposers or seconders, misspelling of names, and the failure to write "none" in the alias column even when the candidate had no other names.[12] Some candidates were disqualified due to mistakes or omissions on one form, which had to be submitted in triplicate, although the other two forms were completed correctly.[13] Among those disqualified were one BN parliamentary candidate and two state candidates, but the rest were from the opposition or independents. The DAP lost seven parliamentary and eighteen state candidates, while a substantial number of PAS candidates were also disqualified.[14] It seemed reasonable to conclude that BN candidates had been forewarned to take special care in filling in the forms and opposition candidates had been caught unprepared.[15] In later elections, disqualification of nominations returned to the low pre-1978 level; and in 1986 the regulations were amended to make disqualification less likely.[16]

After 1974 the government restricted the opposition's prospects of mobilizing support by banning open-air public rallies.[17] The ban favored the BN, which was still able to use government-owned radio and television and had the support of most of the press. The opposition parties had relied most on rallies. Now they were only permitted to hold indoor *ceramah* (talk) sessions with much smaller audiences. The ban was relaxed after UMNO split in the late 1980s to allow Prime Minister Mahathir to address what were called *semarak* (national pride) rallies. According to Deputy Minister for Home Affairs Datuk Megat Junid, these rallies were "not politically-oriented but aimed at enhancing understanding between the various races and instilling in the people a sense of loyalty to the Rulers and the country."[18]

Although the government provided limited time for political parties to campaign on radio, live broadcasts were not permitted and texts had to be submitted in advance. According to the rules, neither the government nor the opposition parties were permitted to campaign on television. In prac-

[12] *Star* 23 June 1978; *NST* 8 September 1978.

[13] *NST* 10 November 1978.

[14] *Star* 24 June 1978.

[15] See Sothi 1993:124–32.

[16] Ibid.:131–32. Twelve parliamentary and seventeen state candidates were disqualified in 1982 and no parliamentary and six state candidates in 1986. But in 1995, Kua Kia Soong, a prominent DAP candidate, was disqualified when one of three copies of his nomination form was not signed by a witness although the other two were properly signed.

[17] Ong 1980:151.

[18] *NST* 12 October 1988.

tice, however, the two government channels and the UMNO-controlled private channel (established in 1983) devoted much of their news programs and election coverage to promoting the government's achievements and pouring scorn on the opposition.

The government, like governments everywhere, was always in a position to make promises to the voters that could not be matched by the opposition. As elections approached, it was normal for the government to promise funds for local development projects such as roads, bridges, electricity, schools, mosques, and so on with the implication that funds would not be made available in constituencies that returned opposition candidates.[19] Although Prime Minister Mahathir assured voters that "we have always carried out development, even in opposition areas," local leaders often created a different impression.[20] In Perak, for example, the Menteri Besar, Tan Sri Ramli Ngah Taib, told voters in one constituency that "if you don't have a Government representative here, you will be left behind while the country progresses."[21] Tengku Razaleigh, who managed the UMNO electoral machine in its contests with PAS in Kelantan, was even more blunt. New development projects would not be carried out in constituencies that elected PAS members, he warned, when he was still in UMNO in 1982.[22]

In 1990 the government amended the Elections Act to enable votes to be counted at polling stations. Under the old system ballot boxes were brought to a central counting hall in each constituency. The government claimed that this change would reduce the possibility of interference with ballot boxes in transit.[23] The Election Commission then decided to increase the number of polling stations so that only seven hundred voters would be enrolled at each station. According to the secretary of the Election Commission, "we do not want the voters to wait in long queues, especially under the burning sun."[24] But the opposition parties were quick to point out that the new arrangements would make it easy for the government to pinpoint areas that had voted for the opposition. Voters might

[19] Dr. Mahathir had lost his seat in the 1969 election but had since made sure that his constituency, Kubang Pasu, located on the Thai-Malaysia border, was not neglected. As the *New Straits Times* pointed out before the 1990 election, "where else in the country can one find a district which has a $580 million university, a polytechnic, a duty-free zone, an industrial training institute, a teacher training institute, a Mardi research centre, a sprawling youth centre, *Pusat Giat Mara,* industries and expressways? And the list continues." *NST* 9 October 1990. The newspaper's comment was intended as praise, not criticism. Mahathir had argued in 1970 that "the most damaging thing about these hand-outs was the discrimination in favour of known party supporters or party strongholds. This blatant partiality evoked the most bitter resentment against the Government and ensured that those opposed to the Government remained permanently so." Mahathir 1970:13.

[20] *NST* 13 January 1985.

[21] *NST* 28 August 1990.

[22] *UM* 25 May 1982.

[23] *Star* 16 March 1990.

[24] *NST* 22 August 1990.

therefore be reluctant to vote against the government for fear of retaliation.

As another incentive to support the BN, the government in the mid-1970s began providing special funds that BN members of Parliament and state assemblies could allocate for "minor projects" in their constituencies. Although proposals had to be made through the district office, the local member effectively controlled allocations for projects such as the construction and repair of minor roads, small bridges, drains, mosques, community halls, and sporting facilities. By the 1980s, funds placed at the discretion of members of Parliament amounted to $200,000, while state assembly members received $75,000–100,000 with an additional $30,000 for religious projects.[25] These funds were not available to opposition party members and were withdrawn from BN members who crossed to the opposition.[26]

UMNO was able to use its control of the government to win votes in other ways. When explaining how UMNO had been able to defeat PAS in the 1978 election, Tengku Razaleigh revealed how recruitment to land projects had been used to increase support for UMNO. For example, "in cases where PAS had a majority of eighty votes in the last election, I brought in one hundred [new UMNO-supporting] families. That's how they lost their majority." He also told how all pro-PAS *penghulu* (local officials) and religious officials were replaced by UMNO supporters after the election.[27] Schoolteachers were vulnerable to transfer to outlying regions or even to East Malaysia if they openly supported opposition parties.

Government machinery at the local level was regularly mobilized during election campaigns. Following the split in UMNO in 1988, the Menteri Besar of Melaka, Datuk Seri Rahim Thamby Chik, warned that penghulus, special-information officers, community-development officers, members of Village Development and Security Committees, and district and municipal councilors would all be replaced if they did not support the new UMNO. In 1990 Minister of Education Anwar Ibrahim said that "all *penghulu* and *penggawa* [local officials] are responsible for explaining to the people about national development, especially rebutting the wild accusations of the opposition."[28] Of particular importance was the Information Ministry. Just before the 1974 election, for example, several UMNO officials were seconded to the special division of the ministry to coordinate civics courses in which government policies were to be explained.[29] In a

---

[25] *NST* 27 June 1983, 10 June 1988. In 1983 these allocations were frozen because of an economic slowdown.

[26] *NST* 9 June 1988.

[27] *UM* 22 April 1981.

[28] *UM* 28 July 1990; *NST* 11 June 1988.

[29] Funston 1980:238. See also Rogers 1992:123–24.

series of three crucial by-elections in 1988 after UMNO split, the government admitted that the Information Ministry had spent $172,000 "to encourage the voters to go to the polls"; and the deputy minister of information added that "the Information Department is also responsible to explain to the public the government's policy to ensure that there is no misunderstanding."[30] The government had plenty of help on its local campaigns from government employees attached to the Community Development Program (Kemas, or Kemajuan Masyarakat) under the Ministry of Rural and National Development. Kemas involved adult-education classes in civics and useful skills such as cooking, nutrition, and hygiene; but in practice Kemas workers were full-time propagandists for the government, and officers were normally party activists.

In an important August 1990 by-election for a state seat (Kijal in Terengganu), UMNO introduced a new tactic in its struggle with the newly formed Semangat '46. Kijal was an almost entirely Malay rural constituency. In the weeks before the by-election the state government sent about two thousand young women who had been participating in a State Economic Planning Unit scheme for unemployed youth to live in the constituency as "adopted daughters" in families considered to be swing voters. The adopted daughters lived with the families, who were compensated with $200 and expected to vote for UMNO. Voters who still seemed doubtful as the day of the election approached were taken to a live-in course at an Inspirational Center (Pusat Pupuk Semangat) and escorted by their adopted daughter to the polling booth on election day.[31] UMNO won the by-election and later used the adopted-daughter strategy in other by-elections in rural east-coast constituencies.

Although the government used its administrative machinery to enhance its electoral prospects, the opposition was nevertheless permitted to field candidates and campaign for them. Only in Sabah during the rule of Tun Mustapha (from 1967 to 1975) were violations of democratic practice so flagrant that elections lost their meaning. When Sabah participated for the first time in a national election in 1969, opposition candidates managed to file nominations in only six of the sixteen constituencies, the rest being disqualified for one reason or another. In 1974 only one opposition candidate succeeded in being nominated. The leaders of an opposition party were said to have been bribed to abandon their challenge while supporters of another party, the peninsula-based Pekemas, were physically intimidated by Mustapha's men. In fact, several potential candidates were ar-

[30] *NST* 10 December 1988.
[31] *Watan* 16 August 1990 (Ahmad Shabery Cheek, "Kijal: Siapakah Yang Boleh Berbangga?"). Ahmad Shabery was the defeated Semangat '46 candidate. The account in *Watan* has been supplemented with details obtained in an interview with Ahmad Shabery in August 1990.

rested on nomination day. The single Pekemas candidate who succeeded in lodging his nomination was "persuaded" to withdraw his candidature before election day, thus enabling the government party to win all sixteen seats unopposed.[32] Competitive elections were only restored in Sabah after Mustapha was dislodged from power in 1975. Nevertheless, some of the practices of the Mustapha era continued. For example, the new Berjaya government under Datuk Harris Salleh used its immigration powers to prevent top DAP leaders from campaigning in the state. During the 1978 election, when DAP leader Lim Kit Siang attempted to defy the ban, he was physically carried back to his airplane after his arrival at Kota Kinabalu airport.[33]

The Opposition Parties

Opposition parties have always maintained solid if limited bases of support in both the Malay and non-Malay communities; but unlike the government parties, they have not been able to work out enduring cooperative arrangements among themselves, although occasional temporary understandings have been reached during particular elections. The essential problem has been that, in order to mobilize votes in a communal society, the parties have had to stress communal issues that by their nature appeal only to one community. Thus, when PAS accused the government of failing to give sufficient emphasis to Islam, it could hardly expect to attract non-Muslim voters. Similarly, when the non-Malay parties opposed the increased use of the Malay language, they naturally alienated Malay voters. Experience suggested that the formation of an enduring opposition alliance in these circumstances was inherently improbable.

In considering the opposition parties we will discuss first the main Malay opposition party, PAS, and then the main non-Malay opposition party, the DAP. Discussion of Semangat '46, founded in 1989 after the UMNO split, will be postponed until Chapter 7.

The Malay Opposition

PAS was formed in 1951. It originated in the religious wing of UMNO but was soon taken over by activists from the religious wing of the banned MNP.[34] PAS (or the Pan-Malayan Islamic Party [PMIP] as it was known then) contested the pre-independence 1955 election and won the opposition's sole seat in northern Perak. In the late 1950s the party expanded its

---

[32] Ross-Larson 1976:112–15, 149, 151.
[33] Ong 1980:166.
[34] See Funston 1980:ch. 4.

base of support in Kelantan and Terengganu, two overwhelmingly Malay states in the northeast, and succeeded in winning power in both during the 1959 election. In 1961, however, UMNO managed to entice several PAS members to cross the floor of the state assembly in Terengganu, with the result that the PAS state government fell and was replaced by the Alliance. Meanwhile, PAS remained in control of the state government in Kelantan until 1977 and continued as a major force in Terengganu while it expanded its influence in Kedah and Perlis, the other northern states with large Malay majorities.[35] In 1973 PAS was persuaded to join a coalition with UMNO and was permitted to retain control of the Kelantan state government while being rewarded with positions in the federal ministry and several state executive councils. But the coalition did not last. In 1977 UMNO exploited rivalries within the Kelantan PAS, which resulted in PAS's expulsion from the BN, the collapse of the state government, and the imposition of emergency rule in the state. A subsequent election in 1978 resulted in an UMNO victory.

PAS remained a substantial force within the Malay community as shown by election results following its 1977 departure from the BN. In the 1978, 1982, and 1986 national elections PAS usually won about half the Malay votes in Kelantan, close to half in Kedah, and at least 40 percent in Terengganu and Perlis.[36] In the other states PAS rarely obtained as many as one-third of Malay votes and often less than one-fifth.[37] A similar analysis of PAS's performance in the 1990 and 1995 elections cannot be made because of the party's alliance with Semangat '46. Under the terms of the pact, the number of seats contested by PAS was greatly reduced while party supporters were urged to vote for Semangat '46 candidates where there was no PAS candidate. As a result, the party's share of votes fell drastically, although it won many more seats, especially in Kelantan.

This pattern of voting behavior lends itself to several explanations. First, one could argue that it is natural for a party stressing religion to be more successful in largely rural communities where traditional values remain strong, levels of modern education are low, and local religious functionaries enjoy high prestige.[38] However, it needs to be noted that the spread of modern education in recent decades has not led to a decline in support for PAS. Second, it is possible that the four northern Malay-majority states have a greater sense of separate identity in contrast with other states with large non-Malay communities. Further, they have all been relatively backward in terms of economic development. Thus, support for PAS might be

---

[35] See Firdaus 1980.

[36] In 1990 Malays constituted 94 percent of voters in Terengganu, 93 percent in Kelantan, 82 percent in Perlis, and 74 percent in Kedah.

[37] On the methodology of these calculations see Crouch 1982:43.

[38] Ratnam 1965:165–69.

interpreted as a demand for recognition and a protest against being taken for granted by UMNO-dominated Kuala Lumpur.[39] Third, it is reasonable to assume that the pressures on the Malay community to remain united politically would be less strong in states where the overwhelming majority is Malay. In such cases non-Malay political domination—at the state level, at least—is simply not a possibility. In the absence of a threatening non-Malay challenge, factionalism among Malays in the large Malay-majority states could more easily be expressed through rival parties. But in the states where the Malay majority is small or Malays are in a minority, factional conflict tends to be contained within the confines of a single party.

Although PAS was ideologically committed to Islam, in practice it usually campaigned (at least before the 1980s) on Malay communal issues, only some of which were directly concerned with Islam. PAS had been a staunch proponent of the view that the Malays were the owners of the land and thus entitled to special privileges. As an opposition party, it claimed that UMNO had betrayed both the Islamic and Malay struggle through its close association with non-Malay partners in the Alliance. Therefore, many PAS activists were dismayed when the party joined the BN and its leader, Datuk Asri Hj Muda, became a minister in the federal cabinet in 1973. A group of dissident candidates in Kelantan won substantial popular support but no seats in the 1974 election. After its expulsion from the BN in 1977 PAS returned to its old themes; but the emergence of a new generation of better-educated leaders was accompanied by greater stress on PAS's Islamic character. The party's "Young Turks" challenged Asri, who eventually resigned in 1982, thus allowing the party to come under the effective control of men who emphasized Islamic rather than Malay issues.[40] Several were admirers of the recent Islamic revolution in Iran. But they were also pragmatic politicians who, under the leadership of Ustaz Fadzil Noor, entered an alliance in 1990 with Semangat '46 and several small Muslim parties, and indirectly with DAP which had formed a separate alliance with Semangat '46.

The cooperation between PAS and Semangat '46 bore fruit in the 1990 election when the coalition deprived UMNO of all its seats in Kelantan, both at the state and national levels. With twenty-four seats compared to Semangat's fourteen in the state assembly, PAS played the dominant role in the state government. Unlike the PAS government in Kelantan in the

[39] According to Kessler, "seeing the benefits of independence concentrated in the more developed and primarily non-Malay west coast, the Kelantanese resented those Malays who enjoyed power in the new order heedless of the peasantry's concerns." Kessler 1978:121.

[40] See Hussin 1990:ch. 4. The campaign waged against Datuk Asri was very bitter. Asri complained that the "false accusations" made against him by the Young Turks were far worse than any made by UMNO leaders. Interview with Datuk Asri, 26 December 1990. The disaffected Asri later joined UMNO.

1960s, which behaved in much the same way as UMNO governments elsewhere, the new PAS government embarked on an Islamization policy that
included the adoption of Islamic criminal law. The new penal code provided for *hudud* penalties such as amputating the hands of thieves and
executing adulterers.[41] But there was little prospect that the hudud laws
would be implemented: the national constitution set limits on the types of
penalties that could be imposed by state law in criminal matters, and the
national government was not willing to change the constitution.[42] Apparently, the PAS-led government did not originally intend to adopt the Islamic criminal code but did so in response to the BN's goading. In this
way the BN hoped to cause a split between PAS and its coalition partner,
Semangat '46, as well as upset the indirect electoral understanding with
the DAP.[43] Although UMNO failed to break the alliance with Semangat
'46, it succeeded in creating a virtually unbridgeable chasm between PAS
and the DAP.

There are few published studies of the sources of PAS's electoral support. Empirical studies tend to downplay the party's religious character
and portray it as appealing to the interests of its supporters in much the
same way as any other party. Because both its leaders and supporters are
Muslim, it naturally expresses itself in Islamic idiom. PAS describes its
ultimate goal as the establishment of an Islamic state in Malaysia, but at
the same time it responds to the more mundane aspirations of its supporters. In practice, the lines of division in rural Malay communities do not
run along religious lines. Scott's observation that PAS members in the
Kedah village he studied "are no more outwardly observant or orthodox
as a group than members of the ruling party" seems valid for most other
areas as well.[44] UMNO and PAS supporters in the villages are much the
same type of people, and there are no strong religious or cultural barriers
preventing UMNO dissidents from switching to PAS or vice versa as local
factional alignments change.

Studies of local Malay politics usually stress the way in which preexist-
ing factional alignments often lay behind the formation of PAS and
UMNO. In his study in the late 1960s of "Jelawat," a small town in Kelantan, Clive Kessler concluded that "the modern politics of Jelawat resulted
from, and perpetuate, antagonisms engendered during the colonial period."[45] In "Sedaka" in Kedah, Scott noted that "the pattern of village
partisanship has its roots in older, family-based factions that existed well

---

[41] Hudud punishments were those specifically stipulated in the Quran.
[42] See Seda-Poulin 1993.
[43] I gained these impressions from interviews with UMNO and PAS officials in Kelantan
in April 1994.
[44] Scott 1985:134.
[45] Kessler 1978:73.

before the formation of political parties."[46] Shamsul, too, in his study of "Mawar," a community in Kuala Selangor, shows how events in the 1920s and 30s shaped contemporary political alignments. He concludes that "there existed underlying locally-based factors, both class and personal, which seemed to have facilitated PAS's entry into Mawar through Kg. Asal."[47]

Empirical studies have identified class distinctions between UMNO and PAS. UMNO is seen as the party of urban government employees, local entrepreneurs, and well-off peasantry while PAS has its roots among the poor peasants. In Kelantan, according to Kessler, the aristocracy took control of the state UMNO and relied on civil servants, government school-teachers, landlords, and the more affluent peasantry to mobilize votes. In contrast, "smallholders, tenants, and smallholder-tenants alike see the source of their anxiety in the acquisition of land by local rentiers and government officials" who were identified with UMNO.[48] In Kuala Selangor Shamsul also found the local UMNO to be dominated by civil servants, village heads, local petty entrepreneurs, and rich landlords. PAS, on the other hand, was the party of at least one part of the peasantry.[49] In his village in Kedah, Scott found that PAS was supported by 54 percent of the poorest half of the households and only 22 percent of the richest half. A small number of well-off peasants supported PAS because of long-standing family rivalries. In the case of poor peasants who supported UMNO, most had "strong ties of blood, marriage or employment to wealthier UMNO households."[50] But despite its poor-peasant base of support, some of the local PAS leaders were large landholders who, according to Nagata, "are no more in favour of land reform than are their UMNO counterparts."[51]

Class identification, however, cannot fully explain why many rural Malays supported PAS. What Shamsul calls "underlying class tensions" were often "obscured" by factors related to intra- and interparty rivalries.[52] Scott refers to PAS's "considerable moral appeal," which was based on "a fusion of class issues, ethnic and religious sentiment, and a populist opposition to government policy and the inequalities it has fostered." He also acknowledges "the element of sheer pride and stubbornness that [kept] PAS members from switching parties, despite the price they [paid] in foregone patronage."[53] A bit more fancifully, perhaps, Kessler believes

[46] Scott 1985:133.
[47] Shamsul 1986a:161.
[48] Kessler 1978:125. See also Kessler 1974.
[49] Shamsul 1986a:237–39.
[50] Scott 1985:132–33.
[51] Nagata 1984:53. Nagata's view is based on data from an unpublished master's thesis at the Universiti Sains Malaysia written by Mansur Othman.
[52] Shamsul 1986a:238.
[53] Scott 1985:134–35.

that for many peasants in Kelantan, voting for PAS, despite its material futility, was a kind of atonement for religious shortcomings. Many Kelantanese peasants "were aware of their own shortcomings as Muslims, in both knowledge and formal observance. But by renouncing at the ballot box what presented themselves as narrow interests and short-term material gains [that is, UMNO promises], PMIP supporters among the peasantry would experience themselves as approaching those ideal standards of disinterested Muslim conduct that ordinarily they remained far from attaining in their own estimation."[54]

In the 1970s and 80s PAS attracted significant support among urban as well as rural Malays. One could hypothesize that the influx under the NEP of Malay migrants from rural areas to towns changed the political outlook of some urban voters. On one hand, migrants might be more traditionally religious and therefore inclined to support PAS. On the other hand, many new migrants in urban squatter areas might feel disoriented and frustrated in their new environment and therefore inclined to support the opposition. There is little evidence to support or refute either proposition. In one study of Malay voting in the Damansara constituency in Kuala Lumpur in 1978, it was clear that PAS had grown rapidly. Nevertheless, its members seemed to be mainly former UMNO supporters who had been alienated by certain UMNO local leaders or particular policies, although some may have been influenced by the growing Islamic consciousness of the 1970s. In this election, PAS campaigned at the local level largely on Malay communal issues.[55]

The Non-Malay Opposition

In contrast to the Malay community, a large majority of which supported UMNO, and the Indians, who gave overwhelming support to the MIC, the political loyalties of the Chinese community were fragmented, with about half the voters regularly supporting the opposition. The Chinese were divided between those who believed that the community had no alternative to accepting Malay political domination and trying to make the best of it by allying with the dominant Malay party and those who believed that the Chinese should assert themselves in defense of their rights.[56] As we saw in Chapter 3, this division made it easy for dissident

---

[54] Kessler 1978:231. Kessler's symbolic-atonement-through-renunciation theory, however, seems at odds with his class theory. According to the former, the peasant gains atonement through renunciation; according to the latter there is nothing to renounce because the peasant would not have benefited from UMNO's policies in any case.

[55] Mohamed Abu Bakar 1980.

[56] Horowitz has suggested that in the case of the Chinese, "subethnic division, such as religion, language, and ancestral place of origin, play important roles in party affiliation." Horowitz 1985:412. He mentions an early tendency for Hakkas and Hailams to support left-

groups within MCA to mobilize support against incumbents. It also made it easy for opposition politicians to rally support against the government.

During the 1960s non-Malay opposition was channeled through several parties: the union-based Labour Party, the Ipoh-based PPP, Lim Chong Eu's following of MCA dissidents in the UDP, and, after the formation of Malaysia, the peninsular branch of the Singapore PAP. Together, however, they won only six seats in the 1964 election. In the 1969 election the non-Malay opposition parties performed much better. Then Gerakan and PPP joined the new BN in the early 1970s while the Labour Party, which had boycotted the election, was disbanded when many of its leaders were detained under the ISA on the alleged grounds that they were Communists. Thus, the DAP, which was the new name of the PAP in Malaysia after the expulsion of Singapore, became the preeminent party of non-Malay dissent.

Although the DAP got most of its support from non-Malays, especially Chinese, it was formally a multiracial party and attracted some Malay support. In its effort to recruit Malay members the DAP was most successful in Perak where some Malays were alienated from UMNO but not attracted to PAS. In the 1974 election thirteen of the party's thirty-one candidates at the state level in Perak were Malays. In 1978 the number increased to twenty-five out of thirty-eight; but the party's Malay candidates were naturally placed in predominantly Malay constituencies where UMNO was strong, and most were defeated.[57] In other states the DAP put forward a sprinkling of Malays among its candidates, but few had any hope of success. The DAP's basic problem in attracting Malay support was the fact that its high standing in the Chinese community resulted from its vociferous championing of non-Malay rights and interests that often conflicted with those of the Malays. During the 1980s the DAP paid less attention to nominating Malay candidates and mobilizing Malay votes, although it had several Malay leaders, including prominent trade unionists. Zainal Rampak, for example, stood as a DAP candidate in 1978 and 1982 but later resigned when he was elected president of the Malaysian Trade Union Congress in 1985. Ahmad Nor, another prominent trade unionist, was the former secretary-general of the government employees union, CUEPACS. He joined the party in 1987 and became the DAP's first Malay member of Parliament when he won a seat in Penang in 1990. In addition, two Malay DAP candidates were successful in the Perak state assembly in 1990.

---

wing parties. By the 1970s and 80s, however, subethnic identity did not seem especially important. Rather, both the MCA and DAP selected candidates according to the constituency being contested. If the constituency was largely Cantonese, for example, both parties put forward Cantonese candidates; if it was largely Hokkien, both nominated Hokkien candidates; and so on.

[57] Ong 1980:143–45, 148–50.

Having failed to mobilize Malay votes on a significant scale, the DAP aligned itself with other parties that could attract Malay votes. In 1982 it worked out an electoral understanding with the small Malay-based Socialist party, Partai Sosialis Rakyat Malaya (PSRM), but the PSRM was too weak to be of much assistance. However, the DAP entered a more promising alliance with Semangat '46 in 1990.

While the DAP campaigned on universal issues such as human rights, corruption, and government maladministration, its main appeal lay in its defense of the rights of non-Malays, especially the Chinese. It openly took up the communal issues that the MCA and Gerakan, constrained by their coalition with UMNO, could not raise in public. The DAP rushed to the defense of Chinese education, language, and culture, calling for the establishment of a Chinese-medium university, increased quotas and scholarships for non-Malays in universities, improved training for teachers in Chinese primary schools, Chinese-language television and radio programs, and so on. It demanded increased recruitment of non-Malays to the civil service, the police, the armed forces, and FELDA schemes. And it supported Chinese businesspeople against the growing controls imposed under the NEP. Even in pursuing its universal issues, the DAP's anti-Malay image was enhanced because the government officials it accused of corruption or civil-rights abuse were often Malays.

It is not easy to estimate the proportion of Chinese who voted for the DAP. In elections since 1974—except in 1995 when its support fell sharply—the party consistently won about 20 percent of the peninsular vote where about 34–37 percent of the registered voters were Chinese. The problem is that we cannot know how many registered Chinese actually voted or how many of the DAP's votes came from Indians and Malays. Assuming that one-quarter of Indian voters and virtually no Malays supported the DAP, it follows that close to half the Chinese voters must have voted for the DAP. If the participation rate of Chinese voters was less than that of the other communities (which is likely), the DAP's share of the Chinese vote would be correspondingly higher.[58] Whatever assumptions we make, it is clear that the DAP normally won at least half the votes of the Chinese community.[59] It is also likely that even more Chinese sympathized with the party: it did not contest all seats, so supporters in uncontested constituencies did not have an opportunity to vote for the party.

---

[58] This is suggested by a comparison of the electoral turnout in urban, predominantly Chinese areas and rural, predominantly Malay areas. For example, in 1990, the turnout in constituencies in predominantly Chinese Kuala Lumpur ranged between 62.1 and 71.3 percent, while in predominantly Malay Terengganu it ranged between 77.7 and 86.8 percent. In largely Chinese Penang, where the state government was Chinese-dominated, the participation rate ranged between 74.3 and 80.8 percent—higher than Kuala Lumpur but lower than Terengganu. Calculated from Election Commission Report 1990.

[59] For a more detailed explanation of these calculations, see Crouch 1982:51–52.

One could surmise that many non-voting Chinese share the DAP's attitudes.

The DAP is particularly strong in urban areas and new villages where the Chinese community constitutes a majority. Chinese in predominantly Malay rural areas are more likely to support the MCA, which is in a better position to help them in their dealings with the government. In areas where the Chinese constitute small minorities, they are unlikely to want to antagonize their Malay neighbors by openly supporting a party viewed as anti-Malay. Despite the common stereotype of the urban Chinese in 1970 only 47 percent of Chinese lived in towns or cities of more than ten thousand people; 23 percent lived in towns with populations between one thousand and ten thousand and 30 percent in concentrations of less than one thousand.[60]

That the DAP's prospects are best in predominantly Chinese urban areas is confirmed by analysis of the ethnic composition of the parliamentary seats it wins. Of the fifteen peninsular parliamentary seats in which Chinese made up more than 60 percent of the voters in 1978, the DAP won thirteen. Chinese made up less than half the voters in only one of the seats won by the DAP—Damansara in Kuala Lumpur. In 1982 demographic change reduced the number of seats in which Chinese made up more than 60 percent of the voters to fourteen; but this time the DAP was less successful, winning only six seats, four of which had Chinese majorities of more than 70 percent. It failed to win any seat where Chinese made up less than 60 percent.[61] Under new electoral boundaries in 1986 there were again fifteen seats with Chinese majorities of more than 60 percent, all of which were won by the DAP. Three more DAP victories were in seats where Chinese made up more than half the voters, and in the remaining seat Chinese constituted 49.3 percent.[62] In 1990 the DAP won all fourteen peninsular seats with Chinese majorities of more than 60 percent, two of the eight seats with Chinese majorities of between 50 and 60 percent and two with less than 50 percent, including the unusual case of Klang where Chinese made up only a quarter of the voters and were outnumbered by Indians, who constituted 29 percent. In 1995, the DAP won only eight of the seventeen peninsular seats with Chinese majorities of more than 60 percent and no seats where the Chinese were less than 60 percent.

There are no published studies examining who exactly supports the DAP in elections. It clearly gets support from Chinese in predominantly Chinese urban areas, presumably among those most concerned about protecting their Chinese identity. But one could equally argue that the pre-

[60] Strauch 1978:1281.
[61] Crouch 1982:50–55.
[62] Calculated from results in Zakry 1986.

dominantly Chinese areas are also the areas where the Chinese working class and those with lower-class occupations are most strongly represented and that the DAP therefore wins most of its support from the Chinese lower class. Similarly, it might be expected that the DAP would win most of its Indian votes in areas where the Indian urban lower class is numerous. Nevertheless, the party draws considerable support from members of the Chinese middle class who are alienated by the government's discriminatory policies.[63]

The DAP's main disadvantage compared with the government's non-Malay parties lies, of course, in its lack of access to the patronage network. Strauch's research in the early 1970s in a rural setting showed how the MCA controlled the distribution of patronage in the Chinese community.[64] In the urban areas, however, direct patronage is less crucial although still important for many voters. But in contrast to rural areas, where the Chinese are usually a small minority and can therefore be more easily reached by the patronage machine and are more dependent on it, it is impossible in urban areas to ensure that most voters get direct benefits. Thus, the number of disappointed voters is much higher and the pool of potential DAP supporters much larger. Moreover, the MCA and Gerakan are often not able to do much to protect the interests of individual Chinese who are having difficulties with the government administration.[65] In any case, urban voters feel less vulnerable to the possible repercussions of supporting the opposition.

Elections

In elections before BN's formation, the Alliance had always won but not always convincingly. In the first post-independence election in 1959 the Alliance won 51.8 percent of the votes and 74 of the 104 seats in the national Parliament, but it was defeated in state elections in Kelantan and Terengganu. The next election was held during the state of emergency declared because of Indonesia's policy of *konfrontasi* against the formation of Malaysia. In this atmosphere of heightened national insecurity, leaders of several opposition parties were detained; and the Alliance was able to increase its vote to 58.4 percent and win 89 of the seats (although it lost

[63] A senior MCA leader estimated in a 1994 interview that 60–70 percent of the Chinese middle class voted for DAP.

[64] Strauch 1981:134, 144–45.

[65] In an interview one former MCA leader said, "In general poor Chinese, like those in New Villages, see little point in supporting the MCA. The MCA does little for them." Referring to one group of urban poor, he admitted, "There is no way in which hawkers who are always in trouble with municipal enforcement officers can be made to vote for the MCA."

once again in Kelantan). But in 1969 the Alliance's share of the vote fell to less than half (48.4 percent). It won only 66 seats (less than two thirds) in the peninsula, while the election, held for the first time in East Malaysia, was postponed.[66] At the state level the Alliance lost in Kelantan and Penang, and its position was in doubt in Selangor and Perak.

After the formation of BN, the ruling coalition usually won about three-fifths of the votes and an overwhelming majority of the seats in parliament. Until 1990 it also kept control of all the state governments except for Sabah in 1985–86. But its share of the national vote dropped in 1990, and it lost the state election in Kelantan. At the same time PBS, the governing party in Sabah, withdrew from the BN.

An examination of election results between 1974 and 1986 shows remarkable consistency. The vote for the BN consistently hovered at 57–60 percent. In terms of seats, it won 88 percent in 1974, 85 percent in 1978, 86 percent in 1982, and 84 percent in 1986. Only in 1990, after the defection of a substantial dissident group from UMNO and the establishment of Semangat '46, did the BN's share of the votes decline to 53.4 percent; and its share of seats fell to 71 percent. In 1995, however, the BN won a record 65.1 percent of the votes and 84 percent of the seats.

Among the opposition parties, the share of seats in Parliament has undergone sharp ups and downs. Votes, however, have usually remained steady. PAS retained its five seats in Parliament when its share in the peninsular vote declined from 17.7 percent to 16.4 percent between 1978 and 1982 but lost four despite a rise in its vote to 17.5 percent in 1986. In the exceptional circumstances of 1990, when an opposition semi-alliance was formed, PAS's share in the peninsular vote fell to 7.8 percent; but it won seven seats. In that election and again in 1995 PAS did not nominate candidates in constituencies contested by its ally, Semangat '46, and directed its supporters to vote for that party. The steady if marginal upward trend in DAP's national vote (from 18.3 to 19.9, 19.6, and 21.1 percent in successive elections up to 1986) was not reflected in the seats it won, which rose from nine to sixteen, and then fell back to nine before leaping to twenty-four in the expanded parliament of 1986. Despite a decline in votes to 18.0 percent in 1990, the DAP retained twenty seats. In 1995, however, the DAP suffered a devastating loss of both votes and seats. The explanation of the difference between votes and seats lies partly in the degree of cooperation between the main opposition parties and also in the role of the small opposition parties—the so-called mosquito parties—which appear or reappear at elections, drawing votes away from the main opposition parties in key constituencies.

[66] Vasil 1972:app. 2.

Table 1. Parliamentary election results

	1974		1978		1982		1986		1990		1995	
	Seats	Votes (%)	Seats	Votes (%)	Seats	Votes (%)	Seats	Votes (%)	Seats	Votes (%)	Seats	Votes (%)
						Malaysia						
BN	135	60.7	131	57.2	132	60.5	148	57.3	127	53.4	162	65.1
PAS	—	—	5	15.5	5	14.5	1	15.5	7	6.7	7	7.3
DAP	9	18.3	16	19.9	9	19.6	24	21.1	20	17.6	9	12.1
Semangat '46									8	15.1	6	10.2
SNAP	9	5.5	—	—	—	—	—	—	—	—	—	—
PBS									14	2.3	8	3.3
Others	1	15.5	2	6.9	8	5.4	4	6.1	4	4.9	0	2.0
TOTAL	154		154		154		177		180		192	
						Peninsula						
BN	104	55.5	94	57.1	103	61.3	112	58.1	99	55.3	123	—[4]
UMNO[1]	(61)		(69)		(70)		(83)		(70)		(79)	
MCA	(19)		(17)		(24)		(17)		(18)		(30)	
MIC	(4)		(3)		(4)		(6)		(6)		(7)	
Gerakan	(5)		(4)		(5)		(5)		(5)		(7)	
PAS[2]	(14)		—		—		—		—		—	
Others[3]	(1)		(1)		(0)		(1)		(0)		(0)	
PAS	—	—	5	17.7	5	16.4	1	17.5	7	7.8	7	—
DAP	9	19.0	15	21.5	6	20.3	19	21.4	18	18.0	8	—
Semangat '46									8	17.5	6	—
Others	1	25.5	0	3.7	0	2.0	0	3.0	0	1.4	0	—
TOTAL	114		114		114		132		132		144	

Sources: Election Commission Reports, 1974, 1978, 1982 and 1990; data from Election Commission, 1995.
1. In 1990 UMNO also won the seat of Labuan in East Malaysia, giving it a total of 71 in the full parliament.
2. PAS was expelled from the BN in 1977.
3. "Others" include PPP in 1994, a former PAS member in 1978, and Hamim, a party of PAS dissidents, in 1986.
4. Not available for 1995.

The Malaysian electoral system could not be described as fair. It was so heavily loaded in favor of the government that it was hard to imagine that the ruling coalition, as long as it remained united, could be defeated in an election. Even in the 1990 election, after UMNO experienced its most serious split and the opposition parties cooperated for the first time in a multicommunal electoral arrangement, the opposition was again defeated. But despite the predictable outcome, elections were held regularly and continued to be vigorously contested by opposition parties, which were able to mobilize substantial shares of the votes and in a few cases win power at the state level. Therefore, the BN could not afford to ignore popular sentiments and grievances but had to respond to issues raised by the opposition parties. Although the BN was unlikely to be removed from government in an election, many individual BN candidates who faced tough fights for their seats pressured the government to take popular feelings into account. Elections could not in practice change the government, but they did make it more responsive than it would have been in their absence.

5 Political Controls

T HE MALAY-DOMINATED RULING ELITE constructed an electoral system that virtually ensured that it could not be removed from power—assuming that it remained united. It was not just the electoral system that favored the ruling elite. That domination was backed by a wide range of political controls that restricted scope for criticism and opposition. The government took the view that because the people elected the government in "democratic" elections, it therefore represented the will of the people. Thus, it was unnecessary for opposition parties and interest groups to "interfere" in the government's work. If the people were unhappy about government policies, they would have their chance again in the next election. In the meantime, to ensure that the opposition did not disrupt the working of the government, political controls were instituted. Often justified as necessary to maintain order in a communally divided society, these controls also hindered the efforts of the opposition to mobilize political support.

Emergency Powers

The most far-reaching powers available to the government are provided in article 150 of the Malaysian constitution which deals with the proclamation of emergency.[1] Clause 1 of article 150 says that the Yang di-Pertuan Agong (king) may issue a proclamation of emergency if he "is satisfied that a grave emergency exists whereby the security, or the economic life, or public order in the Federation or any part thereof is threatened." Clause 2, which was added in a constitutional amendment in 1981,

---

[1] See Jayakumar 1978:328–68; Lee 1986a:135–56.

says that the proclamation "may be issued before the actual occurrence of the event which threatens the security, or the economic life, or public order ... if the Yang di-Pertuan Agong is satisfied that there is imminent danger of the occurrence of such event." A proclamation of emergency is not open to legal challenge. Clause 8, in another amendment added in 1981, says that "the satisfaction of the Yang di-Pertuan Agong ... shall be final and conclusive and shall not be challenged or called in question in any court on any ground." It is understood, of course, that in such cases the Yang di-Pertuan Agong would be acting on the advice of the prime minister.

Once an emergency has been proclaimed, the Yang di-Pertuan Agong has the power to promulgate ordinances that "have the same force and effect as an Act of Parliament" and "may be exercised in relation to any matter with respect to which Parliament has power to make laws, regardless of the legislative or other procedures required to be followed" (clause 2C). While an emergency is in force, Parliament also has an unrestricted power to "make laws with respect to any matter, if it appears to Parliament that the law is required by reason of the emergency" (clause 5). Neither ordinances nor acts passed under the emergency powers can be found "invalid on the ground of inconsistency with any provision of this Constitution" except for provisions relating to religion, citizenship, and language as well as Islamic law and Malay custom in the peninsula and native law and custom in East Malaysia (clauses 6 and 6A).

When Malaya obtained its independence in 1957, the 1948 emergency proclamation issued by the British in response to Communist rebellion was still in force but was lifted in 1960. Since then, four proclamations of emergency have been issued: two covered the whole country, and two applied to particular states. The first national emergency was proclaimed in 1964 after Indonesia launched its policy of confrontation against Malaysia. The second, in 1969, responded to the postelection racial rioting. Neither proclamation was formally withdrawn; and several ordinances, such as the Emergency (Public Order and Crime Prevention) Ordinance, remain in effect based on the 1969 emergency proclamation. Because the grounds for proclaiming or continuing an emergency cannot be challenged in court, it is not necessary for the government to show that a grave emergency in fact existed or continues to exist. The 1964 emergency in effect lapsed with the end of confrontation in 1966, and "normalcy" was restored after the 1969 proclamation when Parliament reconvened in 1971. But the failure to lift the 1969 emergency left the government with far-reaching and legally unchallengeable powers, which can be brought into force at any time without the need to proclaim a new emergency. Nevertheless, the government has not in practice used the full battery of powers available under the emergency provisions.

Emergencies have been proclaimed at the state level on two occasions—in Sarawak in 1966 and Kelantan in 1977. In both cases state governments had fallen under the control of parties that were unacceptable to the central government.[2] In Sarawak the state government was headed by the Iban-based party SNAP, while in Kelantan UMNO leaders of the BN decided to move against their coalition partner, PAS, which controlled the Kelantan state government. In both cases the proclamation of emergency enabled the central government to depose the elected state government; in Kelantan it also took over the administration of the state. In neither case could it be said that "a grave emergency" existed, but in both the emergency proclamations served the purposes of the central government by enabling it to depose an unwanted state government.

Detention without Trial: The Internal Security Act

With the lifting of the first emergency in 1960, the government used powers derived from article 149 of the constitution and immediately introduced the Internal Security Act (ISA), which provided for the indefinite continuation of some emergency powers. Although the armed Communist rebellion had been virtually broken, there was still an active Communist underground, and a large number of Communists were still detained under the emergency provisions. With the passage of the new act, Communist and other detainees were transferred from detention under the emergency provisions to detention under the ISA.

The ISA empowers the minister of home affairs to detain without trial if he "is satisfied that the detention of any person is necessary with a view to preventing him from acting in any manner prejudicial to the security of Malaysia or any part thereof or to the maintenance of essential services therein or to the economic life thereof."[3] In the Karam Singh case in 1969 the federal court held that it was entirely a matter for the executive to decide on the facts of the case and whether or not there was reasonable cause for detention under the act.[4] Reiterating this interpretation in a case in 1988, a judge declared that "it is not competent for the court to inquire into the sufficiency, relevance or otherwise of the allegations of facts. The Minister's finding is a subjective satisfaction and is not subject to judicial review."[5]

In the late 1980s, however, the courts imposed some limits on the executive's prerogative. In 1987 Raja Tan Sri Khalid Raja Harun was detained under the ISA for questioning about loans approved by the Perwira Habib

---

[2] On Sarawak, see Leigh 1974:ch. 3; on Kelantan, see Kamlin 1980 and Chapter 6.
[3] Internal Security Act, section 8(1).
[4] Jayakumar 1978:351–52.
[5] *NST* 15 October 1988.

Bank during his period as a bank director. At the time of his arrest the bank had virtually collapsed. Justice Harun Hashim of the high court ordered his release on the grounds that the application of the ISA was unlawful because the case did not involve national security.[6] In another case, a Malay Christian, Jamaluddin Osman, was detained under the ISA in 1987 because the government claimed that his proselytizing activities among Muslims could have led to increased animosity between Muslims and Christians. While the Supreme Court agreed that it was the executive's prerogative to determine the facts of the case, it held that the court had the prerogative to decide if the grounds for detention fell within the scope of the act. The police claimed that Jamaluddin had participated in various meetings and succeeded in converting six Muslims. But the chief justice of Malaya, Tan Sri Hashim Yeop Sani, in ordering his release in 1989, concluded that "we do not think that mere participation in meetings and seminars can make a person a threat to the security of the country. As regards the alleged conversion of six Malays, even if it was true, it cannot be regarded as a threat to the security of the country."[7] In other contemporary cases, however, courts rejected habeas corpus writs such as that of Kua Kia Soong, who claimed that the allegations against him related to books published in 1985 and speeches in 1986, which were too remote in time to justify his arrest in late 1987.[8]

Although the court decisions freeing ISA detainees did not involve cases with immediate political ramifications, they did have potential political significance. On 8 December 1988 the Singapore Court of Appeal effectively reversed the principle established in the Karam Singh case when it took the view that courts were entitled to review the grounds for arrest under the ISA (Singapore's is similar to Malaysia's) and evaluate the evidence on which the government based its detention orders. The Singapore government reacted immediately by amending its ISA to reaffirm the government's absolute discretion to detain whomever it regarded as security threats. The Malaysian courts took account of precedents established in Singapore cases, and the Malaysian government amended its ISA to limit judicial review to purely procedural matters.[9]

Between 1960 and 1981, 3,102 people were detained at one time or another under the ISA.[10] In the 1960s many detainees were involved in the

---

[6] *NST* 12 February 1987; *AWSJ* 21 February 1987 (here and elsewhere *AWSJ* refers to the *Asian Wall Street Journal*). In justifying their use of the ISA, the police claimed that corruption in the bank could have caused anger in the armed forces, which could have then threatened security because the bank was partly owned by the military pension fund, the Lembaga Tabung Angkatan Tentera.

[7] *NST* 25 February 1989.

[8] *NST* 22 November 1988; Kua 1989:ch. 9.

[9] *NST* 24 June 1989.

[10] *NST* 17 November 1981.

CPM or the Labour Party, including some who were active in radical trade unions. Others had been accused of supporting Indonesia's confrontation campaign. An estimated nine hundred people were under detention in 1979 but in 1981 the number fell to 586 when Dr. Mahathir became prime minister.[11] The Mahathir administration adopted a more liberal approach than its predecessor, especially after the hardline Tan Sri Ghazali Shafie was replaced as minister for home affairs by the relatively liberal Datuk Musa Hitam in 1981. By the end of 1986 the number of detainees had fallen to about forty.[12] After a sharp rise in communal tensions in October 1987, however, the government suddenly arrested 106 people who were all released during the following eighteen months. Further arrests took place from time to time; and by early 1991 the number had grown to 142, 117 of whom were described as adhering to Communist ideology.[13] By December 1993, fifty-two people were under detention, including fourteen Communists.[14] But not all ISA detainees were held for political reasons. According to the deputy minister for home affairs in 1990, some common criminals were also held under the act.[15]

In the 1960s the government justified the ISA's introduction as necessary for the continuing fight against Communist insurgency but later stressed the preservation of intercommunal harmony. In practice, the ISA was also used to block political challenges and intimidate critics. Among the detainees after the 1969 rioting, for example, were DAP leader Lim Kit Siang and trade unionist V. David, who was a member of Gerakan. In Sarawak, a leading member of SNAP, Datuk James Wong, was detained in December 1974, in this case under the Preservation of Public Security Regulations because of his alleged support for Brunei's claim to Limbang.[16] A large number of students were detained in 1974. Others detained during the 1970s included the University of Malaya anthropologist Syed Husin Ali (1974–80); PSRM leader Kassim Ahmad (1976–81); Muslim youth leader Anwar Ibrahim (1974–76); and two DAP members of Parliament, Chan Kok Kit and Chian Heng Kai. Local leaders of the Muslim opposition party, PAS, were detained after peasant demonstrations in Kedah in 1980; and leaders of the Airlines Employees Union were arrested after industrial

[11] Amnesty International 1979:3; calculated from *NST* 5 February 1982.

[12] Letter from Mahathir's press secretary. *FEER* 28 January 1988 (Here and elsewhere *FEER* refers to the *Far Eastern Economic Review*).

[13] *NST* 24 January 1991. The number of detainees was boosted after the surrender of former guerillas following the peace accord between the Malaysian government and the CPM. Of the twenty-five non-Communist detainees, five were described as Muslim extremists, four were alleged Sabah separatists, seven were accused of espionage, eight had forged identity cards and other documents, and one was involved in burning a mosque.

[14] *NST* 9 December 1993.

[15] *NST* 30 July 1990.

[16] *NST* 4 March 1975.

action taken by Malaysian Airlines System workers in 1978–79. Members of the government itself were not exempt from the provisions of the act, as deputy ministers Datuk Abdullah Ahmad and Abdullah Majid and editor of the *New Straits Times,* Samad Ismail, discovered. They found themselves on the wrong side in a factional struggle in 1976 and were not released until 1980. Among the 106 dissidents arrested in 1987 were critics of the government such as Aliran president Chandra Muzaffar, members of environmental groups, and Christian social-welfare activists as well as DAP and PAS politicians.

Following the 1989 amendments to the act that virtually eliminated the possibility of court challenges to detention, the government was no longer compelled to attempt to establish a credible link between a particular detention and a threat to national security. Shortly before the national election in 1990, a DAP member of Parliament and some supporters were detained under the ISA for leading a demonstration against converting a major road in Kuala Lumpur into a toll road.[17] After the election the government used the ISA to detain the brother of the chief minister of Sabah whose party had "betrayed" BN by joining the opposition led by Semangat '46 a few days before the election.[18] In 1994 the government resorted to the ISA to detain leaders of the nonviolent Darul Arqam Islamic organization.

Restrictions on Discussion: The Sedition Act and the Official Secrets Act

Government opponents were also intimidated by other acts. While a case could be made that both the Sedition Act and the Official Secrets Act were necessary to preserve public order and allow the government to perform its duties properly, in practice their implementation restricted the opposition's scope for public criticism.

The most far-reaching restriction on political discussion was contained in the Sedition Act. The original act, adopted by the colonial government in 1948, was directed against offenses such as inciting disaffection against the government, inciting contempt for the administration of justice, and raising discontent among the people. Following the 1969 rioting, the act was amended, widening the concept of sedition to cover matters with "a tendency . . . to promote feelings of ill-will and hostility between different

[17] *NST* 9 September 1990.
[18] Jeffrey Kitingan was accused of planning to take Sabah out of Malaysia. That the government may not have really believed this charge is suggested by Kitingan's appointment as deputy minister in August 1994, six months after his release in December 1993. *NST* 25 June 1994.

races or classes of the population of Malaysia" and proscribe the questioning of "any matter, right, status, position, privilege, sovereignty or prerogative established or protected by the provisions of Part III of the Federal Constitution or Article 152, 153 or 181 of the Federal Constitution."[19] Part 3 of the constitution deals with citizenship, primarily the conditions required for non-Malays. Article 152 establishes Malay as the national language, although it also guarantees that using, teaching, or learning any other language cannot be prohibited or prevented. Article 153 obliges the government "to safeguard the special position" of bumiputeras by reserving for them "reasonable" proportions of appointments in the civil service, scholarships, places in educational institutions, and business licenses and permits; at the same time "the legitimate interests of other communities" must also be respected. Article 181 deals with the sovereignty of the Malay rulers, symbolising Malay dominance of the polity. In 1971 the constitution was amended to extend the application of the Sedition Act to Parliament itself and thus removed parliamentary privilege from discussion of these subjects and other issues considered sensitive.

The effect of the act was to inhibit discussion of some of the country's most controversial political issues. Although one of the earliest cases under the amended act involved Melan Abdullah, editor of the Malay-language newspaper *Utusan Melayu,* who had called for the closure of Chinese and Tamil primary schools, non-Malay politicians, especially those from the DAP, were most affected. The most notable case involved the DAP deputy secretary-general, Fan Yew Teng. As editor of the DAP's periodical, *The Rocket,* he was convicted for publishing a speech by Ooi Kee Saik who, among other things, had stated that the government favored the Malays.[20] DAP member of Parliament, Chan Kok Kit, was charged with publishing seditious posters before the 1974 election, including one that read, "The *Dacing* [scales of justice: BN's election symbol] destroys Chinese education. The Rocket [DAP's symbol] defends Chinese culture."[21] Chan, however, was detained under the ISA before he could face trial under the Sedition Act. Another DAP member of Parliament, Oh Keng Seng, was found guilty in 1978 of uttering seditious words during a by-election campaign in 1972. Oh was alleged to have said that the 13 May riot had been brought about by "racialists" in the government and that the army consisted largely of "their people," implying Malays.[22] But the act seemed to be applied lightly to bumiputeras. In his maiden speech in Parliament in 1978, Mark Koding, a young Kadazan from Sabah, called for the aboli-

---

[19] Sedition Act, sections 3(1)(e) and (f).
[20] NST 8, 14 January 1975. The fine of $2,000 made him ineligible to retain his seat in Parliament.
[21] UM 19 September 1975.
[22] NST 8 September 1976.

tion of Chinese and Tamil schools in Sabah and questioned the use of the two languages on signboards. He was not charged until 1981; and, although Koding was found guilty, the judge described his offense as technical and ordered that no conviction be recorded.[23]

The Official Secrets Act of 1972 was another law tending to restrict the issues that the opposition could raise against the government. Based on the British act of 1911, its scope was broad. Before its amendment in 1986, the act covered the unauthorized publication of any information in the hands of the government, no matter how insignificant or widely known.[24] A major case involved DAP secretary-general Lim Kit Siang, who was found guilty of receiving and revealing information in 1976 about the navy's purchase of ships that appeared to indicate the possibility of corruption.[25]

In response to two cases in 1985 and 1986 involving journalists whose fines had been paid by their employers, the government amended the act to make jail terms of one to fourteen years mandatory for those found guilty. In the 1986 amendment the government also provided more specific guidelines about what constituted official secrets. In the new act official secrets were restricted to cabinet and state executive council documents and those relating to security, defense, and international relations.[26] One effect of the act's broad scope before the 1986 amendment was to make it difficult for the opposition to expose malpractices within the government because such information was normally obtained through leaks, which by their nature were unauthorized. Although the 1986 amendment narrowed the definition of official secrets, the provision for mandatory jail terms enhanced its intimidating effect.

Control of the Press and Other Publications

The mass media were subject to both direct and indirect controls. According to the Printing Presses Ordinance (later an act) introduced by the British at the beginning of the first emergency in 1948, all newspapers and printing presses were required to obtain a license that was to be reviewed annually. In 1971 the act was amended to provide for the license revocation of newspapers that aggravated national sensitivities or failed to serve

[23] *NST* 14 July 1981, 29 May 1982.

[24] In a federal court judgment, Justice Salleh Abas said that a secret document does not "lose its secrecy just because the letter happens to contain information which is already known to the public." If that were so, he said, examination papers could not be kept secret because the information in them was in textbooks. *NST* 23 October 1980.

[25] *NST* 8 November 1978.

[26] *NST* 3, 6 December 1986.

national development goals—criteria broad enough to cover political reasons.[27] After a rise in communal tensions in 1987, the English-medium *Star,* the Chinese *Sin Chew Jit Poh,* and the Malay weekly *Watan* had their licenses revoked and were not allowed to reappear until the following March. Following the 1987 crisis, the government introduced radical changes to the Printing Presses and Publications Act that gave the minister "absolute discretion," which could not be challenged in court, to ban or restrict publications "and future publications of the publisher concerned" that he or she considered to be "prejudicial to public order, morality, security . . . or which is likely to alarm public opinion . . . or is likely to be prejudicial to public interest or national interest." Charges could also be laid against the "printer, publisher, editor and the writer" who "maliciously published any false news" without taking "reasonable measures to verify the truth of the news."[28]

Despite the licensing provisions and the wide discretionary powers in the hands of the minister for home affairs, licenses were liberally awarded. Nevertheless, editors were well aware of the consequences of overstepping boundaries. The three newspapers whose licenses were revoked in 1987 had them restored after a few months; but changes had to be made in their staff, and their editorial tone was subdued. Critical periodicals such as *Aliran Monthly* were normally able to obtain licenses, although their circulations were usually small and they had difficulty finding printers willing to risk being held responsible for the periodicals' contents. Party-affiliated periodicals such as the DAP's monthly *The Rocket* and PAS's biweekly *Harakah* were for a long time permitted to be sold to the public, but in 1991 their publishing licenses were amended to restrict circulation to party members.[29] Opposition-oriented periodicals occasionally lost their licenses; and the government also kept watch over foreign newspapers and journals, occasionally banning particular issues of the *Far Eastern Economic Review, Asiaweek, Time,* the *International Herald Tribune,* and so on.[30]

Control was exercised over the press less directly through ownership.

---

[27] Lent 1974:1.

[28] *AWSJ* 26 November 1987, 7 December 1987. Occasionally, however, editors seem to have been encouraged to publish unverified reports. When the government was disturbed by an Australian television program on Malaysia, editors received a letter dated 12 July 1988 from the Ministry of Information in which they were advised, "We would be pleased if you could take the appropriate action to publish news that would discredit foreign countries in your newspaper." *FEER* 28 July 1988 (Suhaini Aznam, "The Smear Campaign").

[29] Despite the ban, *Harakah* seemed to be freely available in Kelantan when I visited that state in April 1994.

[30] The government's approach to foreign journals was expressed by Deputy Minister for Home Affairs Kassim Ahmad: "People know which magazines the Government doesn't like. They must be vigilant to discard publications which are not in accord with the Government's vision." *NST* 21 March 1984.

The main newspaper group, the New Straits Times Press, published the *New Straits Times* in English and *Berita Harian* in Malay. It was initially owned by Fleet Holdings, one of UMNO's investment arms. Fleet Holdings had been established in 1972 by UMNO treasurer Tengku Razaleigh to take over the Kuala Lumpur edition of the *Straits Times,* which was based in Singapore and controlled by Singaporean and British interests.[31] Razaleigh exercised a strong influence over the *New Straits Times* until 1982. But after his defeat in the 1981 contest for the UMNO deputy presidency, Fleet Holdings was placed under the chairmanship of Prime Minister Mahathir's friend, businessman Daim Zainuddin. In 1993 four senior executives, including the editor, purchased the paper from an UMNO-controlled company. All were closely aligned with Datuk Seri Anwar Ibrahim who was about to launch his challenge to replace Ghafar Baba as deputy prime minister.[32] A second major newspaper group controlled by UMNO interests was the Malay-medium *Utusan Melayu* group, which published *Utusan Melayu* in the *Jawi* script and *Utusan Malaysia* in Roman characters. *Utusan Melayu* had been a major voice of Malay nationalism in the 1940s and 50s, sometimes sympathizing with the radical MNP; but in 1961 it was taken over by a group of UMNO leaders and became "the unofficial voice of UMNO."[33] During the 1970s and 80s, the chairman of the *Utusan Melayu* group and its dominant influence was senior UMNO leader Ghafar Baba. In 1994 Tan Sri Vincent Tan, a Chinese businessman with close UMNO links, launched a new English-medium tabloid, *The Sun.*

The second major English-medium newspaper, *The Star,* emerged in the 1970s when it was transformed from a regional to a national newspaper. Once owned by Tun Mustapha Harun, former chief minister of Sabah and close friend of former Prime Minister Tunku Abdul Rahman, *The Star* was bought in 1977 by Huaren Holdings, a company largely owned by the MCA. Published in tabloid form, it rapidly built up its readership to a point where it challenged the predominance of the *New Straits Times.* The growth of *The Star,* although under the control of a BN party, was not altogether welcomed by the UMNO leadership. The newspaper highlighted issues of concern to Chinese and also published a weekly column by Tunku Abdul Rahman, who was chairman of the newspaper. His views were often not in line with those of current UMNO leaders, especially after his former foes Mahathir and Musa became prime minister and deputy prime minister respectively. In 1987 *The Star*'s license was suspended for

[31] Gomez 1990:52–53.

[32] *FEER* 4 February 1993 (Doug Tsuruoka, "Peace Offering"). The purchase was made through Malaysian Resources Corporation Bhd., a company controlled by Anwar's supporters.

[33] Funston 1980:188.

several months; and when it reappeared in March 1988, Tunku Abdul Rahman's column had been dropped.

The Chinese and Tamil press was also largely controlled by groups linked to the government. Until 1990 the largest shareholder in the Nanyang Press, publisher of *Nanyang Siang Pau,* was the government trading company Pernas. But control eventually passed to Hume Industries, a subsidiary of the Chinese-owned but UMNO-connected Hong Leong group. Meanwhile, in 1985 the *New Straits Times* group had taken over the third-largest Chinese daily, *Shin Min Daily News,* which had previously been controlled by Tan Koon Swan of the MCA. In the Tamil press, different newspapers tended to be aligned with different factions in the MIC's incessant internal struggles. Thus, in the late 1980s *Tamil Nesan* was owned by supporters of the party president, Samy Vellu, while *Tamil Osai* was controlled by supporters of his challenger, Subramaniam.

The fact that the press was largely owned by groups associated with the government meant that news and commentary unfavorable to the government were rare and the activities of opposition parties and government critics were normally presented in an unfavorable light. But this did not mean that only a single point of view was expressed: although uniformly pro-government, newspapers often represented different factions and interests. Thus, while the *New Straits Times* and the *Utusan Melayu* groups were both affiliated with UMNO, they sometimes took different stands on particular issues, especially at times of factional conflict within the party. For example, when Anwar Ibrahim was mobilizing support in 1993 for his challenge to Ghafar Baba as deputy president of UMNO and deputy prime minister, the *New Straits Times* clearly favored Anwar.[34] Similarly, the fact that *The Star* was controlled by a BN party did not prevent it from stressing the interests of the Chinese community or giving a platform to the former prime minister's sniping at the current prime minister.

In contrast to the peninsula, the press in Eastern Malaysia was less strictly controlled. Newspapers were owned by different political groups and used to further particular political interests, especially during election campaigns. In Sabah both Berjaya and USNO were supported by particular newspapers at the time of the 1976 state election. In Sarawak, during the 1987 election campaign, *Utusan Sarawak,* which was aligned with former PBB leader and current Yang di-Pertua Negeri (Governor) Tun Rahman Yaakub, listed timber concessions awarded to friends and relatives of chief minister Datuk Patinggi Amar Taib Mahmud. Taib's supporters at

---

[34] Editors who backed the wrong side were regularly replaced. Noordin Sopiee, the group editor of the *New Straits Times,* was replaced in 1982, apparently for favoring Razaleigh against Musa in the contest for the deputy leadership of UMNO. His successor, Munir Majid, was himself replaced when Musa fell out of favor in 1986. Rehman Rashid 1993:181–82, 207.

The People's Mirror published a similar list of concessions awarded to friends of Tun Rahman Yaakub during his term as chief minister.[35]

Apart from the press, the government through the Ministry of Information had a monopoly over radio and television until 1985 when a private television station was established (although radio remained a government monopoly). News and public-affairs programs on government radio and television were always heavily slanted toward the government, while opposition views were virtually ignored except at election time when very limited opportunities were given to opposition parties to make radio but not television broadcasts.[36] The end of the television monopoly did not provide the political opposition with new opportunities: the private television company, Sistem Televisyen (M) Berhad (popularly known as TV3), was largely owned by the UMNO-controlled Fleet Group and associated companies.[37] In election campaigns, TV3's news programs presented the BN in glowing terms while opposition politicians were often blatantly misrepresented through selective editing.[38]

Control was exercised over other publications as well. The most notable proscribed book was Mahathir Mohamad's *Malay Dilemma,* which remained banned from its publication in 1970 (when the author was expelled from UMNO) until his appointment as prime minister in 1981. Other banned books included *Special Guest* by former Minister for Agriculture Aziz Ishak, who had been detained under the ISA after he left UMNO during the confrontation period, and *The Golden Son of the Kadazans,* a biography of Sabah politician Peter Mojuntin written by a DAP leader, Bernard Sta Maria. Scholarly books on Malaysian politics have also been banned, including Vasil's *Politics in a Plural Society,* von Vorys's *Democracy without Consensus,* and Short's *The Communist Insurrection in Malaya.* On the other hand, strongly critical books have been allowed to circulate such as Lim Kit Siang's *Time Bombs in Malaysia,* Gomez's *UMNO's Corporate Investments,* and Tun Salleh Abas's *May Day for Justice.* In fact, Syed Husin Ali's *Malay Peasant Society and Leadership* was published when the author was in detention under the ISA.

Depoliticization of Potential Opposition

The government took precautionary measures to prevent the emergence of organizations representing potentially significant political forces. In

[35] Ritchie 1987:95–102.

[36] Sothi 1993:169. Under a formula based on the number of candidates in the 1990 election, the BN was permitted nine prerecorded broadcasts, Semangat '46 three, the DAP two, and PAS one.

[37] Gomez 1990:72–78.

[38] Personal observation. In one report Semangat '46 leader Tengku Razaleigh was shown making what appeared to be an anti-Islamic statement. The short excerpt was shown completely out of context.

many Third World countries, opposition to governments has come from universities, workers, and peasants. Of no less importance has been the spread of cause-oriented groups in the educated middle class, which in themselves are often too small to represent a direct threat to governments but can contribute to a general atmosphere that undermines the legitimacy of government claims to rule. While the government in Malaysia generally avoided blatant repression of these potential sources of major discontent, it introduced incremental measures over the years that greatly reduced their scope for political action.

Trade Unions and the Working Class

People in working-class occupations made up slightly more than a quarter of the peninsular work force in 1970 and about the same proportion of the total Malaysian work force in 1990.[39] If plantation labor is included, the proportion is higher. The voice of labor is not strong, however, and has had little political influence.[40]

The trade-union movement's political power reached its peak in the years immediately after World War II when it was based in Singapore. But with the banning of the CPM and many Communist-led unions after the declaration of emergency in 1948, the union movement virtually collapsed. The British colonial government wanted to encourage the development of "responsible" trade unions and sponsored the formation in 1950 of the Malayan Trade Union Council, which later became the Malayan Trade Union Congress (MTUC). The largest union affiliated with the MTUC was the National Union of Plantation Workers (NUPW), which was formed in 1954 (also with British sponsorship) through the amalgamation of several smaller unions. In 1957 the Congress of Unions of Employees in the Public and Civil Services (CUEPACS) was established as a trade-union center for public-sector employees. As might be expected with these origins, the trade-union movement was far from militant: well over half of Malaya's unionists at that time were members of the extremely cooperative NUPW, and another third were government employees affiliated with CUEPACS.[41] Nevertheless, there were signs of growing union militancy during the late 1950s and 60s, and discontented plantation workers with support from the Labour Party made several attempts to establish a new union for plantation workers. Their efforts failed, however, and a number of Labour Party activists who supported their cause were detained for long periods under the ISA.[42]

[39] See Chapter 10.
[40] For a history of the trade unions see Jomo and Todd 1994.
[41] Stenson 1970:237.
[42] Ramasamy 1994:ch. 6.

The government was determined to prevent the growth of a strong trade-union movement that might fall under the influence of the political opposition.[43] The Trade Unions Ordinance of 1959 prevented office bearers or employees of political parties from holding office in trade unions while the Essential (Trade Unions) Regulations, promulgated under the 1969 emergency and consolidated in an ordinance in 1980, made it unlawful for a union to use funds for political objectives. Another provision of the ordinance was intended to prevent the reappearance of large general unions like those banned by the British in the 1940s. It required unions to be based on "particular" or "similar trades, occupations or industries," with *similar* being defined as "similar in the opinion of the Registrar." Thus, it was not possible to form large general unions covering workers in different fields.[44] Due to the similarity requirement, the MTUC itself was not registered under the Trade Unions Ordinance but the Societies Act.

Apart from government controls, other factors also contributed to the weaknesses of the trade-union movement and its lack of political influence. First, the rate of unionization remained low. In 1980 about 25 percent of wage-earning workers were unionized, but by 1990 this figure had fallen to about 17 percent.[45] Second, the trade-union movement lacked political cohesion because its members were drawn from different racial communities. Trade unionism was traditionally associated with Indians who in 1960 made up 62 percent of members. Many prominent trade-union leaders were also Indian.[46] Since then, however, the proportion of Indians in unions has declined, partly because the largely Indian NUPW lost its old preeminence when manufacturing and other industries grew in the 1970s and 80s and employed an increasing number of Malays. By 1980 Malays made up 50.6 percent of union membership while Indians, who constituted 26.9 percent, were still disproportionately represented. Chinese, making up 21.6 percent, were underrepresented compared with their proportion of the population as a whole.[47] By the 1980s, although there were still many Indian trade-union leaders, there were also Chinese and especially Malay leaders. By 1985 61.9 percent of principal officers (president, secretary, treasurer) in trade unions were Malays, 20.7 percent Chinese, and 15.5 percent Indians.[48] But the increased representation of non-Indians did not strengthen the trade-union movement politically because most workers still seemed to give their political loyalty to communal rather than trade-union leaders.[49]

[43] See Arudsothy and Littler 1993.
[44] Wu 1982:ch. 1.
[45] Out of 2.3 million wage earners 580,000 were members of unions in 1980. Pathmanaban 1980:18; *NST* 1 May 1990.
[46] Jomo and Todd 1994:27.
[47] Ministry of Labour 1986:190.
[48] Ibid.:189.
[49] See, for example, Ackerman 1986.

For many years the MTUC was dominated by its president, P. P. Narayanan, the founder and long-serving secretary-general of the biggest union, the NUPW. Narayanan, who in the 1950s had been groomed by the British as a "responsible," anti-Communist unionist, was regarded as a leader who preferred negotiations to confrontation and had good contacts with members of the government, especially in the MIC. In the 1970s, however, several unionists emerged who had political ties with the opposition. In 1978 V. David, the secretary-general of the Transport Workers Union and a DAP member of Parliament, was elected secretary-general of the MTUC. The deputy president elected in 1980, a Malay named Zainal Rampak, had stood unsuccessfully as a DAP candidate in the 1978 election and again in 1982. After taking over as president of the MTUC in 1986, Zainal withdrew from the DAP but in 1990 joined Semangat '46. Another Malay trade unionist, Ahmad Nor, became president of CUEPACS in 1983. He joined the DAP in 1987 after leaving his union post. In 1988 he was elected deputy president of the MTUC and in 1990 won a seat in Parliament as a DAP candidate. Thus, in 1990 the president of the MTUC was a former DAP member who had joined Semangat '46 while the deputy president and secretary-general were both DAP members of Parliament. Yet there is little evidence to suggest that the DAP was able to mobilize political support on a wide scale through its influence in the MTUC.

Rural Organizations and the Peasantry

In Malaysia peasants have generally been politically quiescent. The peasantry is overwhelmingly Malay, including paddy farmers and smallholders growing rubber, palm oil, and other commercial crops. Although poverty has remained widespread, there have been few expressions of serious political discontent. In fact, a strong rural base means that UMNO has been able to maintain its position as the dominant political force in the ruling BN coalition. Although dissident rural Malay voters have supported PAS in elections, UMNO's control of the patronage network has normally ensured that PAS remains in opposition.

During the 1950s and 60s there were a few small, isolated instances of peasant protest, but in 1974 and 1980 large-scale protests took place in Kedah.[50] In November 1974 smallholder demonstrations were held at the small town of Baling in response to a drastic fall in the price of rubber. In January 1980 some ten thousand peasants gathered at the state capital, Alor Setar, to demonstrate against a new system of paying the rice subsidy, which involved an element of forced savings.[51] In both cases the govern-

[50] For details about the protest movement led by Hang Tuah in Selangor in the 1960s, see Husin Ali 1975:157–60.

[51] Scott 1985:275–76.

ment responded with a mixture of concessions and repression. In 1974 it immediately introduced a rubber price-support scheme, while in 1980 the coupon system of paying the subsidy was modified. Ordinary demonstrators were detained temporarily; and in 1980 seven PAS officials, including a state assemblyman, were arrested under the ISA and accused of forming an underground organization, Pertubuhan Angkatan Sabilullah (Holy War Organization) that conveniently had the same initials as the opposition party to which they belonged. In both cases, however, the demonstrations subsided; and no major peasant-based challenge was launched against the government.

There are, in fact, no independent peasant organizations. Although the government encouraged the formation of local cooperatives and farmers' associations to assist in allocating credit, subsidies, fertilizer, and so on, these bodies were actually part of the UMNO patronage network. In 1973 the Farmers' Organization Authority (FOA) was established at the national level to, among other things, "register, control and supervise farmers' organizations and to provide for related matters."[52] The FOA, however, was hardly an independent body representing peasants. Its secretary-general was a civil servant appointed by the government.

Students and the Universities

In the immediate post-independence period universities were not centers of opposition. Expatriates continued to hold many senior academic positions at the University of Malaya, and students were drawn largely from the well-off middle class. But the number of Malay students, including those from rural backgrounds, increased in the late 1960s and especially the early 1970s after the formation of the Malay-medium National University of Malaysia. This change was accompanied by growing politicization that expressed itself largely in communal terms, as in the demand for increased use of Malay and protests against the 1971 visit of the prime minister of Thailand who was perceived as repressing Muslim Malays in southern Thailand. Agitation reached its peak in 1974 when students in Kuala Lumpur demonstrated in September in support of squatters in Johor Baru and then in November in sympathy with the peasants in Baling. Following a large demonstration in Kuala Lumpur in December, more than one thousand students were arrested although soon released.[53] The main student leaders, however, were detained under the ISA for several months. Some students and other government critics, such as a University of Malaya anthropologist and former secretary-general of the PSRM, S. Husin

[52] *Information Malaysia* 1990:112. See also Chee and Khong 1978:222–25.
[53] Funston 1980:278–79; Means 1991:35–38.

Ali, and the leader of ABIM (the Muslim youth movement), Anwar Ibrahim, were held for long periods—Anwar being detained for almost two years and Husin for six.

Following these demonstrations, far-reaching amendments to the Universities and University Colleges Act were introduced by Minister of Education Mahathir in 1975. Students were prohibited from joining or "allying themselves" with political parties, trade unions, or "any other organisation, body or other group" without the written permission of the vice-chancellor. Further, they were not permitted to "say or do anything that could be interpreted as supporting, sympathizing with, or opposing any political party or trade union."[54] Regulations issued under the act also imposed substantial limitations on the rights of university staff to engage in political activity. Although staff were permitted to be members of parties, they were not permitted to hold any position in a party nor contest or even campaign in elections. The regulations expressly prohibited academic staff from making public statements intended to side with any political party or publish any book or paper relating to issues involving political parties, although exception was made for statements in academic seminars (with the written permission of the vice-chancellor) or books and articles based on academic research.[55] Although the rules in regard to the holding of party positions were generally observed, the controls on publications and statements made in seminars were in practice ignored. Nevertheless, the obvious intention of the act and its accompanying regulations served as a strong deterrent to all but the most committed. When S. Husin Ali of the University of Malaya and Sanusi Osman of the National University were elected president and general-secretary respectively of the PRM (the new name for the PSRM) in 1990, both were required to resign their university appointments.

The Educated Middle Class and the Societies Act

The growth of the urban middle class and the spread of tertiary education was accompanied by the emergence of various societies committed to a wide range of causes. Some pursued causes linked to particular communities such as the United Chinese Schools' Committees' Association or the Muslim youth movement, ABIM. Others represented professional interests such as the Bar Council of Malaysia or the Malaysian Medical Association. Still others were concerned more broadly with achieving a "better society," including reformist bodies such as Aliran and Insan, or with re-

---

[54] Universities and University Colleges (Amendment) Act 1975, article 2 (my translation).
[55] Universities and University Colleges Act 1971, National University of Malaysia Regulations (Staff Rules) 1979, article 20.

form in particular areas such as the Consumer Association of Penang or the Environmental Protection Society of Malaysia. Although these bodies usually had little mass support, they had the capacity to raise issues that were often annoying or embarrassing for members of the government.

Since the colonial period, various ordinances have regulated the activities of societies. Consolidated in the Societies Act (1966), these regulations required all societies to be registered with the Registrar of Societies. In 1981 the government introduced a set of amendments in which a distinction was drawn between "political" and other societies. The registrar was also empowered to deregister societies, while a new clause made it impossible to challenge any decision of the minister in court. Although the new controls on so-called political societies were not especially draconian, the creation of a special category seemed to be directed at those societies that had recently been most critical of the government.[56]

In response to the amendments, representatives of various societies formed a committee, headed by ABIM chairman Anwar Ibrahim, to oppose the act. The act had been introduced by Prime Minister Hussein Onn's conservative minister for home affairs, Ghazali Shafie. In the middle of 1981, however, after Mahathir had taken over the prime ministership, Ghazali was replaced by Musa Hitam, who promised a review of the act. In 1982 Anwar Ibrahim was recruited by UMNO and became a successful candidate for the party in that year's election. He was soon appointed as a deputy minister in the government. Finally, in 1983 a new set of amendments were presented to Parliament in which the category of political society was dropped. Nevertheless, many of the old controls on societies remained.

Although Malaysia maintained the institutions of parliamentary democracy, the government acquired a wide range of political controls that could be activated whenever the need arose. The emergency powers gave the government enormous—in effect extraconstitutional—powers that, except in the case of the British-imposed first emergency, were never formally withdrawn despite the passing of the political crises that led to the initial proclamations of emergency. Some of the most important emergency powers were incorporated in the ISA, which was adopted when the first emergency was lifted in 1960 and modified over the years to minimize the possibility of legal challenge to detentions under the act. Other legislation limited the issues that could be raised in political debate while the press was controlled not only through legislation but, perhaps more important, through ownership: all major newspapers were owned by groups linked to BN parties. Finally, the government produced a series of acts or amend-

[56] See Barraclough 1984 and Gurmit Singh 1984.

ments to acts that greatly reduced the scope for political activity among groups that might have challenged the government and supported opposition parties.

While these controls undoubtedly restricted political debate and limited opposition, political freedoms were by no means completely extinguished. Despite the failure of the government to proclaim the end of emergencies, in practice it was selective in using its emergency powers. Unlike its treatment of state governments under opposition control in Sarawak in 1966 and Kelantan in 1978, it refrained from turning to emergency powers when two states fell under opposition control in 1990. Moreover, the numbers detained under the ISA remained quite small, especially after the early 1980s. Although the emergency provisions and the ISA were not used to the full, they nevertheless had a powerful intimidatory effect on potential critics and opponents. Opposition groups were still permitted to publish newspapers and periodicals of limited circulation, but they faced much government harassment and could not expect their views to receive fair coverage in the major newspapers or on radio or television.

The government justified its repressive apparatus largely on the grounds that it was necessary for the maintenance of order in a multicommunal society where racial tensions could flare up and turn into violence at any time. In practice, however, the repressive machinery was used to reduce the scope for political opposition to the government. Although the government permitted a substantial degree of political freedom, it was always ready to intervene whenever opposition rose to the point where it could begin to threaten the government's grip on political power.

6 Contradictory Trends: Incremental Authoritarianism

THE MALAYSIAN POLITICAL SYSTEM exhibited contradictory trends. On one hand, the government resorted to authoritarian measures to keep the opposition in check and perpetuate its own grip on power. On the other hand, democratic political structures were maintained that encouraged, even forced, the government to respond to societal pressures. The government's authoritarian powers were ostensibly acquired to maintain political stability and public order but in reality were also used to preserve the position of the ruling coalition and the dominant faction in its dominant party. The government did not formulate a long-term plan to establish an authoritarian system but instead reacted to political crises in an ad hoc way, resorting to authoritarian measures whenever they promised to be more effective than other means.

The authoritarian character of the regime was enhanced incrementally. This chapter examines its responses to four political crises, beginning with the racial riots of 1969. Whatever the origins of each crisis, in each case authoritarian measures were taken that strengthened the position of the government or particular groups within it.

The 1969 Emergency

The proclamation of emergency in May 1969 was followed by the establishment of an unambiguously authoritarian government for twenty months. Under the emergency provisions, Parliament was suspended and extraordinary powers were placed in the hands of a nine-member National Operations Council (NOC), which ruled until the resumption of Parliament in February 1971. The proclamation of emergency was in response to the racial rioting that broke out three days after the general election on 10 May. According to the official count, 196 people were killed and hundreds more injured, although unofficial estimates were much higher.[1] Clearly the main purpose of the emergency proclamation was to provide the government with sufficient powers to stop the racial rioting and take steps to prevent its recurrence, but newly acquired authoritarian powers also provided opportunities for some politicians to strengthen their positions at the expense of others.

The emergency permitted the Alliance to maintain and consolidate its rule. In the election, the Alliance had experienced a heavy loss of votes, for the first time winning less than half. Although the rural weighting of the electoral system allowed the Alliance to retain a majority of the seats in the peninsula, it was in danger of losing the two-thirds majority that enabled it to alter the constitution at will. The outcome depended on the forty East Malaysian seats, of which the government needed to win thirty. Following the rioting in Kuala Lumpur, however, voting in Sabah and Sarawak was postponed and Parliament was suspended. When the postponed election was held in June and July 1970, the NOC did not object to the chief minister of Sabah's use of blatantly intimidatory tactics to win all sixteen seats. In Sarawak heavy pressure was applied to the leftist Chinese SUPP to convince the party to join the coalition. The government in Kuala Lumpur was thus able to achieve its two-thirds majority.

In the wake of the rioting the government resorted to using both its powers under the ISA and emergency provisions to arrest important opposition leaders, including the DAP leader Lim Kit Siang, prominent Gerakan leader V. David, and many Labour Party activists. Between 13 May and July the number of ISA detainees increased from 251 to 368 while another nine thousand were arrested for various offences ranging from murder and arson to curfew breaking.[2] Political activists detained under the ISA were accused of inciting racial feelings, but their detention also weakened the opposition. Although David was released in July 1969, Lim Kit Siang was held until October 1970.

The emergency also permitted UMNO to strengthen its position vis-à-vis the other parties in the Alliance. Although the Alliance was always dominated by UMNO, the MCA and the MIC had considerable influence and held significant portfolios in the government. Following the large loss of MCA seats in the election and demands by some UMNO leaders that the number of MCA seats in the cabinet be reduced, chastened MCA leaders announced that they were withdrawing from the government. When the NOC was established immediately after the proclamation of the emer-

---

[1] The most complete account is in von Vorys 1975:part 3.
[2] Ibid.:347; NOC 1969:91.

gency, seven of its nine members were Malays; Chinese and Indian communities were represented by the presidents of the MCA and MIC respectively. Although the MCA soon reversed its decision not to participate in the government, its influence was greatly reduced. During the period of NOC rule, the whole thrust of government policy was reoriented toward meeting Malay demands, primarily through the formulation of the NEP and the implementation of Malay as the language of education and government.

The emergency also facilitated the replacement of Tunku Abdul Rahman as prime minister by his deputy, Tun Razak. It seems that Razak had already begun to feel that the Tunku should retire soon. The Tunku had for some time been under criticism from the so-called ultras in UMNO—some of whom were close to Razak—for his accommodating attitude toward non-Malays and his failure to be more assertive on behalf of the Malay community. In the wake of the rioting, the Tunku succeeded in having one of his strongest critics, Dr. Mahathir, expelled from the party and another, Musa Hitam, dismissed as assistant minister. But real power was effectively transferred to Tun Razak as director of the NOC, and in September 1970 the Tunku resigned and was replaced by Razak. While it is likely that the Tunku would have lost his position in any case as a result of UMNO's growing disaffection with his policies, Razak's grip on the government through the NOC made it inevitable.[3]

The proclamation of emergency in 1969 was intended primarily to restore political order and communal harmony. But at the same time it provided substantial political benefits for the dominant group in the government, which was able to use emergency powers to strengthen the Alliance against the opposition, strengthen UMNO against its Alliance partners, and consolidate the power of Razak and his supporters within UMNO. By the time that normalcy was restored in February 1971, the political system had undergone substantial change in an authoritarian direction.

The 1975–77 UMNO Crisis

In contrast to the 1969 crisis, when resort to authoritarian methods of rule was motivated primarily by the government's need to restore public order and only incidentally permitted a shift in the distribution of power within the ruling coalition, authoritarian measures during the 1975–77

[3] In an interview, one of Tun Razak's inner circle of advisors said, "The riots proved a heaven-sent opportunity for Razak to seize power. The NOC was in fact a coup in all but name." December 1990.

UMNO crisis were used to settle a factional struggle within the dominant party despite the absence of any credible threat to public order. Although Tun Razak's domination of UMNO was unchallenged, the change in direction after 1970 gave rise to two types of discontent in the party.[4] First, the Tunku and his supporters became increasingly alienated: they were pushed out of positions of influence, and the pre-NEP policies with which they were associated were abandoned. Second, rivalries developed among Razak's own supporters, especially as it became apparent that his health was declining. In particular, both the Tunku's group and some of Razak's own supporters claimed that Razak's inner circle of political advisors enjoyed excessive influence that they used to the detriment of both the Tunku's allies and their rivals within the Razak camp.

During the 1960s Razak gathered together a group of advisors and assistants who shared his general belief that drastic changes were needed in the 1970s. These advisors were critical of Tunku Abdul Rahman's leadership and believed that more vigorous policies should be pursued to uplift the Malay community. They favored more state intervention in the economy and a more critical approach to foreign investment while asserting that Malaysia should take a more independent stance in foreign affairs.[5]

Among Razak's most prominent supporters were young politicians such as Mahathir Mohamad, Musa Hitam, and Tengku Razaleigh. His staff also included key assistants, most in their early thirties, such as his political secretary, Abdullah Ahmad, and Khalil Akasah, who became the executive secretary of UMNO in the early 1970s. In addition, Razak was receptive to the ideas of a group of leftists who had moved to Malaysia from Singapore in the late 1950s and early 1960s following a series of breaks with Lee Kuan Yew's PAP. The key member of this group was journalist and novelist Samad Ismail, who was placed in charge of the *New Straits Times* when it was taken over by UMNO in 1972. Another was Abdullah Majid who became Razak's press secretary and, after Abdullah's election to Parliament in 1974, the prime minister's parliamentary secretary. Abdullah's brother Wahab became press secretary to Datuk Hussein Onn. During the early 1950s both Samad and Abdullah had been jailed by the British as Communist sympathizers while Wahab had for a time in the 1960s been secretary-general of the Socialist-inclined opposition party, PRM. Lawyers James Puthucheary and Sidney Woodhull, although not Malays and therefore not members of UMNO, were also among the leftists from Singapore whom Razak consulted on political issues.

Tunku Abdul Rahman and his supporters were particularly bitter about the treatment they had received after 1970 and blamed Razak's inner cir-

---

[4] For a more complete account written in the late 1970s, see Crouch 1980.
[5] See Funston 1980:179–83.

cle.[6] The ambitious minister for home affairs, Tan Sri Ghazali Shafie, a former senior civil servant and lifelong friend of Razak, also resented the influence of Razak's advisers. He had originally been associated with the group but became alienated when they undermined his campaign for election as one of UMNO's vice presidents in 1975. Another veteran UMNO leader, Tan Sri Syed Jaafar Albar, a former party secretary-general, had been aligned with the Tunku's critics in the 1960s but had not been given a position of influence in the new regime after 1970. He was outspokenly critical of the "kitchen cabinet."

The rivalries within the UMNO elite grew to critical proportions when Razak decided to take action against the Menteri Besar of Selangor, Datuk Harun Idris. Although a lawyer and bureaucrat by training, Harun proved himself an effective populist politician able to mobilize widespread support among poor Malays in the squatter areas of Kuala Lumpur, which at that time was still part of Selangor. In 1969 he acquired notoriety when the 13 May rioting broke out near his headquarters. In 1971, already in his late forties, he was elected chairman of UMNO Youth, a position that gave him high national visibility.[7] His rising popularity within the party made him a potential threat to Razak's advisers, whose fears were apparently shared by the prime minister.

In the latter half of 1975 Razak decided that Harun had to be stopped. Like most Menteri Besar, Harun's personal wealth seemed to have grown during his period in office; so Razak ordered the government's anticorruption agency, the National Bureau of Investigation, to look into his financial affairs. Nevertheless, with the specter of 13 May 1969 still looming large, the prime minister was anxious to avoid a direct confrontation in which Harun's supporters in UMNO Youth and the squatter *kampongs* of Selangor might rise in his defense. Razak therefore offered Harun appointment as Malaysia's ambassador to the United Nations. Apparently sensing weakness in Razak's offer, however, Harun declined. The prime minister was thus faced with a choice between backing down and arresting Harun. On 24 November 1975, in an atmosphere of great tension with armed troops stationed in the largely deserted streets of the city, Harun was arrested and charged with sixteen counts of corruption.[8]

---

[6] One senior member of the Tunku's group claimed that Samad and Abdullah Majid were the brains in Razak's inner circle while Khalil Akasah was "another snake in the grass." Interview, January 1979. According to the Tunku, "The vicious circle I have referred to, however, decided to carry on with their attacks on me, not directly but indirectly by refusing even to identify me with the old party, let alone with achieving independence of this country. This was indeed a conspiracy by this group of people whose main contention was that Tun Razak should not appear to walk in my shadow." Abdul Rahman 1977:296.

[7] An age limit of forty was imposed on the membership of UMNO Youth, but there was no limit for the chairman.

[8] *NST* 25 November 1975.

The writing seemed to be on the wall for Harun; but the death of Tun Razak from leukemia seven weeks later, in January 1976, offered some hope. Razak was succeeded by his deputy and brother-in-law, Datuk Hussein Onn, who himself had recently suffered a heart attack and was seen by many as a stopgap leader. Therefore, the question of the deputy prime ministership was viewed as one of vital significance. Apparently, Hussein was inclined to appoint Ghazali Shafie; but the three party vice presidents, Ghafar Baba, Mahathir, and Razaleigh, had agreed among themselves that the new deputy should be chosen from among them. Their decision eliminated and apparently embittered Ghazali, who was to play a major role in the events which followed. When Mahathir was selected, Ghafar Baba also showed his disappointment by refusing to serve in the new cabinet although he remained in his position as secretary-general of the BN.

In March, Harun took a leave of absence as Menteri Besar of Selangor and embarked on a nationwide campaign to rally political support. He alleged that certain personalities in the press were engaged in character assassination, and his ally Syed Jaafar Albar claimed that Communist agents had infiltrated the government.[9] Among those named were leading members of Razak's kitchen cabinet, including Samad, the Majid brothers, James Puthucheary, and Sidney Woodhull. A few days later Tunku Abdul Rahman took up the same theme, warning about Communists in the government and the expansion of Soviet influence.[10]

These allegations were welcomed by the minister for home affairs, Ghazali, who apparently blamed Samad's group for persuading Hussein not to appoint him deputy prime minister. Ghazali was the minister in charge of the special branch of the police, which appears to have cooperated closely with its Singapore counterpart. In June 1976, two Malay journalists in Singapore, including the editor of the Singapore *Berita Harian,* were arrested and accused of involvement since 1972 "in a Communist scheme masterminded and directed by Samad Ismail." It was alleged that the journalists had slanted news with the intention of "softening the Malay ground for Communist ideas."[11] Samad had been one of Lee Kuan Yew's enemies in the PAP in the 1950s, and his influence on Tun Razak had been a constant worry for the Singapore prime minister.

In response to the "confessions" in Singapore, the Malaysian minister for home affairs immediately ordered the arrest under the ISA of Samad and another Malay journalist, Samani Mohamad Amin. They were accused of "direct involvement in activities in support of the Communist

[9] *NST* 15 March 1976.
[10] *UM* 22 March 1976; *FEER* 2 April 1976 (Harvey Stockwin, "Harun: Selangor Says No").
[11] *NST* 23 June 1976.

struggle for political power in this country," their activities being "subtly designed to blur public fear of and antagonism towards a possible communist takeover."[12] Two months later, Samad appeared on television to "confess" that the allegations were true. He said that he was able to gain influence with some younger UMNO members and "through them I succeeded in approaching the leadership of UMNO and also through them I succeeded in influencing important UMNO leaders to see issues and solve them in my way."[13] Samad's reference to young UMNO leaders was immediately taken up by the Tunku's and Harun's supporters who demanded that they be uncovered and dealt with. In November 1976, having been presented with "evidence" by his minister for home affairs, the prime minister announced that "there are some UMNO members, whether they realized it or not, who had been influenced by communist activities and ideology." The next day two deputy ministers, Datuk Abdullah Ahmad and Abdullah Majid, were arrested under the ISA together with one MCA official, two DAP members of Parliament, and the chairman of the PSRM.[14] In February 1977 Abdullah Ahmad and Abdullah Majid were also induced, with promises of early release, to make "confessions" on television. Meanwhile, in late 1976 stories circulated that other associates of Tun Razak such as Mahathir, Musa, and Razaleigh were also linked to the Communists.[15]

The new prime minister, Datuk Hussein Onn, was convinced that Harun Idris was corrupt and should pay the penalty. In March 1976 Harun was expelled from UMNO, and heavy pressure was applied to UMNO members of the Selangor legislative assembly to pass a motion of no confidence in the Menteri Besar. Harun was then brought to trial and in May was convicted of receiving a bribe of $250,000 from the Hongkong and Shanghai Banking Corporation for which he was sentenced to two years' imprisonment. Meanwhile, a new charge was laid involving the misuse of $8 million from the Bank Kerjasama Rakyat of which he was chairman. He was again found guilty and sentenced to a further six months in prison, which was later increased to four years on appeal. The arrest of Samad, however, provided new hope for Harun who was still free

---

[12] Ibid.

[13] *UM* 2 September 1976. In an interview Samad said that special branch officers had written his confession for him. He had been held in solitary confinement for some time before. May 1985.

[14] *NST* 4 November 1976.

[15] In interviews, Samad, Abdullah Ahmad, and Abdullah Majid all said that their interrogators attempted to get them to implicate Mahathir and others in alleged pro-Communist activities. Professor Syed Husin Ali, who had been detained under the ISA since 1974, also revealed that he was placed in solitary confinement and underwent intensive interrogation in late 1976. He said that his special branch interrogators "wanted me to admit that I was the middle-man between the communist underground and Dr Mahathir Mohamad and Musa Hitam." Husin Ali 1987:47.

waiting for the hearings of his appeals. His supporters in UMNO Youth claimed that he was a victim of a plot hatched by UMNO's "Communists"; and shortly after Samad's televised "confession," the UMNO Supreme Council yielded to party pressure and readmitted him to party membership.

The arrest of Samad shortly before the UMNO General Assembly in July 1976 also benefited other leaders. Ghazali, who had been badly beaten in his attempt to win a vice president post at the 1975 assembly, was congratulated by the delegates for his vigilance in detecting the "Communists"; and Harun's sixty-two-year-old ally, Syed Jaafar Albar, was elected chairman of UMNO Youth with Harun's nephew, Haji Suhaimi Kamaruddin, as his deputy. During 1977, however, the struggle lost much of its dynamism. Syed Jaafar Albar died in January, and Harun's appeals against his convictions failed. He eventually began his term in Pudu prison in February 1978.

Tan Sri Ghazali Shafie retained his position as minister for home affairs and his extraordinary influence with the prime minister until July 1981 when the UMNO General Assembly, on Datuk Hussein Onn's retirement, unanimously elected Dr. Mahathir as the new party leader and, by convention, prime minister. Mahathir had been acting as prime minister since early in the year when Hussein had undergone a heart operation. After taking over the powers of the prime minister, Mahathir apparently demanded Samad's release. Ghazali agreed only on the condition that Samad make another televised "confession" to show, as Ghazali put it, that "he has responded satisfactorily to rehabilitation and has turned over a new leaf."[16] Several weeks later Abdullah Majid was also released although he was only required to produce a written "confession."[17] Finally, after Mahathir had formally taken over as prime minister and appointed his deputy, Musa Hitam, as minister for home affairs, Abdullah Ahmad, the two DAP detainees, and PSRM chairman Kassim Ahmad were unconditionally released. As a parting shot, however, three days before Mahathir took office, Ghazali arrested his political secretary, Siddiq Mohamed Ghouse, who was alleged to be an agent for the Soviet KGB.[18] Despite the serious nature of the charge he was never tried and was released in 1984. Meanwhile, the three "Communists" were quickly rehabilitated. Samad was appointed editorial advisor to the *New Straits Times* group; Datuk Abdullah Ahmad became a successful businessman, rejoined UMNO, and was reelected to Parliament in 1986; and Abdullah Majid was readmitted to UMNO.

[16] *NST* 1 February 1981; the televised confession was printed in full in *UM* 3 February 1981.
[17] *NST* 22 February 1981.
[18] *UM* 22 July 1981.

The UMNO crisis of the mid-1970s illustrated the way in which authoritarian means were used as weapons in an intraparty struggle for power. The minister for home affairs, with the approval of the prime minister, used ISA powers to detain three UMNO leaders on the ludicrous charge that they assisted the Communists. Not only were they detained for more than four years but they were humiliated by being forced to make absurd confessions on television. That many of their colleagues in the government did not believe the charges was shown by their rapid rehabilitation following the change in leadership in 1981. Yet the power of the minister for home affairs was such that the detainees' friends in the government were apparently inhibited from raising the question as long as Ghazali enjoyed the full confidence of the prime minister.[19]

The moves against Harun also involved the use of authoritarian power because the government clearly intervened in the normal course of criminal investigation to achieve its political purposes. While many people believed that several Menteri Besar were vulnerable to corruption charges, it is highly improbable that the police would have begun investigating such cases on their own initiative. Harun was only investigated when the prime minister intervened. But Tun Razak was not primarily concerned with the problem of corruption. Despite being convinced that Harun was corrupt, he was prepared to appoint him as ambassador to the UN if he would resign voluntarily. The prosecution of Datuk Harun was essentially a political maneuver designed to block a potentially dangerous political challenge when other methods failed.

The 1977–78 Kelantan Emergency

Authoritarian powers were also used to strengthen UMNO vis-à-vis the opposition parties, as the case of the dismissal of the PAS government in the state of Kelantan illustrates. PAS had ruled Kelantan since the 1959 election and remained the dominant force in the state government after the 1973 formation of the coalition with UMNO. The party's long period in control enabled its leaders to consolidate their strength by establishing a patronage network to reward party stalwarts through, among other things, the distribution of appointments and business opportunities in much the same way that UMNO consolidated its control in other states.[20]

[19] In 1976, a few weeks before the arrest of Abdullah Ahmad and Abdullah Majid, I heard a senior UMNO minister say that he would not make comments about Tan Sri Ghazali Shafie "until prison camps are air-conditioned and equipped with massage parlors."

[20] See Funston 1980:246. In an interview in 1975 a senior PAS leader in the Kelantan government admitted that there was little to distinguish between the PAS-led government in Kelantan and UMNO-led governments elsewhere but blamed this on constitutional limitations on the power of state governments.

When the coalition with UMNO was formed, PAS continued to control the Kelantan state government. UMNO was represented on the state executive council while PAS leader Datuk Mohamed Asri Muda joined the federal cabinet.

PAS's continuing domination of the Kelantan state government had been accepted as a reality by most national UMNO leaders but was a source of embarrassment for the Kelantan state UMNO, especially the Kelantanese in Tun Razak's inner circle, such as Razaleigh and Abdullah Ahmad. UMNO's Kelantanese leaders could hardly expect to rise to the highest posts in UMNO as long as they were unable to win their own state from PAS. PAS leaders doubted the commitment of state UMNO leaders to continued cooperation, and PAS was also worried about their influence with Razak. These suspicions became acute in early 1975 when a young Kelantanese journalist with the *New Straits Times* published a book that strongly criticized PAS and its administration in Kelantan.[21] The book's introduction was written by Abdullah Ahmad and it was published by the press of the UMNO-owned newspaper, *Utusan Melayu*. Thus, PAS leaders naturally believed that it confirmed their doubts about UMNO's good faith in pursuing the BN concept.

Signs of friction between PAS and UMNO in the Kelantan state government were soon visible, especially after the 1974 election when Razak insisted on the appointment of Datuk Mohamed Nasir as Menteri Besar. Nasir, who was in his late fifties, had a reputation for honesty but was regarded as politically naive by many of his PAS colleagues. They were soon disturbed by his willingness to work closely with Razaleigh, the head of the Kelantan UMNO. The first crisis in the state occurred in May 1975 after the Menteri Besar revoked a large timber concession and froze an allocation of land believed to contain rich reserves of tin, both of which had been earlier awarded by the PAS government. Tension surfaced again in 1977 when Nasir claimed that the State Economic Development Corporation had guaranteed a large bank loan for a private tobacco company involving "certain people" linked to PAS.[22]

The crisis that led to the proclamation of emergency and the expulsion of PAS from the BN began in September 1977 when twenty of the twenty-two PAS members of the Kelantan legislative assembly announced their intention to introduce a motion of no confidence if the Menteri Besar did not resign immediately.[23] When Datuk Nasir not only refused to resign but allowed his backers, who included many UMNO supporters, to organize several large demonstrations in his support, the national PAS Supreme

---

[21] Alias Muhammad 1975.
[22] *NST* 13 June 1975; Yahya Ismail 1977:13–14.
[23] See Yahya Ismail 1977 and 1978; Alias Muhammad 1978; Kamlin 1980.

Council expelled him from the party. On 15 October the no-confidence motion was adopted by the Kelantan assembly. Several more demonstrations in support of Nasir took place in Kota Baru and other towns; and, after minor damage was done to property on 19 October, police imposed a curfew.

The demonstrations, which were partly sponsored by UMNO, gave the central government the opportunity to intervene. In November the government introduced a bill in Parliament that placed Kelantan under emergency rule, and in December PAS was expelled from the BN. The period of emergency rule lasted for three months and ended with a state election on 11 March 1978. During the emergency period, Datuk Nasir retained the post of Menteri Besar, which gave him prestige and prominence but little power. Encouraged by the BN leaders, he established a new party, Berjasa, consisting of former PAS supporters. Although Berjasa clearly cooperated with UMNO, it did not immediately join the BN because Tengku Razaleigh's strategy was aimed at splitting the PAS vote. The strategy worked, with the BN winning twenty-three and Berjasa eleven seats. PAS was thus reduced to two seats in the thirty-six-seat assembly, and its percentage of the overall vote fell to thirty-three percent compared to 52 percent in 1969 when it last contested independently of the BN. Following the election, a new UMNO-Berjasa coalition was formed, and Datuk Nasir was rewarded with an appointment as senator and minister in the central government. Berjasa later joined the BN.

In the Kelantan case, political rivalries between factions and parties were not allowed to play themselves out in the normal democratic way. When the Kelantan assembly passed a vote of no confidence in the Menteri Besar, he did not resign but stayed in his position with central government support. The Menteri Besar could not call the assembly into session again because twenty of its thirty-six members wanted a change in leadership. The federal government therefore introduced emergency rule in Kelantan, using the large demonstrations in support of Nasir as the pretext. In fact, the Kelantan UMNO encouraged and participated in the demonstrations. Although the demonstrations caused some minor damage to property, there was no serious threat to security. The emergency declaration was intended primarily to remove PAS from control of the Kelantan state government, thus benefiting UMNO as well as the main planner of the move, Tengku Razaleigh, whose prestige in the party rose enormously. Having toppled the long-established PAS regime, Razaleigh was in a position three years later to contest the deputy leadership of the party, something he could hardly have done if he were unable to control his own state.

The UMNO Split and Operasi Lalang

In 1987 the Malaysian economy was in decline due to the world recession. Business bankruptcies were common, and unemployment was rising.

In such circumstances, it was not surprising that ethnic issues came to the surface; each ethnic group felt insecure and tended to see other groups as the cause of its difficulties. Moreover, in 1986–87 the general communal tensions arising from economic decline were aggravated by political rivalries within the Malay and Chinese communities.

As I will explain in Chapter 7, Dr. Mahathir's grip on the government was by no means firm after his narrow defeat of Razaleigh's challenge for the party leadership. For the first time, factional rivalries within UMNO were threatening the coherence of the party. At all levels rival groups were pitted against each other. While UMNO had always emphasized its Malay character, the demands of its electoral alliance with non-Malay parties usually compelled it to tone down its stand on ethnic issues. But the internal split in the party put UMNO leaders in the position of losing party support if they did not take a strong line on ethnic issues. Leaders in both factions increasingly portrayed themselves as champions of the Malays. For some this meant compromising multicommunal principles, but for others it allowed them to say what they really felt.

Similar pressures operated on the Chinese side. In the 1986 election, the opposition DAP performed very well at the expense of the MCA and Gerakan. Moreover, the reputation of the MCA was at a very low ebb because of the conviction of its former president, Tan Koon Swan, for business crimes in Singapore. Several other top MCA leaders were facing charges related to the collapse of deposit-taking cooperatives involving the savings of some six hundred thousand depositors, who were mainly Chinese and had invested over $1.5 billion.[24] The MCA was under great pressure to reassert itself as the representative of the Chinese community, and to a lesser extent Gerakan was under similar pressure. The DAP, however, was intent on driving home its advantage.

During late 1986 and 1987, several issues stirred ethnic emotions among Malays and non-Malays, especially the Chinese. In November 1986 an MCA convention enraged Malays by adopting a resolution that declared, "Malaysia's three major races are originated from other countries. Therefore, none of them should brand the other as immigrants and claim themselves as natives."[25] In July 1987 the University of Malaya decided that optional courses in the departments of Chinese and Tamil studies should be taught in Malay. This disturbed non-Malays who feared further encroachments on the use of languages other than Malay. In August three DAP leaders led a protest demonstration at the entrance of the university, which was followed by a counterdemonstration by Malay students a few days later.[26]

[24] Gomez 1991:ch. 3.
[25] *Asiaweek* 23 November 1986; Towards Preserving National Security 1988:15.
[26] Towards Preserving National Security 1988:10–11; *FEER* 30 July 1987 (Suhaini Aznam, "Of Races and Tongues"); *Asiaweek* 16 August 1987.

The final issue was the government's appointment of more than one hundred Chinese teachers as senior assistants and afternoon supervisors in Chinese primary schools. The problem was that the new appointees, although Chinese, did not possess qualifications in Mandarin. The deputy minister of education, Woon See Chin of the MCA, explained that the government had advertised twice but failed to attract sufficient applications. Nevertheless, many Chinese saw the appointments as a subtle move to undermine the status of the Chinese-medium primary schools. The DAP, supported by the Chinese school association, the Chinese school-teachers' association, and the umbrella organization for the Chinese community in Selangor known as the Selangor Chinese Assembly Hall, led the protest. Fearing that the party was being outflanked by the DAP and no doubt genuinely concerned about the long-term implications of the policy, the MCA, represented by its deputy president, Datuk Lee Kim Sai, participated in a protest meeting at the Thean Hou Temple in Kuala Lumpur on 11 October. During the meeting he sat next to the DAP leader Lim Kit Siang. Gerakan was also represented at the meeting. Although the government had already decided to reassign teachers, the meeting called for a boycott of schools if the appointments were not withdrawn by 14 October. On 15 October the boycott began.[27]

The MCA's participation with the DAP in a protest on behalf of the Chinese community gave the UMNO Youth movement an opportunity to present itself as the champion of the Malays. The movement's acting leader, Datuk Najib Tun Razak, was in particular need of establishing his credibility; he had recently switched to the Mahathir camp after initially being aligned with the challengers.[28] A huge rally was held at the Jalan Raja Muda Stadium on 17 October. Speakers, including the Menteri Besar of Selangor, Datuk Haji Muhammad Haji Muhammad Taib, condemned the attitude of the MCA and the Chinese in general, while some demanded the expulsion of Lee Kim Sai from the cabinet. Banners and posters carried anti-Chinese slogans such as "Chinese are Rascals," "Chinese Go Back to Mainland," "Close down Chinese and Tamil Primary Schools," "Revoke the Citizenship of Those Who Opposed the Malay Rulers," and "Lee Kim Sai Is [CPM leader] Chin Peng's Descendant." Other, more ominous slogans included "May 13 Has Begun," "Oct. 17: Second May 13" and "Soak It [the Malay dagger] with Chinese Blood."[29] Some of the youths

[27] *FEER* 29 October 1987 (Suhaini Aznam, "The Language of Politics"); *Asiaweek* 23 October 1987.

[28] In September, Najib had warned that UMNO Youth would lodge police reports against any politican who "incites the feelings or challenges the rights, dignity and sovereignty of the Malays." *Asiaweek* 6 September 1987.

[29] *FEER* 29 October 1987; *Asiaweek* 30 October 1987; Towards Preserving National Security 1988:16–17; DAP 1988:16–17.

wanted to present Najib with a *parang* (a sword or long knife) and burn Lee Kim Sai in effigy at the rally, but Najib refused to give them his permission.[30] Meanwhile, on the evening of 18 October, a deranged Malay soldier went on a shooting spree in the Chow Kit area of Kuala Lumpur, not far from where the 13 May rioting had begun in 1969. Several people were hit by bullets, and one—a Malay—was killed before the soldier surrendered. Although the incident was unrelated to political developments, it had an electrifying impact; and people in Kuala Lumpur began to stock food.

These developments took place while the prime minister was abroad. In his absence, Sanusi Junid, the party secretary-general, and several other UMNO leaders apparently decided to take advantage of the situation by calling a mammoth rally in Kuala Lumpur on 1 November "to prove to the world" that the Malays were united, as Sanusi put it. He called on UMNO supporters to "spread the word that all Malays must come to the rally whether they have to travel here by car, bus, train or plane."[31] UMNO leaders claimed that the rally would be attended by about half a million Malays, although the stadium in which it was to be held could take only sixty thousand. The rally had originally been intended to be held in Johor Baru, the birthplace of UMNO, as part of Mahathir's campaign against the UMNO dissidents led by Razaleigh. In his absence, however, his lieutenants felt that it would now have a bigger impact if held in Kuala Lumpur. The possibility of the rally's precipitating a racial riot was apparently not given much consideration.

On his return to Kuala Lumpur, the prime minister quickly called off the UMNO rally and gave his approval to the police to arrest 106 dissidents (the number later rose to 119). The arrests took place under the ISA between 27 October and 14 November in what was called Operasi Lalang (Tall Grass Operation). At the same time, assemblies and rallies were prohibited and three newspapers were suspended. During the next few months most of the detainees were released, but forty-nine were served with two-year detention orders. Most of these were also gradually released during 1988, the last being freed in April 1989.

Some of the detainees had clearly been involved in debating the communal issues that lay behind much of the tension in October 1987.[32] Among them were sixteen members of the DAP, of whom ten were members of Parliament, including the leader of the opposition, Lim Kit Siang. Four were members of state assemblies. At least five members of the Chinese education movement were detained. In addition, eight members of the

---

[30] *FEER* 19 November 1987 (Suhaini Aznam, "The Double-edged Sword").
[31] *Star* 26 October 1987, cited in DAP 1988:18.
[32] They denied, however, that they had been "stirring up racial tensions." See DAP 1988; Kua 1989.

MCA and five members of Gerakan were detained. Lee Kim Sai went on an extended visit to see his children who were studying in Australia, and the Sultan of Selangor withdrew his datukship. Although the rise in ethnic tension had followed the UMNO Youth rally and civics course as well as the announcement of the huge UMNO rally planned for 1 November, only four UMNO members were arrested. One was closely aligned to Mahathir and, according to rumour, was detained by the police at Subang International Airport for reasons unconnected with the racial situation. The other three were prominent supporters of Tengku Razaleigh in UMNO Youth. All the UMNO, MCA, and Gerakan detainees were released fairly quickly, while seven DAP and five Chinese education-movement detainees were among those given two-year detention orders.[33]

In justifying the communal imbalance in the detentions, Mahathir explained the background.[34] Referring to the planned UMNO rally, he said that "somebody tried to change it from an UMNO rally to a Malay rally against the Chinese. There was even talk about fighting, about coming with weapons." But it was not those people whom the government arrested. "I could say, stop the rally, but that would inflame Malays further because they would say the other people have been making all this noise but you haven't done anything. So I have to do both: stop the rally and take action against the people who have been provoking the Malays."[35] It seemed that the detention of Chinese was a kind of quid pro quo for UMNO leaders who had not been permitted to go ahead with their rally.

Although the rise in communal tensions in October 1987 provided the occasion for the mass arrests, most of the detainees had no connection with the developments in Kuala Lumpur. At least nine were members of PAS who were accused of aggravating communal tensions by making wild claims about Christians converting Malays. Several members of the First Baptist Church in Petaling Jaya were also detained and accused of converting seven Malays.[36] Many of the detainees, however, could not be credibly accused of contributing to the rise in communal tensions in any way. On the contrary, they were associated with organizations concerned with broad social issues of importance to all communities. One of the detainees was Chandra Muzaffar, the founder and chairman of the multicommunal Aliran organization whose philosophy was based on intercommunal cooperation. Others were associated with Insan, a social-reformist organization that regularly publicized issues involving abuse and exploitation of the poor, and the Environment Protection Society of Malaysia, which had

[33] CARPA 1988:76–77; *AWSJ* 28, 29, 30–31 October 1987 (articles by Stephen Duthie).
[34] Of the first eighty-eight arrested, fifty-nine were Chinese and only twenty were Malays. *Asiaweek* 6 November 1987.
[35] *Asiaweek* 20 November 1987.
[36] Towards Preserving National Security 1988:18, 20.

been advising residents in small towns and villages in Perak who were protesting against the siting of a radioactive waste dump. In Sarawak, Harrison Ngau, who led members of the small Penan tribe in protests against the logging of their traditional area, was arrested. The detainees also included activists in the Catholic National Office of Human Development and the Protestant Christian Conference of Asia who were alleged to be adherents of "the 'Liberation Theology' concept upheld by the Marxist group."[37]

There seems to be little doubt that racial tensions had risen to a high point during October 1987; fears that "May 13 Ha[d] Begun", were by no means unfounded. In these circumstances it was hardly surprising that the government resorted to arrests under the ISA to prevent the situation from worsening. Indeed, many residents in Kuala Lumpur felt a great sense of relief when the government acted firmly to bring the situation under control. But the government's critics claimed that the real culprits were the UMNO leaders who had called the UMNO Youth rally and the planned mass rally on 1 November. They, however, were not arrested.

The nature of the arrests suggested that other motives were also involved. Critics claimed that the government deliberately allowed—even encouraged—the rise in racial tensions to gain an excuse for clamping down on the opposition and thus preserving the position of the Mahathir faction in UMNO. Another explanation lay in the political challenges faced by both UMNO and MCA leaders, which "forced" both them and their challengers to turn to racial issues to mobilize support. Both Mahathir's supporters and his challengers presented themselves as the true upholders of Malay dominance, and each group sought to outdo its rivals. Similarly, MCA leaders had to publicly espouse Chinese issues to restore some of their damaged credibility in the Chinese community and meet the DAP challenge.

Although the government was faced with the threat of the outbreak of communal conflict, it also used the situation to achieve other goals. By arresting DAP leaders it not only removed the most vigorous campaigners for Chinese interests but also silenced some of the government's most effective critics on other sensitive issues—in particular, the awarding of a huge road-building contract to United Engineers (M) Berhad, which was controlled by Hatibudi, an UMNO-affiliated company in which the prime minister and other UMNO leaders were trustees. In early October, Lim Kit Siang and Karpal Singh had successfully persuaded the high court to issue an injunction against the signing of the contract. In the cases of Chandra Muzaffar of Aliran and the Insan group, there was no serious claim that they had been involved in stirring up racial feelings. Nevertheless,

[37] Ibid.:26.

they, too, had been active in exposing government corruption and misuse of power. Several of the other detainees were linked to organizations that regularly raised issues that embarrassed the government and tended to undermine its legitimacy, such as the movement against the dumping of radioactive waste, the supporters of the Penans, and the various church organizations.

While most of these organizations were hardly more than irritants to the government in normal times, their significance was greatly enhanced in circumstances where the ruling party was internally divided and the prime minister's grip on power threatened. By raising issues involving corruption, misuse of power, and suppression of human rights, the DAP and the small dissident organizations were providing ammunition for UMNO dissidents in their campaign against Mahathir. In many cases the dissidents were not in a position to raise such issues themselves because of their recent close association with the government, but they benefited whenever embarrassing revelations were made by others. By repressing these organizations and their leaders, the dominant UMNO faction may have hoped to protect itself against damaging criticism that could be exploited by its UMNO rivals. Presumably, the government also calculated that the mass arrests would have a deterrent effect on UMNO dissidents.

Although the introduction of authoritarian measures was in some cases primarily motivated by the perceived need to deal with challenges to political order and stability, the measures also strengthened the political position of those in power. Moreover, authoritarian powers were sometimes used mainly to strengthen the government against the opposition or even one government faction against another.

The proclamation of the 1969 emergency was a case where the primary purpose of authoritarian measures was to restore order. The ISA detentions in 1987 were also a response to a serious threat to order (as well as a result of the behavior of UMNO leaders themselves) and seemed to have succeeded in reducing the level of communal tension. But the senior UMNO members arrested under the ISA in 1976 had not even remotely constituted a threat to order or security. The disturbances that preceded the introduction of emergency rule in Kelantan were, in fact, largely perpetrated by government supporters to provide a pretext for central government intervention.

In all four cases the dominant group of UMNO leaders benefited from the use of authoritarian measures. In 1969, the emergency enabled UMNO to ward off an electoral challenge by the opposition parties and strengthen UMNO's position vis-à-vis its coalition partners. It also helped Tun Razak to replace the Tunku as prime minister and push aside the Tunku's main party allies. The 1977 emergency in Kelantan allowed UMNO to rid itself of a troublesome partner in the BN and defeat PAS soundly in the 1978 state election. At the same time, this success greatly enhanced the reputation of its chief strategist, Razaleigh, who thus acquired a base from which to launch his bid for the deputy prime ministership in 1981. In 1987, Mahathir, while having good reason to take firm action to prevent communal disorders, did not arrest the main instigators among his own supporters but used the opportunity to detain some of his most damaging critics and thus prop up his position, which was being challenged by rivals within UMNO. Finally, the 1976 detentions under the ISA were the most blatant use of authoritarian powers for purely intraparty factional purposes.

7 Contradictory Trends: The UMNO *Split and the 1990 Election*

Despite the UMNO leaders' easy recourse to authoritarian means to preserve their hold on power, the formal constitutional framework remained essentially democratic in character. In accordance with the constitution, competitive elections were held at regular intervals to elect the national and state Parliaments to which governments were responsible. Therefore, it was theoretically possible for the government to be defeated in elections; and, on a few occasions, this did happen at the state level. In practice, however, the electoral system was weighted heavily in favor of the incumbents who routinely used their governmental authority to reinforce their political domination. But this domination depended on the continued strength and coherence of UMNO. As long as it was united, UMNO could control the system; but the durability of BN rule was threatened when its core party suffered severe factional conflict and eventually split in two.

Regular competitive elections, even when the victory of the governing coalition seemed inevitable, had always forced the government to take some account of popular pressures from below. But after the UMNO split and the establishment of Semangat '46 by UMNO dissidents, political competition intensified as the new Malay party allied itself with other opposition parties, both Malay and non-Malay. The challenge could not easily be repressed by authoritarian means, partly because its leaders had the same links with the bureaucracy, police, and other constituents of the Malay establishment as the majority faction in UMNO had. The government was thus confronted with a major electoral challenge to which it responded by redoubling its efforts to win votes. In other words, electoral competition forced the government to broaden its electoral appeal to voters.

The UMNO Split

As I outlined in Chapter 3, the 1970s and 80s had seen an important change in the social composition of UMNO, which in turn reflected change in Malay society as a whole. Economic growth had been accompanied by the growth of the middle class, especially under the NEP, as increasing numbers of Malay youths gained access to secondary and tertiary education. While UMNO continued to rest on a solid rural base, its old leaders with their aristocratic and bureaucratic backgrounds were joined by the products of the expanding educational system, many of whom had humble rural backgrounds. The new socially mobile recruits to the middle class were more ready to question and criticize their leaders than were their parents in the villages. Moreover, for many, politics offered a road for further social mobility. The NEP also resulted in an influx of Malay businesspeople into UMNO, most of whom believed that links with UMNO leaders were essential for business success.

By the 1980s the educated middle class and NEP-produced businesspeople were playing a major role in UMNO, and candidates spent huge sums to ensure victory in party elections. While the Malaysian economy was growing in the 1970s and early 1980s, UMNO was easily able to reward its business supporters. But when the economy contracted in the mid-1980s, it became increasingly difficult to satisfy all of them. Not everyone could get the contracts, licenses, and concessions that they wanted, with the result that many were disappointed. Therefore, the factional struggle within UMNO increasingly took on a life-or-death quality, and many losers faced backruptcy. In these circumstances there was a ready pool of support for dissidents in the UMNO leadership.

The UMNO split was preceded by increasing factional conflict during the first half of the 1980s. Early in 1981 Datuk Hussein underwent heart surgery and in effect left the leadership of the country in the hands of his deputy, Dr. Mahathir, until his resignation on 16 July. Rather than formally nominate his successor, Hussein preferred to leave the choice to the party, which, as he expected, elected Mahathir unanimously as party president and therefore prime minister. But while the transfer of power from Hussein to Mahathir was smooth, a bitter struggle took place over the deputy presidency of the party and therefore, according to custom, the deputy prime ministership. The combatants were the minister of education, Dutak Musa Hitam, and the minister of finance, Tengku Razaleigh Hamzah.[1] While Musa's personal financial resources were no match for

---

[1] For a biography of Musa Hitam, see Gale 1982. For Razaleigh's biography, see Gill 1987.

those of the aristocrat Razaleigh, both campaigns were well financed.[2] Mahathir maintained a facade of neutrality between the two contestants, but it was no secret that he supported Musa who won a narrow victory with 722 votes to 517.[3] During the next three years both sides concentrated on organizing their forces. In 1984 another bitterly fought contest was again won by Musa with a slightly increased majority of 744 to 501. Datuk Harun, now released from prison, got 34.[4] With the party sharply divided at all levels between supporters of the rival camps, the prime minister decided to keep Razaleigh in the cabinet, although he was moved from the Ministry of Finance to the Ministry of Trade and Industry.

The Musa-Razaleigh contest in 1984 was complicated by the emergence of a rising new leader in UMNO, former Muslim youth leader Anwar Ibrahim. The son of a UMNO parliamentary secretary during the Tunku's era, Anwar had been a prominent student leader at the University of Malaya in the late 1960s, fighting for the Malay cause championed at that time by UMNO dissident Mahathir. After graduation Anwar set up a Muslim youth movement, Angkatan Belia Islam Malaysia (Malaysian Islamic Youth Movement, or ABIM) that called for a return to what it saw as true Islamic values. Anwar's activities in the early 1970s brought him into conflict with the government, and he was detained for almost two years under ISA after student demonstrations in December 1974. In the 1978 election Anwar and other ABIM leaders had campaigned for PAS, so it was a surprise to virtually all observers when Anwar's old friend Mahathir persuaded him to become an UMNO candidate in the 1982 election.

Anwar's rise in UMNO was meteoric. After winning his seat in the mainland part of Penang, the thirty-four-year-old was immediately appointed deputy minister in the Prime Minister's Department. Later that year he contested the leadership of UMNO Youth against the incumbent, Datuk Suhaimi Kamaruddin, who was also a deputy minister, defeating him by a mere ten votes. As leader of UMNO Youth, Anwar automatically became one of the vice presidents of UMNO itself and in 1983 was appointed to full membership of the cabinet as minister for youth, sports, and culture.

Anwar's rapid rise was naturally resented by many of the party's younger leaders who had previously given their full support to the Mahathir-Musa leadership. Leaders of Anwar's generation who had loyally served the party for many years and had gradually risen to membership of

---

[2] During a talk at the National University of Malaysia on 17 December 1988, Musa confided that most of his funds were obtained from the prime minister.

[3] *UM* 27 June 1981.

[4] *NST* 26 May 1984.

the party's Supreme Council and been appointed ministers suddenly found their road to further advancement blocked by a man who, during the decade before 1982, had been one of UMNO's most devastating critics. Many of these leaders increasingly turned to Musa with their complaints, and he apparently sympathized with them.

During 1983 rumors began to circulate about tension between Mahathir and Musa, but it was not until February 1986 that the rift became public. Musa suddenly announced his resignation from his position as deputy prime minister and deputy president of the party. In a confidential letter addressed to Mahathir on 26 February Musa said that he was resigning because Mahathir no longer trusted him. According to Musa, Mahathir had believed untrue reports from "senior government officials and journalists" that Musa and "Musa's boys" were spreading stories about Mahathir's being "a dictator, corrupt and the richest [prime minister] in the world." Because the prime minister no longer trusted him, Musa felt that he had to leave the government.[5] Although Musa went ahead with his plan to resign, he was persuaded by his supporters to retain his party position.

In retrospect, it seems that the rift between the prime minister and his deputy first became serious immediately after Musa defeated Razaleigh for the deputy presidency in 1984. Musa had asked Mahathir not to reappoint Razaleigh to the cabinet, arguing that Razaleigh's presence in the leadership would only perpetuate the growing split within the party. But Mahathir took the view that dropping Razaleigh from the cabinet would free him to mobilize his forces for a bigger challenge later, so he moved him from Finance to Trade and Industry. After Razaleigh's appointment as minister of trade and industry, Musa wrote a letter to the prime minister "with a heavy heart and the greatest reluctance" to "register my strongest views against TR's appointment at MTI." In particular, he pointed to the enormous patronage opportunities available to Razaleigh in that ministry.[6] Musa was also apparently unhappy when Mahathir decided to appoint his close friend, millionaire Malay businessman Daim Zainuddin, as minister of finance. During the next year-and-a-half the relationship between Musa and Mahathir deteriorated further.

Although there was no large ideological gap between the two men, a number of Musa's supporters made accusations against the prime minister. He was seen as too impetuous and unwilling to consult his colleagues while tending to equate any criticism of his policies with treachery. Thus,

---

[5] Photocopy of letter from Dato' Musa Hitam to YAB Datuk Seri Mahathir Mohamad, 26 February 1986. Although the letter is stamped *rahsia* (confidential), copies were also sent to all members of UMNO's supreme council. Photocopies were soon circulating widely in Kuala Lumpur.

[6] Musa's letter, dated 5 July 1984, is reproduced in Muhammad Azree and Sudirman Hj Ahmad 1987 and referred to in Chapter 3.

the industrialization program, especially the Malaysian car project, and the "Look East" policy, were adopted without sufficient preparation and without making thorough economic calculations. Further, Mahathir was criticized for being too close personally to several big Malay businessmen, including Daim Zainuddin and Tan Sri Ibrahim Mohamad, whose financial success had depended heavily on facilities provided by the government. Moreover, his own sister-in-law had been awarded huge construction projects.[7] On the other hand, Mahathir's supporters criticized Musa for his impatience and untrustworthiness. Musa was seen as unwilling to bide his time until Mahathir resigned but was instead attempting to undermine the prime minister's position from within.[8]

By the next party election in April 1987, bitter rivals Razaleigh and Musa had papered over their earlier antagonism and agreed that Razaleigh would run for the party presidency against Mahathir while Musa would attempt to retain the deputy presidency. For his running mate, Mahathir teamed up with party veteran Ghafar Baba, a proven vote winner who had been a party vice president since 1962 but left the cabinet in 1976 in a fit of pique when Hussein Onn had selected Mahathir as deputy prime minister. Since then, he had continued to be active in party affairs and had also become a wealthy businessman who, like other bumiputera businesspeople, was heavily dependent on government patronage. Ghafar had been politically close to Tengku Razaleigh, but his commercial dependence on the goodwill of the government made it unlikely that he would ever side with Mahathir's critics.

The hard-fought election resulted in a narrow victory for the Mahathir-Ghafar team. Mahathir won 761 (51.45 percent) of the votes against Razaleigh's 718, a margin of only 43; Ghafar won 739 against Musa's 699, a majority of 40 with an additional 41 ballots being spoilt. In the contest for the three elected vice-presidential positions, Mahathir's candidates, Wan Mokhtar Ahmad, the veteran Terengganu Menteri Besar, and Anwar Ibrahim came first and third while a Musa supporter, Abdullah Ahmad Badawi, came second. Of the twenty-five elected positions on the party's Supreme Council, supporters of either Razaleigh or Musa won eight.[9] Following his victory in the party election, the prime minister purged his cabinet of the remaining supporters of Razaleigh and Musa.

Although Mahathir had established his control of the party and the government, his position was far from secure: about half the party member-

---

[7] Interview with a cabinet minister in Musa's camp, April 1986.

[8] An anonymous twenty-eight-page statement detailing Musa's weaknesses was circulated by Mahathir's supporters in March 1986. Similar allegations were made by a senior UMNO official in the Mahathir camp in an interview in April 1986.

[9] For details of voting at the assembly, see Shamsul 1988:182–3. See also Means 1991:199–206.

ship was ranged against him. But his opponents, popularly called "Team B" as opposed to Mahathir's "Team A," continued to be sharply divided among themselves. Razaleigh and Musa had worked together in their effort to topple Mahathir but, having failed in that endeavour, remained rivals. The legacy of earlier struggles between them, which had divided the party into rival camps at all levels, made it difficult for their supporters to be reconciled. While Razaleigh remained adamantly opposed to compromise with Mahathir, some of Musa's supporters were inclined to look for a modus vivendi.

Meanwhile, a group of Razaleigh supporters filed a suit in the high court in which they claimed that delegates from several unregistered branches of the party had voted in the party elections. The Societies Act stated that "no registered society shall establish a branch without the prior approval of the registrar." Thus, it was not enough that a society be registered; each branch had to be registered individually. Because branches in four divisions that sent forty-four delegates to the assembly were found to be unregistered, their votes could have affected the outcome—the winning margin was only forty-three votes. Therefore, the plaintiffs called on the court to declare the party election "unconstitutional, illegal and null and void" and to order that fresh party elections be held. When the case was heard in February 1988, UMNO's lawyers, realizing that they could not hope for a favorable judgment, were instructed to opt for what the dissidents' lawyer called a *"kamikaze* defense." Another section of the Societies Act, framed no doubt with parties and organizations other than UMNO in mind, stated that "where a registered society established a branch without the prior approval of the registrar, such registered society and the branch so established shall be deemed to be unlawful societies."[10] Relying on this section, Justice Harun Hashim declared the UMNO election to be null and void and concluded that UMNO was an illegal organization. Having deemed the organization to be illegal, he did not grant the plaintiffs' request for an order that new party elections be held.[11] The plaintiffs, who had only sought the voiding of the old elections and the holding of new elections, then appealed to the Supreme Court.

Despite this setback, the dissidents immediately attempted to exploit the judgment by applying to register a new party called UMNO Malaysia. Neither Razaleigh nor Musa were directly associated with the new party, but its proposed secretary-general was Musa's ally, the former foreign minister Datuk Rais Yatim. In addition, the dissidents recruited to their

[10] This section of the act was amended in March 1988. Under the amendment unregistered branches were deemed illegal but not the parent organization.

[11] *AWSJ* 3, 4, 5–6 February 1988 (Stephen Duthie, "Malaysia's Ruling Party Declared Illegal").

cause Malaysia's two living ex-prime ministers: octogenarian Tunku Abdul Rahman, who was proposed as the new party's president, and Tun Hussein Onn, proposed as deputy president. The registrar of societies, however, rejected the application on the grounds that a new organization was not permitted to have a name similar to an existing organization. The old UMNO, although declared illegal by the court, had not yet been administratively removed from the register of societies. Immediately after the registration of the old UMNO was officially canceled two days later, Mahathir's group successfully applied to register its new party, called UMNO Baru (New UMNO).[12] Because the registrar of societies is part of the Ministry for Home Affairs (of which Mahathir was minister), it can be assumed that his group had inside information about the timing of the removal of the illegal UMNO from the register and was able to pre-empt the rival group and retain UMNO as part of its name.

The dissidents' appeal to the Supreme Court had enormous political significance because a judgment in their favor would have not only reinstated the old UMNO legally but required that new party elections be held in circumstances unfavorable to the prime minister. At this point the legal battle for control of UMNO became entwined with a growing conflict between Mahathir and leading members of the judiciary, which resulted in the dismissal of the lord president of the Supreme Court and the suspension of five Supreme Court judges (see Chapter 8). The hearing of the UMNO case was in the meantime postponed until early August 1988 when a five-judge bench (including two high court judges temporarily promoted to make up the numbers of the depleted Supreme Court) ruled against the dissidents.[13]

The struggle between the UMNO factions could now only be settled on the political level. Which group would be able to win the loyalties of the old UMNO's claimed 1.4 million members? A major issue was the question of the old party's assets. In March, before the final court decision on the legality of the old UMNO, the government had amended the Societies Act to facilitate the transfer of the old party's assets to UMNO Baru. According to the amendments, the assets of a defunct organization could be transferred to a new organization if the new organization's constitution closely resembled that of the old one and a majority of members joined it. As a disincentive to dissidents, the amendments, while allowing members who refused to join the new party to claim their share of the assets before the transfer, made them responsible for their share of any debts that might be uncovered during the next six years.[14]

---

[12] *AWSJ* 9 February 1988, 11–12 March 1988.

[13] *NST* 10 August 1988.

[14] *AWSJ* 16 March 1988. UMNO Secretary-General Datuk Mohammed Rahmat claimed, "Our debts are large, we cannot pay them off, the banks want their money back, that is all

Having set up UMNO Baru, Mahathir called on old UMNO members to join the new party. All would be welcome, he said, except "less than one hundred" who had been involved in the abortive attempt to establish UMNO Malaysia.[15] By the middle of the year only sixteen of UMNO's eighty-three members of Parliament and ten members of state assemblies had openly sided with the dissidents, although many more were wavering.[16] During the latter part of 1988 the prime minister's supporters continued to exploit the differences between Razaleigh and Musa and eventually succeeded in enticing Musa to join UMNO Baru early in 1989. The defection of Musa and his supporters reduced the number of dissident seats in Parliament from sixteen to twelve. Of crucial importance was UMNO Baru's control over government patronage, which persuaded many of the waverers that they could not afford openly to join the dissidents.[17]

Having failed in his attempt to have the original UMNO restored and having lost Musa and many of his supporters, Razaleigh decided to establish a new party to "continue the struggle of the old UMNO." Unable under the Societies Act to use a name similar to UMNO Baru—which increasingly called itself simply UMNO—the Razaleigh group called themselves Semangat '46 (Spirit of '46), referring to the year of UMNO's foundation in 1946. The new party held its inaugural general assembly in October 1989, electing Tengku Razaleigh as president and Datuk Rais Yatim as deputy president.

The Opposition Alliance and the 1990 Election

Before Musa's defection, UMNO dissidents had calculated that they had the support of roughly half the old UMNO membership and, by extension, half the UMNO voters. But half would not be sufficient to defeat UMNO Baru in elections as long as its coalition partners in the BN remained loyal and mobilized supporters to tip the balance in UMNO Baru's favor. Semangat was therefore faced with two alternatives. It could stress its Malay character and attempt to outflank UMNO Baru by accusing it of not doing enough for the Malays, or it could attempt to forge its own multicommu-

---

there is to it." He therefore advised that "Former members who did not join UMNO would most likely be faced with the burden of paying off some of the debts personally." *NST* 30 December 1989. In fact, no member ever had to contribute to paying off these debts.

[15] *AWSJ* 15 March 1988.

[16] *NST* 11 June 1988.

[17] One dissident leader said in an interview (in December 1990), "I was very fortunate that I did not have a large overdraft." According to him, it only took a telephone call from the minister of finance, Daim Zainuddin, to have an outstanding bank loan called in. Others faced the threat of possible investigation for corruption.

nal alliance with the opposition parties, especially DAP. It opted for the second alternative. In addition to cultivating DAP, it also sought an alliance with PAS, which regularly won between 40 and 50 percent of Malay votes in Kelantan, Terengganu, and Kedah. By forming simultaneous alliances with both the DAP and PAS, Semangat believed it could defeat the BN.

The alliance strategy, however, was by no means easy to implement. First, much of the Malay community considered the DAP as chauvinist and anti-Malay. Moreover, as the main opposition party, the DAP had a long record of attacking UMNO leaders, including those who now led Semangat. Tengku Razaleigh, for example, had been a prominent target of DAP's attempt to expose the massive Bank Bumiputera scandal of the early 1980s. By aligning itself with the DAP, Semangat opened itself to accusations that it was betraying the Malays. Second, there had been decades of rivalry between UMNO and PAS. In particular, Tengku Razaleigh had been the key figure in the overthrow of the PAS-dominated government in Kelantan in 1977–78. Finally, while it was no easy task to work out cooperative relations with either the DAP or PAS individually, it was extremely difficult to do so with both simultaneously. Nevertheless, during 1989 and 1990 Semangat worked toward this goal.

The advantages of seeking an electoral understanding with DAP had been underlined during a series of by-elections. In August 1988 (before the open rift between the Razaleigh and Musa camps) Musa's protégé, the former minister for federal territories, Datuk Shahrir Samad, challenged the government by resigning from and recontesting his parliamentary seat in Johor Baru. Running as an independent but with the backing of Tunku Abdul Rahman, Musa, and Razaleigh, he secured the DAP's support for a seat where Malays made up only 48 percent of the voters. Shahrir won an overwhelming victory, attracting more than double the votes of the UMNO Baru candidate. His huge winning margin was due in large part to strong support from Chinese voters mobilized by the DAP, which saw Shahrir as the lesser evil, while the Malay vote was evenly divided. Shahrir's victory demonstrated the importance of Chinese votes for Malay candidates; and, in response, the BN made a special attempt to win back Chinese voters. In several by-elections in 1989 and 1990 Chinese votes seemed decisive in tipping the balance in UMNO's favour.

In the middle of 1989 Semangat established a front called the Angkatan Perpaduan Ummah (APU, or Muslim Unity Movement) with PAS and two small Islamic parties, Berjasa and Hamim.[18] Without such an alliance, Semangat faced the probability that the split in UMNO would simply allow PAS to take power in Kelantan, possibly Terengganu, and even

---

[18] Both Berjasa and Hamim were parties of PAS dissidents who had left PAS, joined the BN, and later withdrawn from the BN.

Kedah. Therefore, it was crucial for Tengku Razaleigh, whose home base was in Kelantan, that PAS be brought into an electoral arrangement with Semangat. APU was based on the understanding that Semangat would support PAS in its endeavor to regain control of the Kelantan state government while PAS would support Tengku Razaleigh at the federal level.

While Semangat worked out a formal alliance with Muslim parties that had their main strength in the Malay-majority states of the north and northeast, it also tried to reach an understanding with the DAP, which had its base among the urban Chinese, especially in the west-coast states. The by-elections between 1988 and 1990 had shown how crucial Chinese votes were for the competing Malay parties. Semangat's understanding with DAP was not formalized until just before the 1990 general election when Semangat formed a second alliance, called Gagasan Rakyat (People's Concept), with the DAP, the small Malay party PRM, and another small party of MIC dissidents.[19] The basis of this arrangement was the understanding that Semangat would support the DAP goal of taking over the state government in Penang while the DAP pledged support to Tengku Razaleigh as prime minister.

Although Tengku Razaleigh seemed reasonably comfortable with both his major allies individually, they were not comfortable with each other. The DAP leaders declared that they could not accept the PAS goal to establish an Islamic state in Malaysia and would not be able to cooperate with that party if it did not abandon that aim.[20] PAS, of course, had no intention of abandoning its fundamental, even if largely symbolic, goal. Its leaders denied that the party had any association with the DAP; and its treasurer, Haji Mustafa Ali, declared that "PAS has never and will not work with DAP as long as it remains a secular party and opposes PAS' aspirations for the creation of an Islamic state."[21] The pact with Semangat in APU, however, had avoided the term "Islamic state" and instead referred to the aim of "upholding Islam as a way of life based on truth, justice, freedom and good values."[22]

Although the DAP and PAS leaders took contradictory public stands, their political cooperation may have been quite close. By taking a strongly anti-DAP stand in public, PAS was able to rally its rural Malay supporters. Similarly, by declaring its total opposition to the idea of an Islamic state,

[19] Strangely, in the English-language press Gagasan Rakyat was erroneously translated as "People's Power," echoing the movement that had recently overthrown President Marcos in the Philippines. The PRM had reverted to its 1960s name by dropping the word "Socialist" from PSRM.

[20] See the statements by DAP Vice President Karpal Singh (*NST* 11 December 1989) and Secretary-General Lim Kit Siang (*NST* 6 May 1990).

[21] *NST* 12 April 1990. See also statements by PAS deputy president, Ustaz Hadi Awang. *NST* 15 February 1990, 13 May 1990.

[22] See Tengku Razaleigh's statement. *NST* 13 October 1990.

the DAP was appealing to its urban Chinese and Indian supporters. Nevertheless, the obvious conflict between Semangat's two most important allies was exploited by the BN in its efforts to show that the coalition led by Tengku Razaleigh was unfit to govern.

Despite contradictions between their components, Razaleigh's two overlapping alliances offered an unprecedented challenge to the BN. In previous elections UMNO had enjoyed strong support from the Malay community while the Chinese were divided between government and opposition. As a result, UMNO normally won an overwhelming majority of the predominantly Malay constituencies; and victories by non-Malay BN parties usually depended on Malay support channeled to the BN through UMNO. But with UMNO split, the party for the first time was depending on non-Malay, especially Chinese, votes in predominantly Malay constituencies. In the overwhelmingly Malay seats, which had previously been considered UMNO strongholds, the Chinese minority suddenly became very important. Among the 132 seats in the peninsula, Chinese made up 10–20 percent in nineteen and 20–30 percent in twenty-six.[23]

As a consequence, the BN was forced to appeal to Chinese interests and feelings. In the past, for example, the government had adopted a negative attitude to manifestations of Chinese culture: restrictions on the performance of the lion dance symbolized the government's attitude. But in 1990, two months before the general election, the prime minister himself opened a lion-dance competition at the Stadium Negara in Kuala Lumpur before a crowd of five thousand. In his speech he promised that the government would promote multiculturalism and claimed that the competition itself proved that "the Malaysian tradition of cultural tolerance was alive and thriving."[24] A fortnight later, the deputy prime minister opened a Chinese cultural festival attended by fifty thousand people in the Seremban municipal stadium at which nine dragon-dance and fourteen lion-dance troupes performed.[25]

The government also liberalized its policy on visits to China. Previously only those over sixty years old were allowed to make social visits to China, and tourists had to be more than fifty-five. But in May 1989, just before a by-election, the age limit for social visits was reduced to fifty and for tourists to thirty (although tourists had to go in organized groups for not more than fourteen days). Finally, in the month before the general election in October 1990, all restrictions on visits to China were removed.

The tone that UMNO leaders used to speak about Chinese education also changed dramatically. Government spokespeople assured the Chinese

[23] *NST* 8 May 1990.
[24] *NST* 22 August 1990.
[25] *NST* 2 October 1990.

community that the government was committed to the preservation of Chinese primary schools, and a new Education Act was proposed by the minister for education, Anwar Ibrahim. In the new act the controversial section 21(2) of the old act, enabling the minister to convert Chinese or Tamil schools to Malay-medium, would be abolished.[26] Building grants were given to various Chinese schools and the MCA-sponsored Tunku Abdul Rahman College. Nine graduation certificates awarded by the college were recognized for the purpose of government employment.

The general election was held in October 1990 for 180 seats—132 in the peninsula and 48 in East Malaysia.[27] The electoral pacts between the main opposition parties in the peninsula resulted in a drastic decline in the number of opposition candidates. In contrast to previous elections, only one major opposition candidate was nominated in all but one of the peninsular parliamentary constituencies, although in several state constituencies the DAP and PAS both nominated candidates. The main opposition party, Semangat '46, contested fifty-nine peninsular seats, the DAP thirty-four, PAS thirty-one, and PRM three. Only seventeen (of which seven were in Kelantan) of the 132 peninsular constituencies were contested by more than two candidates.

The opposition was dramatically strengthened several days after nominations closed when PBS, the Kadazan-based ruling party in Sabah, announced its withdrawal from the BN and its support for the opposition. PBS had apparently calculated that the opposition was likely to win. By withdrawing after nominations had closed, it deprived the BN of the opportunity to put up its own candidates in the fourteen BN seats allocated to PBS. Moreover, it became clear that independents nominated in seats allocated to USNO were, in fact, PBS-supported. Immediately after PBS's defection, the prime minister said that he had not been able to accept PBS's demands for an increase in the petroleum royalty, a special TV station in Sabah, and a state university; but the relationship between PBS and the central government had never been warm. It was no secret that UMNO preferred to work with fellow Muslims in USNO rather than the Christians who were predominant in PBS.

On the eve of the election the combined opposition fronts were confident that they would at least deprive the BN of its two-thirds majority. Some leaders, especially after the defection of PBS, even believed that victory was not completely out of reach. But the BN once again scored an overwhelming victory in terms of seats in Parliament, winning 127 of the 180 seats, seven more than it needed for a two-thirds majority (although

---

[26] NST 14 November 1989. This promise, however, was never implemented.
[27] This discussion of the 1990 election is based on Crouch 1992:35–39. See also Khong 1991.

twenty-one less than it had gained in the 177-seat Parliament elected in 1986). Its performance in terms of votes was less impressive, falling to 53.4 percent of the valid votes compared to 57.3 percent in 1986. Moreover, the BN suffered a devastating defeat in the state election in Kelantan and won only narrowly in Penang. Although an election at the state level was not held in Sabah, the defection of PBS meant that the BN no longer controlled that state. The DAP continued to be the largest opposition party with twenty seats, Semangat had eight, and PAS had seven, while PBS contributed fourteen. In the peninsula the BN's share of the votes fell from 58.1 to 55.3 percent, but the decline in support for the DAP from 21.4 to 18.0 percent and for PAS from 17.5 to 7.8 percent did not represent setbacks for those parties. Although Semangat '46 attracted 17.4 percent, it is likely that a substantial part of its votes came from DAP and PAS supporters who voted for common opposition candidates.

The most spectacular progress by the opposition was made in Kelantan where APU, the front based on Semangat '46 and PAS, won all seats for both Parliament and the state assembly. But APU performed poorly elsewhere. The victories of the other opposition front, based on Semangat's alliance with the DAP, were almost entirely won by the DAP. At the state level, however, the DAP failed narrowly in its bid to take over the government in Penang. Although it clearly had the support of a majority of non-Malay voters, and its leader, Lim Kit Siang, defeated the long-entrenched chief minister, Lim Chong Eu, the DAP's Malay partners in the Gagasan Rakyat (Semangat and PRM) as well as PAS lost in all their contests with UMNO, leaving the DAP three short of a majority in the state assembly.

Why did the Malay opposition fail to win more seats? In the Malay-majority states of the north and northeast, the opposition had assumed that PAS would maintain its usual share of the Malay votes, ranging from 40 to 50 percent, to which would be added a substantial share of the votes previously won by UMNO but now directed to Semangat. This is indeed what happened in Kelantan, where virtually half the Malay voters were already committed to PAS and about 40 percent of UMNO's old supporters switched to Semangat.[28] In the other states with large Malay majorities, however, the defections from UMNO were much fewer and not sufficient to boost the opposition vote substantially.

Why did Semangat fail to live up to its expectations? Part of the answer lies in the nature of patronage politics in UMNO. Semangat's supporters had all been part of the UMNO patronage network before the UMNO split. Indeed, the split itself had revolved to a large extent around control

---

[28] This rough estimate was reached as follows: The BN's share (that is, UMNO's) in the total votes for Parliament in Kelantan declined from 54 percent in 1986 to 33 percent in 1990, a drop of twenty-one percentage points or 39 percent.

of the patronage machine. In the 1987 contest for the presidency of UMNO, the two sides were evenly balanced; and in the by-elections of 1988 Semangat seemed to be attracting about half the Malay votes. The patronage network was in disarray as a result of the split, and it was still not clear which side would come out on top. But the advantages of incumbency made themselves felt during 1989 and 1990 with the result that dissidents at all levels gradually moved back to UMNO. Businesspeople who were dependent on government licenses, credit, or contracts; politicians with big personal loans from banks; schoolteachers who did not want to be transferred to an outlying district or another state; and villagers who were applying for land all felt that they had no choice but to return to UMNO. After all, many had joined UMNO in the first place to get access to the patronage network and had supported Semangat because they thought that the dissidents were about to take control of it. Now that Semangat's chances were not so bright, it was safer to return to UMNO. Only in Tengku Razaleigh's home state of Kelantan did the alliance with PAS seemed assured of winning and therefore controlling patronage at the state level. Thus, UMNO voters in that state shifted their loyalties in large numbers to Semangat '46.

In the weeks before the election it still seemed that the opposition would do well, and many observers predicted that the government would lose its two-thirds majority, especially after the defection of PBS from the BN. But the government, which monopolized the English and Malay daily newspapers and television, was able to turn threatened defeat into clear victory after the PBS defection by suggesting that Tengku Razaleigh was supporting Christianity against Islam. On a visit to Sabah, Tengku Razaleigh was photographed wearing a traditional Kadazan headdress decorated with what looked like a cross! That photograph appeared throughout the mass media, and the opposition believed that it swayed many Malay voters at the last moment.[29]

The BN's victory had a demoralizing impact on the opposition. While both the DAP and PAS had mobilized their supporters behind the opposition fronts, UMNO dissidents in Semangat had performed poorly except in Tengku Razaleigh's home state of Kelantan. In the aftermath of the election, chastened Semangat supporters gradually drifted back to UMNO with the hope of reintegrating themselves into the patronage network.

In 1995 when the next national election was held, the BN not only regained the ground that it lost in 1990 but surpassed its performance in earlier elections. Although the Semangat-PAS coalition easily retained control of the Kelantan state government, the BN obtained 65.1 percent of the national votes—its highest-ever share. Outside Kelantan Semangat '46

[29] See the photograph in *NST* 19 October 1990.

won no seats while PAS won only one parliamentary and a few state seats. Although PAS increased its share of the national vote slightly to 7.3 percent, it is likely that most of the 10.2 percent won by Semangat in fact came from PAS supporters. A serious setback was also experienced by the DAP which had withdrawn from the Gagasan Rakyat coalition with Semangat '46. The party won only 12.1 percent of the votes, a decline of almost one-third compared to 1990 and its worst-ever performance. The success of the BN in attracting Chinese voters was due in part to the rapid growth of the economy. In each of the previous seven years the growth rate had exceeded 8 percent with the result that both Malays and non-Malays were enjoying unprecedented prosperity. Chinese business was flourishing and unemployment had been virtually eliminated. Liberal policies in education, including the re-introduction of English for some university subjects, also won non-Malay approval.

Political developments during the 1980s showed that the Malaysian political system retained much of its competitiveness despite the authoritarian powers exercised by the government. As I argued earlier, the electoral system has always forced the government to take some account of popular sentiments and interests. But the split in UMNO and the formation of interlocking opposition fronts made the system more competitive and more responsive.

The UMNO split was due in the first instance to personal and factional rivalries involving Mahathir, Musa, and Razaleigh. The party was divided into two as rivalries at the top intermeshed with the normal factionalism at the grassroots level. While there may have been differences in emphasis between the top leaders in regard to policy, the main issue revolved around the question of eventual succession to the prime ministership. At the middle and lower levels of the party, the driving force behind factional conflict was the struggle for access to patronage. The struggle intensified in the mid-1980s as the economy moved into recession and resources for patronage distribution dried up.

Before the 1990 election voters had seen for the first time the formation of an alternative semi-alliance consisting of all the major opposition parties representing both Malays and non-Malays. With the prospect of power dangling before their eyes, Malay and non-Malay leaders who had never worked together before found it possible to make compromises—albeit very limited ones—in the interest of defeating the BN. The tensions between the opposition parties were obvious and prevented the formation of a single front, but the parties were still able to nominate common candidates in all but one of the peninsular parliamentary seats and almost all the state seats. Despite increased votes for the opposition, however, the parties did not capture a large number of additional seats except in Kelantan.

The large, although reduced, majority obtained by the BN in the 1990 election was an indication of the durability of the Malaysian political system and the effectiveness of its dominant party, UMNO. The BN's convincing victory brought an end to speculation that the political system was about to undergo a major transformation. Nevertheless, the election illustrated the significance of electoral competition in the Malaysian system. As long as the BN—in particular, UMNO—was united and the opposition split along communal lines, government victory was assured in each election. But the UMNO split and the steps toward the formation of a multi-communal opposition front raised the level of competitiveness in the system and forced the government to respond to pressures from below to secure its victory.

8 *The Institutional Pillars of the State*

Umno's domination of the political system was backed by the Malay elite's domination of the institutional pillars of the state: the bureaucracy, the armed forces and the police, the judiciary, and, at the symbolic peak, the monarchy. While UMNO, the bureaucracy, the military, and the judiciary each had its own functions and interests, these elites were all parts of a common Malay elite. They often came from the same family backgrounds and had gone to the same types of schools: and it was not uncommon for them to be related through blood or marriage.

In the 1960s the Malay elite was still very small and tight-knit and drawn largely from the upper reaches of Malay society. A significant number had royal connections while many had known each other since schooldays or had worked together at early stages in their careers. But the expansion of educational opportunities for Malays after independence, especially in the 1970s, increased the size of the Malay elite and allowed Malays with more varied backgrounds to move into elite positions. While some sons of peasants and fishermen managed to achieve elite status during the early period, most new members came from the middle levels of Malay society, which had easy access to the key to advancement—an English education. Among the most prominent of these schools were the Malay College in Kuala Kangsar, the English College in Johor Baru, the Penang Free School, the Victoria Institution in Kuala Lumpur, and the Sultan Abdul Hamid College in Alor Setar. Some students went on to tertiary education in England, often in law, while most received their tertiary education in Malaysia. In the 1970s and 80s the broadening process continued as the elite institutions gradually opened their doors to the Malay-educated (although by the 1990s these recruits had yet to rise to senior positions). Nevertheless, as a result of the broadening base of recruitment,

130

Malays from relatively humble backgrounds were able to rise in the civil service, the military, the police, and, to some extent, the judiciary, although the royal families were immune to this process.

The similar backgrounds of the members of the Malay elite did not guarantee complete harmony between and within its various branches, but it did mean that they had a common outlook on questions relating to the broad features of the political system. There were rivalries and disputes within the elite, but its essential coherence rested on solid foundations.

The Bureaucracy

During the colonial era, the elite branch of the civil service, the Malayan Civil Service (MCS), had been largely a British preserve although small numbers of Malays were occasionally promoted into it from the junior Malay Administrative Service (MAS). The MAS had been established at the beginning of the century to provide clerical and lower-level administrative support to the MCS and consisted entirely of upper-class Malays, many of whom had aristocratic or royal family backgrounds.[1] After World War II the number of Malays appointed to the MCS increased, but it remained closed to Chinese and Indians until the 1950s. As the British prepared to grant independence to a multicommunal Malaya, they decided to appoint a sprinkling of non-Malays to the MCS with the proviso that a minimum of 80 percent of positions would be reserved for Malays. In the immediate post-independence period, British officials continued to dominate the civil service. Of the 360 members of the MCS in 1957, 67 percent were British as were 61 percent of the 2,761 Division One officials.[2] In the following years, however, a program of "Malayanization" was implemented. Although British officials were phased out, by 1962 there were still twenty-six British MCS officers, making up 9 percent of the service, and 409 British Division One officials, constituting 14 percent.[3] Only in the late 1960s were British officials finally replaced.

During the 1970s the MCS, now called the Administrative and Diplomatic Service (Perkhidmatan Tadbir dan Diplomatik, or PTD), expanded very rapidly. The implementation of the NEP required more administrators while the expansion of the universities produced more Malay graduates looking for jobs. In 1970 the PTD had 696 members, 86.6 percent of whom were Malays.[4] By 1975 it had grown to 1,568 members of whom

[1] See Khasnor 1984.
[2] Tilman 1964:70, 73.
[3] Ibid.:68–69.
[4] Puthucheary 1978:54.

85.6 percent were Malays.[5] By 1984 it numbered about 2,500.[6] In the early 1980s it was taking in 200–250 recruits a year, nearly all of whom were Malays, although the intake fell to about one hundred annually in later years.[7]

Because the PTD was dominated by Malays, they held most of the top positions in the bureaucracy. The post of chief secretary to the government was always held by a Malay while most departmental secretaries-general (permanent heads) were also Malay. Of twenty-two departmental secretaries-general in 1980, eighteen were Malay, three Chinese, and one Indian.[8] In 1989, nineteen were Malay, two were Chinese, and one was Indian, while 88 percent of the deputy secretaries-general were Malays.[9]

Although Malays dominated the small elite administrative service, they had originally been outnumbered by non-Malays in the managerial and professional Division One of the civil service. In 1970 Malays held only 39.3 percent of 4,744 such posts compared to 34.5 percent held by Chinese, 20.3 percent by Indians, and 5.9 percent by others.[10] During the 1970s the number of positions in the renamed Group A increased rapidly to more than thirty-four thousand, and the Malay share in such positions increased sharply to 49 percent in 1978.[11] Overall, however, within the entire civil service, Malays made up 61 percent of the federal service in 1969 and 62 percent of employment in government services in 1985.[12] Lower-level clerical and manual occupational categories were largely filled by Malays.

The civil-service elite always enjoyed close links with UMNO. Unlike many countries where nationalist movements regarded indigenous colonial civil servants as traitors to the nationalist cause, UMNO, as the major force of Malay nationalism, was formed by Malay civil servants employed by the British. The first leader of UMNO, Datuk Onn Jaafar, was a civil servant as were seven of the eleven members of the original UMNO executive committee in 1946. When the first national election was held, in 1955, twenty-eight of UMNO's thirty-five candidates were former civil servants; and when Malaya obtained independence in 1957 six of the seven Malay

[5] *UM* 21 January 1976.

[6] *NST* 12 August 1984.

[7] One senior non-Malay member of the PTD, Datuk Ramon Navaratnam, contrasted the large 1980s intake with the ten to fifteen recruited each year in the 1960s, saying that this "raised questions about the quality, calibre, educational background, attitudes, and racial make-up of these recruits." *NST* 29 July 1984. Senior Malay civil servants also confided to me their dismay at the quality of new PTD recruits.

[8] MCA 1982:26.

[9] MCA 1990:83.

[10] Puthucheary 1978:55.

[11] *NST* 25 September 1981, 15 November 1978.

[12] Puthucheary 1978:57; 5MP:102.

members of the cabinet, including the prime minister, were former civil servants.[13]

Civil service regulations prohibited civil servants in Division One/Group A from actively participating in politics. Although they were permitted to be party members, they were not allowed to contest elections, hold office in parties, or openly campaign for candidates in elections. By 1990 the number of Group A civil servants had risen to fifty-eight thousand out of a total of almost seventy hundred thousand civil servants.[14] On the other hand, lower-level civil servants could apply for permission to participate actively in political party activities. In practice, government leaders often called on government employees to join parties—meaning, of course, UMNO.[15]

In general, the regulations prohibiting Group A officers from political involvement seem to have been implemented in a fairly relaxed way, especially when civil servants were active in government parties. In 1981 the minister of finance, Tengku Razaleigh, addressing civil servants at the civil-service training institute in the presence of the chief secretary to the government, said that "officers and other government employees are not permitted to be neutral in politics but should support and defend government policies."[16] In Johor in 1981 the UMNO state liaison secretary even boasted about the role played by civil servants in the party, pointing to the case of the Kota Tinggi district officer who was elected chairman of UMNO Youth in his division.[17] Similarly, in 1980 the deputy state secretary of Selangor won the UMNO Youth divisional leadership in Temerloh, Pahang.[18] During the 1980s it became increasingly common for civil servants to contest positions in UMNO and other government parties, but by the late 1980s the government felt compelled to take action against flagrant breaches of regulations. The change in policy took place in the context of the UMNO split when many civil servants in UMNO may have sympathized with the prime minister's opponents. In 1989 it was revealed that 272 Group A civil servants held leadership positions in party organizations, 184 in UMNO, 48 in the MCA, 18 in the MIC, and 10 in Gerakan. Twelve were active in the opposition party, PAS. Of the 272, 247 were employed in the Education Ministry. But by the end of 1989, only six had resigned from government service while another nine gave up their party posts. In answer to a question in Parliament, a deputy minister explained that "action was still being taken" in the case of the rest.[19]

[13] Puthucheary 1978:34.
[14] *NST* 22 April 1990.
[15] See, for example, the call by the Kedah Menteri Besar. *NST* 20 May 1985.
[16] *UM* 22 April 1981.
[17] *NST* 22 July 1981.
[18] *NST* 1 June 1980.
[19] *NST* 5 December 1989.

Civil-service and other government employment was a major recruiting ground for UMNO, and many of its senior leaders began their careers as civil servants. In an analysis of members of UMNO's national executive committee up to 1969, Funston found that nearly half had bureaucratic backgrounds.[20] In 1980 seven of the thirteen UMNO members of the federal cabinet, including the prime minister, had served at one time or another in either the administrative or legal service (while two more had been employed by the government—one as a government doctor and the other with Radio Malaysia).[21] By 1987, however, the predominance of ex-civil servants was declining, only three of fourteen UMNO ministers having previously served as civil servants (although three had experience in state corporations).[22]

The Military

Like the bureaucracy, the military was established during the British period, the Royal Malay Regiment tracing its origins back to an experimental corps set up in 1934.[23] As its name implies, the regiment was comprised entirely of Malays. In the early 1950s, at the time when the MCS was being opened to a small number of non-Malays, the military established a multi-ethnic reconnaissance corps; but the number of non-Malay officers and soldiers remained small. During the early post-independence period the military continued to be commanded by seconded British officers. In 1961 a Malaysian was finally appointed head of the army, but the position of chief of armed forces staff was not transferred to a Malaysian general until 1964. (That change took place during Indonesia's confrontation campaign when Indonesia was portraying Malaysia as a British "neo-colonial project.") The navy and air force remained under British chiefs of staff until 1967. In 1966 there were still 336 British officers and 316 other ranks serving with the Malaysian Armed Forces, but by 1970 the forces had been almost fully Malayanized.[24]

The Malaysian armed forces remained quite small until the 1970s. During the campaign against the Communist guerillas and then against Indonesia's confrontation, the main brunt of operations was borne by British forces, especially Gurkha troops. Among domestic forces the Police Field Force rather than the army was most prominent. After the 1969 emergency, the army expanded rapidly, especially the Malay Regiment, which

---

[20] Funston 1980:106.
[21] Morais 1980.
[22] See *Information Malaysia* 1990:374–78.
[23] This section is based in part on Crouch 1991. See also Zakaria 1988; Chandran 1988.
[24] Chandran 1980:73.

increased from ten to sixteen battalions in 1969–70 and then grew to twenty-six by the mid-1980s. At the same time the number of multiracial ranger battalions increased to ten. The military was primarily a counterinsurgency force carrying out small-scale operations against a low-key Communist insurgency, but the buildup after 1969 was a response to racial rioting in that year.[25] The government expanded the army as an overwhelmingly Malay force to back up the government in the event of further communal conflict.

Like the government and the bureaucracy, the military was a Malay-dominated institution. In its report on the 1969 racial riot, the National Operations Council revealed that in that year Malays made up 64.5 percent of the armed forces officer corps.[26] The Malay Regiment, which formed the backbone of the army, was entirely Malay. In 1971 Prime Minister Tun Razak revealed that Malays made up 84 percent of the other ranks and 50 percent of the officers in the multicommunal ranger battalions. In comparison with the army, the navy and air force were more multi-ethnic. According to Razak, Malays made up only 51 percent of the officers and 74 percent of other ranks in the navy, and 46 percent of officers and 59 percent of other ranks in the air force.[27]

The racial balance within the armed forces tipped further in favor of the Malays during the next decade. According to a Defense Ministry spokesman in 1981, in the armed forces as a whole, 74.6 percent of officers and 84.8 percent of the other ranks were Malay. Chinese made up 16.2 percent of the officer corps and only 6.1 percent of the other ranks, while Indians constituted 6.2 percent of officers and 6.4 percent of other ranks. A further 2.7 percent of the other ranks were classified as "other."[28] That this pattern was likely to continue was indicated by statistics for recruitment to the armed forces. Malays made up 86 percent of officer recruits in 1979 and 91 percent in 1981 while they constituted 92 percent of rank-and-file recruits in 1979 and 93 percent in 1981. Of a total of 8,125 rank-and-file recruits in 1981, only thirty-five were Chinese.[29]

Malay domination was also evident in appointments to key commands. The positions of chief of defense forces (previously chief of armed forces staff) and chief of the army (previously chief of general staff) were always held by Malays as was command of the air force. In the case of the navy, the first Malaysian commander was of Indian descent, but all his successors were Malay. In 1990 the chief of defense forces and all service chiefs

---

[25] The insurgency finally ended in 1989 when a peace agreement was signed by the Malaysian government and the MCP. See Sebastian 1991.

[26] NOC 1969:23.

[27] Chandran 1980:66–67.

[28] *NST* 18 December 1981.

[29] *NST* 20 October 1981.

and their deputies were Malay as were the army corps commander and the army chief of staff. All five army divisions (including the reserve) were under Malay commanders, although one of the twelve infantry brigades was commanded by a non-Malay. In the early 1980s, however, one of the divisions was commanded by an Indian officer; and at several times there were one or two Indian or Chinese brigade commanders. Thus, there was no question that Malays were in control, particularly of infantry forces that might be needed to back up the government in a domestic political crisis.

Military officers were linked to the civilian elite through more than their Malayness. Officers often came from the same sorts of families that produced civil servants and UMNO politicians. In the 1960s both the military and civilian elites tended to originate in the small upper and middle strata of Malay society; but as opportunities for higher education extended to the lower levels of Malay society after 1970, Malays of humble background were able to join the elite service in the bureaucracy and also rise in the military.

At the highest levels, the links between the civilian and military leadership were very close. The first Malaysian chief of general staff and then chief of armed forces staff, General Tunku Osman Jewa, was a member of the Kedah royal family and nephew of the first prime minister, Tunku Abdul Rahman. The chief of general staff, Major General Abdul Hamid Bidin, was related to the deputy prime minister, Tun Razak. The chief of general staff in the early 1970s, General Ungku Nazaruddin Ungku Mohamed, had attended the Malay College in Kuala Kangsar with Tun Razak. In 1981, Prime Minister Datuk Hussein Onn promoted his brother-in-law, General Tan Sri Ghazali Seth, as chief of armed forces staff and his brother, Lieutenant General Datuk Jaafar Onn, as deputy chief of staff of the army. In 1983, Lieutenant General Jaafar was replaced by Lieutenant General Datuk Hashim Mohamed Ali, the brother-in-law of the new prime minister, Datuk Seri Mahathir Mohamad. Lieutenant General Hashim was also a brother of both the governor of the central bank and the Menteri Besar of Selangor. Mahathir later appointed General Hashim to command the army and then, in 1987, the armed forces.

Since independence, Malaysia has experienced only one political crisis of the sort that might possibly trigger a military coup. When a state of emergency was declared in the aftermath of the 1969 racial rioting, government power for almost two years was in the hands of the National Operations Council dominated by senior Malay politicians and bureaucrats but also including the chief of armed forces staff and the inspector-general of police. Another senior army officer served as chief executive officer of the council. Although military officers in effect joined the government, they did so by invitation of UMNO. There was never any suggestion that they desired to take full control of the government themselves; and there was no hint of military resistance to the return to normalcy in February 1971 and the resumption of Parliament. As part of the Malay elite, the military leadership had no reason to be dissatisfied with Malay-dominated civilian rule.

The police also played a role in backing up the authority of the state. In addition to normal police functions, the Malaysian police force included the paramilitary Police Field Force (PFF), which in the 1980s consisted of twenty-one battalions with about twenty thousand personnel. The PFF received training in jungle warfare and had armor similar to the army's. In addition, the police had the 2,500 members of the Federal Reserve Unit trained to meet emergencies such as demonstrations, strikes, or riots. Moreover, the police special branch controlled internal political intelligence. Unlike some neighboring countries, Malaysia did not make its police force part of the armed forces but placed it under the Ministry for Home Affairs.

Like the military leadership, the senior police leaders came from much the same Malay socioeconomic background as the civilian elite, although there were more non-Malays among its officers. During the British period, while the army was overwhelmingly Malay, non-Malays were recruited into the police force, which many believed needed to ethnically represent the populace with which it worked. Thus, in 1968, Malays made up only 45.1 percent of police officers and some 39 percent of the total police force.[30] Malay participation in the police force increased sharply during the 1970s and 80s with the result that by 1989 Chinese made up only 4.6 percent of the force's 75,957 members. Of the Chinese members, 1,808 were officers. Non-Malays in general seemed to make up 30–40 percent of officers.[31] The lower ranks, however, were overwhelmingly Malay except for certain specialized areas such as criminal investigation. In 1988 the deputy home minister complained that the quota of eight hundred places for non-Malay police recruits had not been met in 1987 and that the response had been particularly weak among Chinese.[32]

The Judiciary

The judiciary, like the bureaucracy and the military, continued to be dominated by British expatriates in the early years after independence. At

[30] Gibbons and Zakaria 1971:341; Enloe 1978:280.

[31] *NST* 12 October 1989. Cursory examination of published lists of police promotions suggests that 60–70 percent of officers are Malay. See, for example, *UM* 12 November 1983; *NST* 14 March 1984.

[32] *NST* 22 August 1988.

that time only two of the fourteen judges were Malayans, but by 1959 the number had risen to five. In 1966 the last English lord president (chief justice of Malaysia) retired, and the last expatriate judge retired in 1969.[33] Drawn largely from the same social classes as the bureaucracy and the military, the judiciary was mainly a Malay institution despite the overwhelming preponderance of non-Malays in the legal profession as a whole. At the beginning of 1980 six of the eight members of the Federal Court (renamed the Supreme Court in 1985 following the abolition of appeals to the Privy Council in London), including the lord president, were Malays as were nine of the fifteen high court judges in peninsular Malaysia. (Another two were Indian Muslims.) In contrast, only one of the five high court judges in East Malaysia was a Malay.[34] Unlike civil servants and military officers, judges did not retire at age fifty-five but were allowed to continue until sixty-five with the result that the composition of the judiciary was at first less affected by the broadening base of recruitment in the Malay elite. Nevertheless, a few judges, such as Tun Salleh Abas, had quite humble origins.

On the whole, the judges shared the broad conservative outlook of the rest of the Malay elite. Although from time to time the courts handed down decisions unfavorable to the government, in general the judges rarely showed interest in reinterpreting the law in ways that might restrict the prerogatives of the government and its bureaucracy. For example, the courts rarely questioned the government's powers under the emergency provisions or the ISA and hardly ever found legislation to be in conflict with the constitution.[35]

The Malaysian constitution was not, in fact, a substantial check on government power. It provided for easy amendment, requiring only a two-thirds majority in both houses of Parliament except in the case of certain entrenched provisions (relating to, among other things, Malay special rights and citizenship) that also required the assent of the conference of rulers (the state sultans). Because the Alliance and the BN always had two-thirds majorities in both houses of Parliament, amendment of the constitution was a simple matter. Between 1957 and 1994 thirty-four constitutional amendment acts were passed, each often containing numerous individual amendments.[36] In 1970, Dr. Mahathir wrote that "the manner, the frequency and the trivial reasons for altering the constitution reduced this supreme law of the nation to a useless scrap of paper."[37] Nevertheless,

---

[33] Mohamed Suffian 1978:239.
[34] Morais 1980.
[35] Shad 1987:110.
[36] Federal Constitution (List of Amendments). The 1988 amendment act, for example, amended ten articles and one schedule of the constitution.
[37] Mahathir 1970:11.

under his prime ministership, constitutional amendment acts were passed in 1981, 1983, twice in 1984, 1985, 1988, 1990, 1992, 1993, and 1994.

The relationship between the government and the judiciary had been close until the appointment of Mahathir as prime minister. Earlier prime ministers had similar social backgrounds to the Malay judges and mixed with them socially. Indeed, links were so close that prime ministers sometimes consulted certain judges about proposed legislation before it was taken to Parliament.[38] But the relationship became more brittle during Mahathir's prime ministership partly because of his personal opinion about the proper role of the judiciary and his feelings toward some of the judges.[39] Unlike earlier prime ministers who had their origins in the upper reaches of Malay society, Mahathir, the son of a schoolteacher, had risen into the elite through education and politics and lacked close personal ties with the leaders of the legal profession. Moreover, unlike earlier prime ministers who had been trained in law in England, Mahathir was a Singapore-trained medical doctor who seemed to have only a partial understanding of the way in which judges arrived at their judgments.[40]

In 1986 and 1987 the courts brought down a series of judgments that invalidated several government actions. There was no suggestion that the courts had deliberately sought a confrontation with the government; but it was clear that the prime minister was irritated, particularly because the more controversial judgments involved the Ministry for Home Affairs, which he also held. In one case, the Supreme Court, believing that "natural justice" had been denied to two correspondents of the *Asian Wall Street Journal,* held that the Ministry for Home Affairs' withdrawal of the journalists' work permits was invalid because they had not been given an opportunity to defend their case.[41] In another case Justice Peh Swee Chin overruled a detention order made by the minister for home affairs under the ISA for DAP politician Karpal Singh on the ground that it was "made without proper care, caution and a proper sense of responsibility."[42] And in October 1987, the high court issued an injunction against the signing of a huge contract awarded to an UMNO-linked company.[43]

[38] Salleh Abas with K. Das 1989:19.

[39] In a speech in Hongkong in October 1988, former Deputy Prime Minister Datuk Musa Hitam said, "Mahathir was continuously upset with the Judiciary. One of his favourite slogans was 'Hang The Lawyers! Hang the Judges!' " Cited in Salleh Abas with K. Das 1989:18.

[40] Tunku Abdul Rahman, Tun Razak, and Datuk Hussein Onn had all studied law in England. The Tunku and Tun Razak had been students together with Tun Mohamed Suffian, the lord president of the federal court, from 1974 to 1984. See Abdul Rahman 1977:295, 300.

[41] *AWSJ,* reports between 29 September and 14 November 1986.

[42] *AWSJ* 10 March 1988. The judge ordered Karpal's release; but he was arrested on new charges, again under the ISA, a few hours later.

[43] The injunction had been sought by DAP leaders Lim Kit Siang and Karpal Singh who were both arrested in Operation Lalang several weeks after the high court injunction. In January 1988 the injunction was overruled by the Supreme Court in a 3–2 decision. *AWSJ* 18 January 1988.

Finally, a case of great political significance was decided in a way that at first seemed to harm the interests of the prime minister but that he turned to his own advantage. As I discussed in Chapter 7, Mahathir's re-election as UMNO president in 1987 was challenged by Tengku Razaleigh's supporters who sought to invalidate the party election. Justice Harun, in a surprise decision in February 1988, found that the presence of illegal branches within UMNO meant that the party itself was an illegal organization and therefore had to be dissolved. The prime minister quickly established a new party, UMNO Baru, with his own supporters in control. The dissidents appealed to the Supreme Court against the decision. If the court took the view that only the unregistered branches were illegal but not the party as a whole and then ordered the holding of a new election, Razaleigh might win and replace Mahathir as prime minister.

In view of the importance of the case, the lord president of the Supreme Court, Tun Salleh Abas, decided on 23 May 1987 that the appeal would be heard by a panel consisting of nine Supreme Court judges—the first time an appeal had ever been heard by the full court. The appeal was fixed for 13 June. Another crucial appeal was fixed for two days later—that of the attorney general against Justice Peh Swee Chin's order to release Karpal Singh. The stakes in these cases were clearly high, but the cases were not heard as planned. As Tun Salleh said, "My decision to fix these two cases appeared to have precipitated the events that followed."[44] On 26 May the Yang di-Pertuan Agong suspended Tun Salleh from his office as lord president and on 27 May the registrar of the Supreme Court postponed hearing of the cases involving UMNO and Karpal Singh.[45]

The suspension of Tun Salleh as lord president was the culmination of a period of growing tension between the prime minister and members of the judiciary. Following an unfavorable court decision in 1986, an angry Mahathir complained, "The judiciary says [to us], 'Although you passed a law with a certain thing in mind, we think that your mind is wrong, and

[44] Salleh Abas 1989:16. Later Tun Salleh wrote, "When I decided in Ipoh on 23 May 1988, a Monday, and instructed my Senior Assistant Registrar to fix the same UMNO case to be heard on June 13, the entire Government machine seems to have been rocked, rattled and shaken, and awoken with a terrible start. And gone into frenzied action." Salleh Abas with K. Das 1989:290.

[45] It is sometimes suggested that the Yang di-Pertuan Agong may have had a personal grudge against Tun Salleh. In January 1973 when the Yang di-Pertuan Agong was still a prince in Johor, he had been convicted of assault. The successful prosecutor in the case was the future lord president, Salleh Abas. Salleh Abas with K. Das 1989:314. We should also note, however, that in another case in 1977 the prince had been convicted of manslaughter and sentenced to six months imprisonment. The judge in that case was Tun Salleh's successor, Tan Sri Abdul Hamid Omar. Williams 1990:217. Tun Salleh's account of these developments is found in Salleh Abbas 1989 and Salleh Abas with K. Das 1989. Tun Salleh's account is strongly criticized in Williams 1990. Williams's account, however, shows little understanding of the political context—for example, on p. 64 he seems to think that the UMNO case was irrelevant.

we want to give our interpretation.' "[46] In a speech in Parliament at the end of 1987 he argued that the trouble with the judiciary was their use of unwritten law such as English common law, precedents from other countries, and the concept of natural justice. He claimed that "judicial review gives unlimited power to the interpreters of laws who can obstruct the implementation of any laws at all" while "natural justice can be interpreted in various ways according to the discretion of the judge." In an attempt to buttress his argument, he cited the example of sodomy, which he said is considered natural in England but not in Malaysia. "Thus," he concluded, "we should not use this British concept of natural justice. It is not natural for us." If judicial review persists, he went on, "the government is no longer the executive. Another group has taken over its role."[47]

Following Tun Salleh's suspension, the government set up a tribunal consisting of two judges of the Supreme Court, including the new acting lord president, Tan Sri Abdul Hamid Omar, who was appointed chairman of the tribunal; two retired judges; and two foreign judges—one from Singapore, the other from Sri Lanka—to consider whether the lord president should be dismissed. In essence, Tun Salleh was accused of being biased against the government. The tribunal, whose hearings were held in camera, came to the conclusion that he was guilty of misbehavior, and on 8 August he was dismissed as lord president.[48]

Meanwhile, in late June Tun Salleh sought leave from the high court to commence proceedings to prohibit the tribunal from carrying out its work on the grounds that it was improperly constituted. No decision had been made before 2 July, a Saturday, when the tribunal was completing its report. Fearing that the report would be handed to the Yang di-Pertuan Agong before the following Monday, Tun Salleh's counsel sought a temporary stay from the Supreme Court. Because the lord president was under suspension and the acting lord president was a member of the tribunal, the initiative was taken by the most senior judge, Wan Sulaiman Pawan Teh, who quickly established a five-member panel that issued the stay. All five were immediately suspended by the Yang di-Pertuan Agong, acting on the recommendation of the acting lord president, for conspiring to hold a special sitting of the court without the acting lord president's permission. Another tribunal was established that resulted in the dismissal of two of the judges, although the other three were reinstated.[49] Thus, the government

[46] *Time* 24 November 1986, cited in Salleh Abas 1989:9.

[47] Mahathir's speech on the Act to Amend the Printing Presses and Publications Act in Parliament, 3 December 1987. The speech is reproduced as an appendix in Hanafiah A. Samad 1989:292–98 (my translation).

[48] By coincidence or otherwise, the Supreme Court commenced its hearing of the UMNO dissidents' appeal on this day. Apart from Tun Salleh, five more Supreme Court judges were under suspension at that time, as we shall see. On the following day, 9 August, the court rejected the appeal.

[49] *NST* 7 October 1988.

was able to rid itself of three judges who had shown a readiness to hand down decisions unfavorable to the government. It may also have been expected that the dismissals might have an intimidatory effect on other judges.

Despite the fears of many, the judicial crisis of 1988 did not completely destroy the independence of the judiciary. Since then, the courts have continued to hand down occasional decisions that have been unfavorable to the government. Nevertheless, any tendency to interpret the law in ways that impose stricter limits on government prerogatives has been nipped in the bud. When court decisions have threatened fundamental government interests, the government has taken whatever action necessary to defend its position. It is inaccurate, however, to see the 1988 crisis as a conscious challenge on the part of the judges to the government. The judges continue to be essentially conservative custodians of a political system dominated by the Malay elite to which most judges belong. The crisis arose in part because of the prime minister's lack of understanding of legal tradition and seems to be largely a by-product of the UMNO crisis. With the passing of that crisis, government-judiciary relations were allowed to fall back into their old mold.

The Sultans

The Federation of Malaysia consists of thirteen states, two of which were formerly part of the colonial Straits Settlements (Melaka and Penang) while another two (Sabah and Sarawak) are the East Malaysian states that joined Malaysia in 1963. The other nine are the traditional Malay states of the peninsula headed by sultans (Raja in the case of Perlis; Yang di-Pertuan Besar in Negeri Sembilan) whose lineages stretched back to the pre-British era. When independence was achieved in 1957, the institution of the sultanate was not only preserved at the state level but embodied in a new form at the national level. The independence constitution created the position of Yang di-Pertuan Agong, the head of state who continued to symbolize Malay dominance.

Because it was impossible to give precedence to one of the nine sultans without alienating the rest, the monarchy took a unique rotating form. The sultans, through their conference of rulers, elected one of themselves to be Yang di-Pertuan Agong for five years after which he was replaced by another sultan elected in the same way. It was understood among the sultans that each state would eventually be given its turn to supply the Yang di-Pertuan Agong.[50]

[50] Trinidade 1978:101–22.

The Malaysian monarchy was constitutional, and the scope for the king's exercise of discretion was strictly limited. At the state level, however, several state Menteri Besar had experienced problems with their sultans. In the mid-1970s the sultan of Perak made no secret of his dislike for the Menteri Besar, Tan Sri Ghazali Jawi. He not only refused to attend the opening of the state legislative council but vowed that he would not shave until Ghazali was removed from office. Only when the Menteri Besar resigned in 1977 did the sultan shave his beard.[51] In Johor, Tunku Mahmood Iskandar also had bad relations with the Menteri Besar, Tan Sri Othman Saat. After ascending to the throne in 1981, he ordered the Menteri Besar to vacate his offices because he, the sultan, wanted an office in the state administrative building.[52] In another case, the Menteri Besar of Selangor, Tan Sri Muhammad Haji Muhammad Taib, fell out of the sultan's favor when he secretly took the sultan's daughter as a second wife.[53] For a week after the 1990 election the sultan refused to approve the reappointment of Muhammad.[54] Following the split in UMNO in the mid-1980s, the sultan of Kelantan sided with the dissidents led by his wife's relative, Tengku Razaleigh. In 1988 he refused to allow the Menteri Besar to make the traditional oath of allegiance and attempted to transfer senior state civil servants without the state government's approval. Then, on his birthday in 1989, he bestowed awards on the five judges accused of misbehavior in the Salleh Abas affair.[55]

In one case the breakdown in relations between state government and sultan virtually stopped the effective working of the government. Following the 1978 election, the sultan of Pahang objected to the appointment of Datuk Abdul Rahim Abu Baker as Menteri Besar in preference to his own candidate. Rahim seems to have been handpicked by the prime minister, Hussein, who was concerned about the excessive distribution of timber and land concessions under the previous Menteri Besar, who had enjoyed excellent relations with the sultan. The conflict between the sultan and the new Menteri Besar escalated when Rahim rejected the sultan's application for a large timber concession and was further exacerbated by his rejection of the sultan's application for land for a commercial housing project and his request that a new palace be built. In 1979 the sultan of Pahang was elected Yang di-Pertuan Agong; but his son, as regent of Pahang, continued the war with the Menteri Besar by refusing to give assent to two bills passed by the state legislative assembly—one concerned with the salaries

[51] Abdul Rahman 1981:30.
[52] Azlan Shah 1986:80–81.
[53] *NST* 23 February 1990.
[54] *Star* 31 October 1990.
[55] *FEER* 26 January 1989 (Rodney Tasker and Suhaini Aznam, "A Judge As King"); *NST* 25 December 1988, 30 March 1989.

of the Menteri Besar and members of his executive council, the other with timber. Hussein Onn continued to support his protégé. But after Hussein's resignation as prime minister in June 1981, Rahim lost his protector and was forced by Prime Minister Mahathir to resign later in the year.[56]

Many of the state royal families were engaged in commercial ventures and often needed grants of land, timber concessions, and other facilities from the government at both state and federal levels. Several royal families succeeded in developing substantial enterprises of which Antah Holdings, owned by the Negeri Sembilan royal family, was the most prominent in the 1980s.[57] The Pahang royal family also had extensive business interests centred around TAS Holdings and Apera Holdings.[58] Sometimes the financial affairs of members of the royal families were embarrassing and expensive for the state governments. It was well known that one state government had to bail out its sultan on several occasions because of the huge gambling debts that he contracted while most of the other sultans were notorious for their extravagance.

In 1983 the government was confronted with a dilemma as the sultan of Pahang's term as Yang di-Pertuan Agong drew to a close. The only two states that had yet to supply a Yang di-Pertuan Agong were Perak and Johor. But there were objections to the sultans of both states. Sultan Idris of Perak had previously not wanted to become Yang di-Pertuan Agong because, as one report euphemistically put it, he "was not at all sure in the past that he would still be able to lead the sort of life he liked to lead if he were king."[59] In the 1970s he had clashed with his Menteri Besar and in 1982 had again shown his independence by declaring the end of the Muslim fasting month in Perak one day earlier than the rest of the country. Sultan Mahmood Iskandar of Johor, on the other hand, was no less strong-willed; in addition, he had a criminal record. Although convicted in 1973 for assault and in 1977 for manslaughter, he was pardoned on both occasions by his father, then sultan, and did not actually serve a term in jail. With the prospect of either the sultan of Perak or the sultan of Johor on the throne in Kuala Lumpur, and having just experienced the unwillingness of the regent of Pahang to give his assent to legislation, the government decided to introduce constitutional amendments to further reduce the scope for royal discretion.

The amendments were passed in July and August 1983 but, not surprisingly, failed to obtain the assent of the Yang di-Pertuan Agong. In effect, they removed the necessity for royal assent. Instead, the Yang di-Pertuan

[56] Shafruddin 1987:ch. 9; *FEER* 30 June 1983 (David Jenkins, "Sultans As Symbols").
[57] See Cheong 1990a:1–5.
[58] *FEER* 26 January 1989 (Nick Seaward, "The Merchant Princes").
[59] *FEER* 30 June 1983. (David Jenkins, "Princes and Palaces, and a Possible Battle Royal").

Agong (and each state ruler) would be allowed fifteen days to give assent. If he failed to do so, "he shall be deemed to have assented to the Bill." Apparently out of fear of a unilateral emergency proclamation, article 150, relating to the proclamation of emergency, was also amended. Under the existing provision, an emergency could be proclaimed if the Yang di-Pertuan Agong were satisfied that it was necessary—of course, on the understanding that he would act in accordance with the advice of the prime minister. But the constitution did not actually say that the Yang di-Pertuan Agong was bound by the prime minister's advice. To remove ambiguity, therefore, the article was amended to give the prime minister sole discretion to determine whether or not to proclaim an emergency.[60]

The Yang di-Pertuan Agong brought on a constitutional crisis by refusing to sign the constitutional amendment bill. In response Mahathir launched a nationwide campaign in support of the amendment. Nevertheless, the Yang di-Pertuan Agong had the full support of the other sultans, who were probably most concerned with the amendment that related to their own powers at the state level. In the middle of the crisis the Yang di-Pertuan Agong had a heart attack and was temporarily replaced by his deputy, the Yang di-Pertuan Besar of Negeri Sembilan. After extended negotiations, the acting Yang di-Pertuan Agong signed the amendment bill in December 1983 but only on the understanding that further amendments would be introduced immediately.

In the new bill adopted in January 1984, the amendment dealing with assent was further amended to allow a period of thirty days for the Yang di-Pertuan Agong to give his assent. If he failed to give assent within that period, the bill would be deemed to have been given assent. Within the thirty-days period, however, the Yang di-Pertuan Agong could send a non-money bill back to the houses of Parliament with a statement of his objections for reconsideration. The two houses would then return the bill to him, and his assent would have to be given within thirty days. Thus, as one commentator put it, "the suggested reality of the situation is that the Yang di-Pertuan Agong has simply been given an enlarged period to delay giving the royal assent."[61] While the Yang di-Pertuan Agong's power to withhold assent remained severely limited, the amendment limiting the powers of the state sultans was completely withdrawn. According to the prime minister, however, the sultans gave a "verbal undertaking," which, while not announced, was understood to mean that they agreed not to withhold assent.[62] Finally, the article relating to the proclamation of emer-

---

[60] Lee 1986b:238–39.

[61] Ibid.:247. In May 1994 a further constitutional amendment eliminated the Yang di-Pertuan Agong's right to send back legislation for reconsideration. The amendment made it clear that the Yang di-Pertuan Agong always had to follow the advice of the government. *NST* 10 May 1994.

[62] *NST* 17 December 1983.

gency was restored to its wording before the 1983 amendment but again on the understanding that the Yang di-Pertuan Agong would always follow the prime minister's advice.[63] Although the government had backed down in terms of the formal wording of the constitution, it appeared to have gained an informal understanding among the sultans on the limitations of their power.

Following the resolution of the constitutional crisis, the sultans elected the sultan of Johor after the sultan of Perak suddenly died. Despite the events that preceded his reign—events that had, in fact, been precipitated by the prospect that he would become king—Sultan Mahmood Iskandar seemed to develop an excellent relationship with the prime minister. Although he preferred to remain in his palace in Johor Baru rather than reside in Kuala Lumpur, he did nothing to undermine the government. During the crisis over the fate of the suspended lord president, he even played a crucial role in allowing the prime minister to rid himself of the lord president.[64]

The question of the sultans arose again following the 1990 election when the sultan of Kelantan was alleged to have favored Semangat '46 led by his wife's relative, Tengku Razaleigh. But dissatisfaction was not limited to this single case. In the UMNO assemblies of 1990 and 1991 delegates were unusually open in accusing the sultans of using their positions to further private business interests. This was followed by pressure on the sultans from UMNO (represented by one of its vice presidents, Datuk Seri Anwar Ibrahim) to adopt a code of conduct in which they would agree to accept as Menteri Besar whoever had majority support in legislative assemblies and refrain from involvement in business except through trusts. Only six of the nine sultans were willing to accept the code. Part of the discontent in UMNO apparently arose because members of royal families were competing with UMNO members for business opportunities.[65]

The behavior of Sultan Mahmood Iskandar after his return to Johor ignited a new clash between the government and the sultans at the end of 1992. After he had assaulted a school hockey coach, the government reacted by passing legislation in January 1993 to amend the constitution

---

[63] Lee 1986b:248–49.

[64] His behavior, however, had given rise to some disquiet. In 1987, following an incident involving the Yang di-Pertuan Agong on a golf course, Tunku Abdul Rahman called attention to the position of the sultans "who are above the law, which means that they are free to commit crime without being subject to prosecution under the law." Abdul Rahman 1987:20. He was also reported to have said, "You can't allow the ruler to come and knock somebody's head off with his golf stick and break open his head and kill him and go scot free." *FEER* 3 September 1987 (Suhaini Aznam, "Princes, Power, People"). The prime minister took no public action in this case, although it had led to the death of a caddy.

[65] See *FEER* 12 March 1992 (Michael Vatikiotis, "A Code for the Royals") and 16 July 1992 (Michael Vatikiotis, "Code of Conduct").

to limit both immunity from prosecution and the power to bestow royal pardons. When the sultans refused to endorse the constitutional changes, the government withdrew all privileges accorded to them and launched a public campaign in which the press revealed tales of extraordinary royal extravagance.[66] In the end, the sultans backed down and agreed to the amendments after the government gave minor concessions. The constitutional amendment bill was finally passed in March 1993.

Thus the 1980s saw a significant diminution of the role played by the sultans in Malay society. At the time of independence in 1957 the sultans had symbolized Malay domination of the state, which was perceived as being under threat. But by the 1980s there was no question that Malay domination would be undermined, so the Malay community felt less need for the traditional protection offered by the sultans. If protection was needed, the Malay community looked to UMNO rather than the sultans. At the same time the rising level of education among Malays made many people increasingly critical of the royal life-styles, and the growing Malay business class felt alienated by what they saw as unfair competition from businesses linked to royalty. But the moves launched by Mahathir to restrict the powers of the sultans were not intended to abolish the institution. The sultans continued to symbolize Malay political dominance.

In the immediate post-independence period, the pillars of the state—the bureaucracy, the military, and the judiciary (although not the sultans)— remained under British control. But by the 1960s the British had been replaced by Malaysians mainly drawn from the Malay elite. During the post-independence era the Malay establishment grew in size and was recruited from a wider social base, but it retained its essential coherence. The Malay-dominated bureaucracy was loyal to the Malay-dominated government, and there were no indications of serious dissatisfaction within the Malay-dominated armed forces and police. The crisis involving the judiciary created a good deal of acrimony and personal animosity but did not involve fundamental alienation of the judges from the Malay-dominated system. Rather, the conservative judges wanted to maintain the harmonious relationship between the judiciary and the government that had characterized the pre-Mahathir era. The crises involving the sultans arose less from opposition to the monarchy and all that it symbolized than from the behavior of many members of the royal families and, in the 1983 case, the feared consequences of allowing particular individuals to ascend to the national throne.

[66] See *NST* 20–24 January 1993. The UMNO-controlled press also hinted at the possible overthrow of the monarchy. See, for example, the list of "monarchs deposed or who abdicated since end of World War II." *NST* 20 January 1993.

Although the Malay establishment preserved its essential coherence, there were, of course, conflicts and rivalries within the elite. But they revolved around immediate issues and personalities and did not involve basic challenges to the Malay-dominated system. The crises caused by conflicts between the government and the sultans and the government and some of the judges were settled fairly quickly. In fact, the strength and durability of the system meant that these conflicts did not seriously undermine the long-term authority of the government or the dominant position of the Malay elite.

PART THREE

SOCIETY AND POLITICS

Wᴡʜɪʟᴇ Mᴀʟᴀʏsɪᴀ ʀᴇᴛᴀɪɴᴇᴅ a democratic constitutional framework, the system gradually acquired a widening range of authoritarian characteristics. But the democratic structure was more than a mere facade. Although the scope for legitimate opposition activity had been restricted, it had certainly not been eliminated. Therefore, the authoritarian character of the system was tempered by democratic opportunities that allowed nongovernment groups to put forward demands and criticisms to which the government was often forced to respond. The political system was certainly not democratic in the Western sense, but it was far from fully authoritarian.

In their attempts to explain the development of political systems, many political scientists have emphasized the importance of socioeconomic or society-centered factors.[1] While few would claim that socioeconomic factors actually determine the nature of the political system, many argue that social and economic conditions can favor the development of one type of political system while obstructing the development of a different one. Thus, it is plausible to expect that there will be substantial congruence between polity and society. In Part 3 I turn my attention to three areas of potential congruence. I argue that in the Malaysian case pressures emanating from society have often been ambiguous in their effects and have tended to push simultaneously in democratic and authoritarian directions.

One area where the character of society might be expected to influence the nature of the political system involves ethnicity. It has often been argued that in societies sharply divided along ethnic lines, the ever-present danger of communal upheaval makes it difficult for democratic govern-

[1] For a critique of this approach, see Skocpol 1985.

149

ment to survive long. In the context of ethnic rivalry, each major ethnic community will feel compelled to establish its own predominance because it cannot risk the possibility of rival communities' taking power. Once in power, the predominant community has to resort to authoritarian means to consolidate its position. On the other hand, one can hypothesize that the presence of several major ethnic communities, each organized to protect and advance its interests, would make it extremely difficult for an authoritarian government dominated by one community to rule effectively. The presence of rival ethnic communities might contribute to a balance of power that favors governmental responsiveness and promotes intercommunal bargaining and negotiation. In Malaysia, both hypotheses seem valid. One ethnic group has established its predominance while the continuing threat of ethnic conflict has provided a justification for repressive measures of control. On the other hand, the presence of distinct ethnic communities has encouraged bargaining and government responsiveness.

A second area of possible congruence between society and polity lies in the class structure. Economic development inevitably brings about changes in the class structure as people leave rural occupations and join the modern sector of the economy. An increasing proportion of the population becomes urbanized, educational levels are raised, and the urban middle and working classes expand. As the social structure becomes more complex, various groups organize to protect and advance their distinctive interests. One likely consequence is an increase in class conflict when rival groups perceive their interests as being threatened. While governments might respond to rising class conflict by becoming more authoritarian, the development in the long run of a more complex class structure can also be favorable for democratization. Governments, which were in the habit of brushing aside the demands and complaints of the rural masses, are less able to ignore and repress organizations representing the interests of the expanding middle and working classes. In Malaysia the evolution of a modern class structure as a result of economic development could be expected to favor increasing democratization, but this process has been complicated by crosscutting communal cleavages. As a result, class interests have been more commonly manifested within ethnic communities rather than in crosscommunal forms.

Of particular importance is the private business class—the bourgeoisie—which pioneered the process of democratization in Europe. But Third World economies are often dominated by foreign and state capital with the result that the domestic business class has little political weight. In many cases domestic businesspeople are little more than pliant clients of corrupt politicians and bureaucrats. But as economic growth proceeds, we can expect that private business will grow and develop interests that are distinct from those of its patrons in the state apparatus. In Malaysia, however, the composition of the capitalist class is especially complex. Foreign capital, which was predominant before 1970, maintains a large presence while the state sector expanded enormously during the 1970s and 80s. The domestic capitalist class is still mainly Chinese, but a new class of Malay capitalists was produced by the New Economic Policy. For different reasons, however, both the Chinese and Malay capitalist classes have been inhibited from acting as checks on government power and have not played a strong democratizing role.

A third, functionalist, approach to the link between society and the political system concerns the political requirements of various stages of economic growth. Rapid economic growth, especially the transition to industrialization, has often been associated in the Third World with authoritarianism. In East Asia, in particular, the transition from import-substitution to export-oriented industrialization seems, in several countries, to have required authoritarian political controls for its success. Some have argued that heavy industrialization also often requires authoritarian rule. In Malaysia, however, although the transition to export-oriented industrialization and the later launching of heavy industries were associated with authoritarian political controls, these controls were far less repressive than in South Korea, Taiwan, or Singapore and continued to permit a significant degree of democratic practice.

Pressures emanating from society, therefore, tended to be contradictory and their impact ambiguous. Communal politics both facilitated and obstructed pressures toward authoritarianism and democracy. Economic growth brought about changes in the class structure that could be expected to make the government more democratic and responsive. At the same time, however, the demands of the industrialization process seemed to require stronger authoritarian controls while the new class structure lacked a strong and independent bourgeoisie. Therefore, it is hardly surprising that socioeconomic change led to neither full democracy nor full authoritarianism.

9   *Communal Identity and Consociationalism*

IN WHAT WAYS does the communal composition of a country affect the nature of its political system? The argument for the proposition that democracy cannot work in ethnically divided societies is based on the assumption that severe ethnic antagonisms cannot be resolved by democratic means.[1] The central political issues in ethnically divided societies always involve questions that polarize politics along ethnic lines. In a democracy, ethnic politicians cannot avoid taking ethnic stands on ethnic issues. To mobilize ethnic votes, they have little choice but to give voice to sentiments felt deeply by their constituents while there is a strong incentive to stir up ethnic feelings further in order to outbid rival politicians from the same ethnic group. In circumstances where politicians from all communities feel compelled to adopt rigid policies on ethnic issues, compromise becomes almost impossible to achieve with the result that multi-ethnic coalitions either break apart or cannot be formed in the first place. Ethnic antagonisms continue to grow; and, in the end, multi-ethnic democratic government is likely to be replaced by a regime dominated by a single ethnic group that resorts to authoritarian means to consolidate its power.

But authoritarian rule by a single ethnic group is not inevitable in multi-communal societies. While he accepts that ethnic conflict is likely to remain serious in many societies, Lijphart argues that political order might be maintained through arrangements of a consociational nature in which the main ethnic communities are all represented in the government.[2] In contrast to the confrontation between government and opposition in Anglo-American democracy, the central feature of consociational democ-

[1] See Rabushka and Shepsle 1972; Nordlinger 1972:33–36.
[2] Lijphart 1977; see also Nordlinger 1972.

racy is a grand coalition consisting of the leaders of each major ethnic community. The ethnic parties of the consociational regime have to reach decisions by consensus, taking into account the disparate and conflicting ethnic interests that they represent. Moreover, the principle of proportionality should be observed in areas such as political representation, civil-service appointments, and the distribution of public funds to assure each community that its interests are truly being served.

Apart from their willingness to cooperate with the leaders of other ethnic communities, a key requirement for ethnic elites is their capacity to retain the loyalty of their own followers. As long as the masses are docile and deferential and are prepared to entrust their leaders with the responsibility to safeguard the community's interests, the leaders have sufficient scope to deal with the leaders of the other communities. Such deals naturally result in sacrifices as well as benefits. But if compromises include a leader's sacrificing some of his or her own community's interests, it is likely that some followers will be alienated, making the leader vulnerable to accusations of betrayal. Given the ease with which politicians can rally support on ethnic issues, there is no guarantee that the masses will remain passive and loyal to leaders who seem more willing to give concessions to other ethnic interests than defend their own ethnic group's interests.

The willingness of ethnic leaders to give concessions takes on a further dimension in the context of a society where one ethnic group is clearly stronger than the others. One of Lijphart's favorable conditions for the practice of consociational democracy is the presence of a multiple balance of power between ethnic groups. Ideally there should be three or four ethnic groups where none constitutes a near majority. But in cases where one ethnic group makes up the majority, the concessions given by leaders of minority ethnic groups are even more likely to be perceived by group members as the result of betrayal rather than compromise.[3] If significant parts of minority ethnic groups see themselves as victims of oppression by an illegitimate regime, the government might feel the need to turn to overt forms of authoritarian control.

Horowitz, however, has argued that even in cases where one ethnic group is larger than the rest, consociational-like arrangements can still be preserved provided that an appropriate "political incentive structure" is in place; in other words, ethnic parties need incentives to form cooperative arrangements with parties representing other ethnic groups.[4] There are plenty of examples of unfavorable incentive structures. Two-party democ-

---

[3] Lustick argues that consociationalism might really mean control. "A 'control' model is appropriate to the extent that stability in a vertically segmented society is the result of the sustained manipulation of subordinate segment(s) by a superordinate segment." Lustick 1979:330.

[4] Horowitz 1985:ch. 10.

racy where each party represents its own ethnic community is likely to produce a permanent majority for one party and a permanently alienated minority. Even worse is a situation where two or more parties fight for the votes of each ethnic community because each party will have an incentive to outbid the other by adopting ever more aggressive positions on ethnic issues. But in some circumstances strong rivalries within ethnic communities can result in an ethnic party's having an incentive to align with a party representing the other ethnic group despite its likely vulnerability to outbidding. Thus, in a parliamentary system, an ethnic party might have insufficient seats to form a government and, due to its antagonism towards its fellow ethnic competitor, prefer to take as a partner a party representing the other ethnic group to secure a parliamentary majority. It is even better if the electoral system is organized in such a way as to make politicians dependent on the votes of members of ethnic groups other than their own—for example, through highly heterogeneous constituencies. The formation of multi-ethnic alliances in such circumstances does not depend on a common outlook toward ethnic issues but only requires each party to see sufficient advantage for itself to outweigh the risks of losing support in its own community. There is nothing automatic about this process, as Horowitz emphasizes, and much depends on particular circumstances, the personal judgments of leaders and chance.

But it is not only a question of electoral incentives. While it is undeniable that severe ethnic conflict often leads to the establishment of authoritarian regimes, the presence of distinct ethnic communities, each with its own strong sense of identity, can itself constitute an obstacle to authoritarianism. In countries where there is a balance between ethnic groups with no group overwhelmingly predominant, it is difficult to establish authoritarian rule under the control of a single community. The presence of other large groups—especially if they have economic strength—encourages the dominant group to work out cooperative arrangements with the minorities.[5] In these circumstances consociational or semi-consociational power-sharing arrangements are more likely to be established. The outcome may not be democracy, but it need not be authoritarianism.

As I described in Part 1, the Malaysian political system exhibits some of the characteristics of consociationalism, although the system is backed by considerable authoritarian powers. In this chapter I discuss some of the major ethnic issues dividing Malaysian society to see whether policy outcomes conform to the expectations of consociational theory. The discussion will illustrate the wide gap between the Malays and non-Malays on crucial ethnic issues and the potential that ethnic differences have to bring about social disintegration. But ethnic tensions, while remaining serious,

---

[5] Diamond 1989:18–22; Crouch and Morley 1993:293–95. The case of India is relevant.

have been more or less kept in check. Part of the explanation lies in the political system, which allows for the representation of minority ethnic groups in the government while providing the government with substantial authoritarian powers. Although the ethnic-minority parties in the government have been less than full partners, they have nevertheless been more than token representatives. The government has been able to work out compromises that, while unquestionably favoring the Malay community, have generally been regarded as unpalatable but tolerable by many non-Malays. I suggest that the capacity of the hybrid political system to reach ethnic compromises that would have been less likely under fully democratic or straightforward authoritarian rule helps to explain the system's durability.

Ethnic issues have two aspects. In part the struggle between ethnic groups is over political power and the material benefits that flow from it. The ethnic group that wins political power is likely to use it in the interests of its own constituents. Ethnic leaders will use political power to ensure that their group gets privileged access to bureaucratic appointments, commercial opportunities, and higher education while developmental projects will be carried out disproportionately in the regions where members of their group live. But ethnic conflict also involves the question of identity. Who are the owners of the country? What are the symbols of national identity? What is the meaning of the nation's history? While the question of identity is often closely linked to that of material benefits, it is nevertheless separate and has a dynamic of its own.

Horowitz has argued that "in the modern state . . . the sources of ethnic conflict reside, above all, in the struggle for relative group worth" which determines ethnic self-esteem. Ethnic conflict often arises from the resentments felt by economically and socially backward groups toward advanced groups, especially when the backward group is indigenous and the advanced group alien. Indigenous ethnic groups often respond by claiming "ethnic identification with the polity" in ways that exclude other ethnic groups. This, Horowitz says, explains "the highly symbolic content of ethnic politics" where the objective is "a public affirmation of legitimacy where legitimacy is contested." While some symbolic claims—the language of education and administration, for example—also involve material benefits, many "have no direct effect on the distribution of tangible resources among the contending groups, but they usually connote something about future treatment: who will be discriminated against and who preferred." Political struggle over symbols, however, is dangerous for the polity because "symbolic claims are not readily amenable to compromise."[6]

This chapter considers ethnic issues that involve a strong symbolic ele-

---

[6] Horowitz 1985:143, 185, 186, 216, 217, 223.

ment. In Chapters 10 and 11, I discuss the question of ethnicity in the economy (where the symbolic element also involves the distribution of material benefits) in the context of a broader discussion of the evolving class structure. My focus here, however, is on the apparently irreconcilable contrast in perceptions of the character of the Malaysian state, involving issues such as language and education, culture, religion, and population composition. The compromise reached in each case has overwhelmingly favored the Malay community, but the interests of the non-Malay communities have by no means been ignored.

Perceptions of the State

Politics in communally divided societies involves contrasting perceptions of the nature of the state and the role of the citizen, reflecting the distinctive cultures, values, and interests of the rival ethnic groups. Unlike economic disparities, which can be tackled by concrete measures to reduce the disparity, and political rivalries, which can be tempered by the sharing of positions and perquisites, cultural perceptions are far less susceptible to bargaining and compromise. For example, it is easier to reach compromise agreements on the distribution of commercial licenses or the allocation of seats in a cabinet than on the language to be used in education or the religion of the state. The roots of communal conflict in Malaysia do not lie in economic imbalances or political rivalries alone but also involve the struggle to preserve and project ethnic identity—the aspirations of Malays as the indigenous community to project their culture and values onto the state and the determination of non-Malays to preserve their distinctive cultural identities.

One of the most influential statements of the Malay perception was written in 1970 by an UMNO dissident who had recently been expelled from the party. The author, Mahathir Mohamad, later rejoined UMNO and eventually became its leader as well as prime minister in 1981. In *The Malay Dilemma,* which was banned from the time of its publication until the author's appointment as prime minister, Mahathir found the root of the Malay dilemma in the Malay sense of being dispossessed in one's own land.[7] In the pre-British era, Chinese, Indian, Arab, and other traders had come to the Malay peninsula where they spoke Malay, adopted Malay customs, and married Malays. As a result, they were eventually fully absorbed into the Malay community. The author, who himself is of part-

---

[7] See Mahathir 1970. The book was banned apparently because the government feared that it would stir up communal feelings. It was also severely critical of the government and Tunku Abdul Rahman's leadership.

Indian descent and, perhaps because of his medical training, was worried about a tendency toward inbreeding in the Malay community, believes that this infusion of new blood was beneficial. But massive immigration during the colonial period created separate self-sufficient communities that had little inclination to conform to the established traditions of what Mahathir calls the "definitive people." Instead, with their numerical and economic strength, the immigrants threatened to become the dominant community in the homeland of the Malays who feared being reduced to the status of the American Indians.

Malays commonly refer to Malaysia, especially peninsular Malaysia, as Tanah Melayu (the Land of the Malays); and the Malays and other indigenous peoples are described as bumiputera or "sons of the soil." In popular parlance Chinese and Indians are still often called orang asing (foreigners). In practice, there was no choice but to accept the reality of the presence of a large number of non-Malays. Nevertheless, Malays expected the immigrant Chinese and Indians to conform to terms set by the Malays. In the negotiations that led to the granting of independence in 1957, the leaders of the three communities represented by UMNO, the MCA, and MIC reached an understanding, the essence of which was that Malays would be dominant in government while the non-Malays were granted citizenship and assured that their position in the economy would not be disturbed. Although unwritten, this informal bargain or social contract continues to be the basis for Malay dominance in an essentially Malay state.[8] It was agreed that the symbols of the new state would be Malay—the Yang di-Pertuan Agong as head of state, Islam as the state religion, and Malay as the national language.

The perceptions of non-Malays differed sharply from the typical Malay perception. By the post-independence period most non-Malays regarded Malaysia as their own homeland, and many had little sense of attachment to the country from which their forebears had come. These non-Malays naturally resented the establishment of a state based on the premise that Malays, as the indigenous people, had a claim to the privileges of citizenship stronger than those who had merely been born in Malaysia. Why, they asked, should the descendants of immigrants from Indonesia be granted superior status to the descendants of immigrants from China or India? Non-Malays, especially the young, asked why they should feel bound by the pre-independence understanding to which the leaders of the MCA and the MIC had committed themselves without seriously consulting the communities they claimed to represent. Non-Malays believed that they had as much right to belong to Malaysia as did the Malays and felt

---

[8] See, for example, the controversial speech given in Singapore in 1986 by a prominent UMNO leader, Datuk Abdullah Ahmad, and hostile non-Malay reactions to it. Das 1987.

little attachment to the Malay symbols of the state. Non-Malays aspired to a nondiscriminatory state where all citizens of whatever race would have the same rights and opportunities. Long after the expulsion of Singapore from the federation in 1965, the PAP's call for a "Malaysian Malaysia" continued to encapsulate the sentiments of most non-Malays who resented what they perceived as their second-class-citizen status.

Although the constitution implemented in 1957 symbolized Malay dominance, its provisions were not especially onerous for non-Malays who were gratified by the citizenship rights granted to them. Moreover, the symbols of Malay predominance did not in practice greatly affect the daily lives of non-Malays. The king was a constitutional monarch; the establishment of Islam as the state religion was balanced by a guarantee of freedom for other religions; and the national language, Malay, was accompanied by English, which was designated as an official language to be used until 1967 in administration, the courts, and a large part of the educational system.

The failure of the government to give more substance to the symbols of Malay dominance, however, produced growing anger and frustration in a large part of the Malay community. As a result, cultural issues, affecting not only the interests but also the sense of identity of each ethnic community, loomed large in the politics of the 1960s before exploding in the riots of 1969. In response to the events of 1969, UMNO took steps to strengthen the Malay identity of the state. The NEP was directed at the redistribution of material benefits between the Malay and non-Malay communities, but it also constituted an unambiguous symbol of Malay dominance. Apart from the NEP, communal tensions during the 1970s and 80s were regularly exacerbated by government measures in the sensitive areas of language and education, national culture, religion, and population policy, all of which—whatever their material implications—also stood as symbols of the nature of the state.

Language and Education

Language and education are not simply cultural issues but also have crucial economic importance. As I will show in Chapter 10, the medium of instruction in Malaysia facilitated or blocked access to education for significant parts of the population. As long as English remained as the main medium in secondary and tertiary education, access was limited to those proficient in that language—predominantly urban dwellers and non-Malays. After 1970 high schools and universities switched to Malay, which, combined with racial quotas for university entrance, benefited Malays and disadvantaged non-Malays. But the issue of language and education was not just a matter of who had access to higher education and the economic benefits that went with it. The "sovereignty of the Malay language," in the words of many Malays, was generally considered a symbol of the Malay nature of the state and Malay predominance in it. The debate over language and education policy, therefore, involved incompatible conceptions of the nature of the state and the obligations of its citizens.[9]

Starting from Mahathir's premise that the Malays were the definitive people of Malaysia, the champions of the Malay language argued that national unity required all citizens to speak a common language—Malay. They rejected the continued use of English on the grounds that most Malays (and, they could have added, many non-Malays) could not understand the language and were therefore excluded from participation in key state institutions while non-Malays, who had better access to English education, in effect were favored. They also rejected the continued use of Chinese and Tamil in the education system on the grounds that it perpetuated non-Malay exclusiveness and obstructed the formation of a truly national community. Naturally, they were also aware that the change to Malay would open enormous opportunities to Malays because non-Malays unable to communicate effectively in Malay would be displaced. But the symbolic satisfaction that the adoption of the language afforded was no less important: it showed that Malays, who once feared disposession, had been restored to their true status as masters of their own land.

The non-Malay elite, and indeed some members of the Malay elite, favored the retention of English—the international language—on the grounds that it would facilitate Malaysia's access to the world community. Many also doubted that sophisticated concepts could be handled in Malay. Of course, the full adoption of Malay also threatened their own elite status, which was based in part on their mastery of English. At the same time, some Chinese and Tamils feared the loss of cultural identity that they expected to accompany the decline in Chinese and Tamil education. The change to Malay, however, stimulated renewed interest in Chinese-medium education. Many Chinese who had earlier been prepared to accept English as the main language of education rejected Malay and turned to Chinese schools instead. Although Chinese spokespeople sometimes argued that English was necessary for higher education or that mother-tongue instruction was desirable at the primary level, it was hard to escape the feeling that their key problem was an unwillingness to accept what the adoption of Malay symbolized rather than what it actually meant in the

---

[9] Horowitz noted a neon sign in Kuala Lumpur bearing the message, "Jayakan Bahasa Kebangsaan" (Glorify the National Language). "It may seem odd to persuade people to glorify a language," he comments, but the point is that "more than just language was at stake. . . . Language . . . is a symbol of domination." Horowitz 1985:219.

schools. The much smaller Tamil community, which accepted the reality of domination in any case, found it much easier to accept the government's language policy and the implied Malay dominance.

Until the end of the 1960s, English was the medium of instruction for the middle class of all races. The children of urban middle-class parents went to English primary and secondary schools. Some children from urban lower-class families also went to English schools, although most began their education in Malay, Chinese, or Tamil-medium primary schools. In the 1960s government pressure resulted in the conversion of many Chinese secondary schools to English and the closure of the few Tamil high schools. Nevertheless, some independent Chinese schools continued outside the government-financed national system. Within the national system the English schools remained the most popular; 71 percent of high school students attended English schools in 1969, but only 29 percent attended Malay schools.[10] Although non-Malay students predominated in the English schools, urban Malay parents also preferred to send their children to English schools, which offered the best prospects for employment and further education. At the tertiary level, the University of Malaya was the only university and conducted virtually all its courses in English.

Following the communal upheaval in 1969, a new education policy was introduced. English-medium schools were converted year by year to Malay, beginning in the first year of primary school in 1970 and ending with the last year of high school in 1982. The universities, which by then numbered six, were to follow in the years after 1983. Meanwhile, the National University of Malaysia was established in 1970 with Malay as its sole medium of instruction. In the heightened communal atmosphere of the 1970s much teaching in the other universities was also converted to Malay well before the deadline. Resistance from non-Malay parties and organizations was mainly unsuccessful except at the primary level, where the old Chinese and Tamil primary schools, which in the 1960s had catered mainly to non-Malay lower classes, remained intact.

Although non-Malay organizations had not been able to prevent the change in education policy, non-Malay parents, especially the Chinese, continued to resist it. One unexpected consequence of the new policy was a rapid expansion in the number of children attending Chinese primary schools. When the policy was introduced, many non-Malay children, especially in urban areas, went to English-medium primary schools. But instead of enrolling their children in the same schools under a different medium of instruction, Chinese parents increasingly sent them to the remaining Chinese-medium schools. Between 1971 and 1978 the proportion of Chinese children attending Chinese primary schools increased from 78

[10] Lee 1972:18.

to 88 percent.[11] Apparently parents who had not been worried about their children's losing their Chinese culture at English-medium schools suddenly became champions of Chinese traditions and converts to the theory that primary education was best conducted in the mother tongue when the alternative was education in Malay.[12]

On several occasions communal tensions rose to dangerous levels over educational issues. In 1973 the Chinese community was outraged by the huge number of failures among Chinese students who were taking the compulsory Malay language paper in the Malaysia Certificate of Education (MCE, form 5) examinations.[13] In 1982 the focus was on a new primary school syllabus that placed greater emphasis on fundamental skills: the three Rs—reading, writing, and arithmetic (known in Malay as the 3-M). The initial teaching materials were in Malay and seemed to downgrade Chinese culture—for example, by teaching Malay but not Chinese songs. Although the government claimed that the Chinese materials would be supplied later and that it had no intention of changing the character of the Chinese schools, Chinese pupils boycotted school; and the 3-M reform became an emotional issue in the 1982 election campaign.[14] In 1987 ethnic passions were again inflamed when, as I discussed in Chapter 6, the government appointed non-Mandarin-educated teachers as senior administrators in Chinese schools. The furor over both the 3-M and the appointment of the non-Mandarin teachers could not be understood purely on the merits of the issues but had to be considered in terms of what the issues symbolized.[15]

While most Chinese parents and students reluctantly came to the conclusion that the national-system secondary schools offered the most promising path to further educational opportunities and employment, some sought alternatives. During the 1970s there was a revival of the independent Chinese schools with their own curricula but without government financing, and by the late 1970s about 11 percent of Chinese high school students were attending such schools.[16] Meanwhile it became increasingly common for Chinese parents to send their children overseas for secondary and tertiary education—normally to English-speaking countries rather

[11] Calculated from Ministry of Education (Kementrian Pelajaran Malaysia) 1979:Jadual (Table) 5A (opposite p. 16). Among Indians the proportion attending Tamil schools dropped from 52 to 49 percent.

[12] During the same period but in a quite different political context, Chinese parents in Singapore were moving their children from Chinese- to English-medium schools.

[13] *FEER* 30 April 1973 (M. G. G. Pillai, "The MCE Drama").

[14] This issue received extensive press coverage in January 1982. See also Mead 1988:28–33.

[15] As Horowitz points out, often "what might have been seen as a minor issue involved deeper disputes over group status." Horowitz 1985:216.

[16] *NST* 13 December 1978. See Tan Liok Ee 1992:192–95.

than Taiwan, where one would expect them to go if concern for the maintenance of Chinese culture was the main problem.[17] This option was obviously not open to all Chinese parents. Nevertheless, even lower-middle-class families seemed able to maintain one or more children overseas, especially at the tertiary level. The preference for overseas education led, in the late 1980s, to the proliferation of English-medium private colleges preparing mainly Chinese students for entrance examinations to foreign universities and the development of "twinning" arrangements between these institutions and foreign universities under which the first few years of an overseas course could be taken locally at much lower cost to the student. Non-Malays opted, when they could afford it, for overseas tertiary education partly because they believed that an overseas degree was of higher value than a local one but also because the racial quotas set by the domestic universities, especially in the 1970s, meant that many academically qualified Chinese were excluded despite having higher marks than those of Malay applicants.[18]

In the 1960s various Chinese organizations unsuccessfully demanded government approval to set up a Chinese-medium university called Merdeka (Independence) University. Widespread popular support in the Chinese community placed the MCA, as a component of the government, in a very awkward position. Partly to restore MCA's credibility, the government permitted the establishment, under the auspices of the MCA, of the Tunku Abdul Rahman College. Because its students sat for foreign professional examinations, the college used English as its medium of instruction. But as the movement toward the use of Malay in the universities spread in the 1970s and entrance quotas heavily favored Malay students, leaders of the Chinese community once again demanded the right to found Merdeka University. The government again rejected their demand.[19] Although a legal challenge to the government's decision failed, the agitation of the Chinese community finally brought some results in 1978 when UMNO and MCA leaders agreed to increase gradually the non-Malay quota for university entrance.

The implementation of the quota system for university entrance was the most important educational issue causing Chinese indignation and alienation in the 1970s. The quota system was intended to "correct" the imbalance between the communities in tertiary education where Malays had been substantially underrepresented in the past. In 1963 Malays made up only 20.6 percent of the students at the only university, the University of

---

[17] Another reason, of course, for not choosing universities in Taiwan or the Chinese-medium Nanyang University in Singapore was the refusal of the government to recognize degrees from them.

[18] Foreign degrees were also preferred because such qualifications were internationally accepted and therefore more valuable for those who emigrated from Malaysia.

[19] See Kua 1985a:150–80; Aliran 1979.

Malaya.[20] The imbalance was especially marked in the sciences: in 1970 Malays constituted only 1.3 percent of engineering students, 12.4 percent of science students, and 17.2 percent of medical students.[21] In 1977 Prime Minister Hussein Onn pointed out that during the previous eighteen years only twelve of the 1,126 graduates of the University of Malaya's engineering faculty were Malays and only 249 among 3,272 science graduates.[22] To increase the number of Malay students, the government set different requirements for Malay and non-Malay applicants. For example, the cutoff score in 1978 for bumiputeras in arts was only 36 compared to the 44 required by non-bumiputeras. In the sciences non-bumiputeras needed 54 whereas all bumiputera applicants with a minimal pass were accepted.[23] As a result, 74.9 percent of new students accepted by the five local universities in 1977 were bumiputeras, 19.9 percent were Chinese, and 5.2 percent were Indian and other.[24]

The deteriorating prospects of qualified non-Malay applicants gaining admission to the local universities was one reason for a resurgence of support for the proposal to establish Merdeka University, and it also contributed to the poor performance of the MCA in the 1978 election. The MCA badly needed to show evidence that its special relationship with UMNO could bring some benefits to the Chinese community. While still determined to block the Merdeka University proposal, the UMNO leaders were apparently worried about declining support for their coalition partner and were therefore willing to make some concessions. Therefore, in 1978 the quota for bumiputeras was drastically reduced to 65.5 percent.[25] Moreover, an agreement was reached between UMNO and the MCA in December 1978 to increase the total number of places while decreasing the bumiputera quota by about 2 percent annually until a ratio of 55 to 45 was achieved, roughly reflecting the makeup of the population.[26] The details of the agreement were not announced immediately, apparently for fear of alienating Malay opinion. The minister of education, Musa Hitam, merely said that "the Government trusts that this will reduce frustration and disappointment among non-bumiputeras and will be received with good will and understanding by bumiputeras."[27] By the late-1980s the target ratio had been achieved.[28]

[20] Hussin 1990:58.
[21] Mead 1988:25.
[22] *NST* 2 April 1977.
[23] *NST* 17 October 1978.
[24] *UM* 12 July 1977.
[25] *NST* 11 October 1978.
[26] *NST* 14 November 1980.
[27] *NST* 2 February 1979. In reaction, an outraged Malay professor in one university introduced final-year courses that required students to read documents in the *Jawi* (Arabic) script to dissuade Chinese students from continuing in his department.
[28] In 1988, however, an MCA member of Parliament, citing official figures, claimed that the ratio was only 63 to 37. Minister for Education Anwar Ibrahim explained that the official

In the early 1990s the government appeared to give another concession to the Chinese who were still unhappy with the language policy. In December 1993 Prime Minister Mahathir announced the government's intention to permit the use of English in Malaysian universities to teach subjects in science, technology, and medicine. Although the Chinese community welcomed this policy change, it was not primarily a result of Chinese pressure but rather the government's belief that Malaysia's progress toward full economic development required mastery of English as an international language. Mahathir seemed to be particularly concerned about the poor standard of English among graduates of local universities. Despite protests from Malay academics and others, the new policy was implemented.[29]

Medium-of-instruction policy obviously affected the material prospects of Malay and non-Malay students differently, but it was also symbolic of a broader issue—the whole question of the ethnic identity of the state and the position of minority communities. Language policy in education symbolized the Malay nature of the state by placing Malay culture in a higher position relative to other cultures. During the 1970s and 80s many issues aroused strong passions on both sides. These passions, however, seemed out of proportion to their intrinsic significance. In essence, non-Malays felt that not only their material interests but also their sense of identity was under threat, while many Malays viewed non-Malay resistance as evidence of the unwillingness of the Chinese community to identify fully with Malaysia. Nevertheless, although Malay predominance was established unambiguously, non-Malay representatives in the government, responding to non-Malay pressures in society, were able to defend some of their own educational symbols, especially the Chinese primary schools, and modify the adverse consequences of some of the government's pro-Malay policies.

Culture

The question of national culture was closely connected to the issues of language and education. It did not directly involve the distribution of economic benefits, however, but fully revolved around the question of identity. One might argue that it did not really matter what the government decided was the national culture because the various ethnic communities continued to live their lives in their accustomed ways. But different perceptions of national culture implied different perceptions of the state and different senses of belonging. While Malays never doubted that they belonged

---

figures included Malay students who were taking special matriculation classes sponsored by the universities. According to the minister, the ratio for actual university students was 55 to 45. *NST* 23 November 1988.

[29] *NST* 28 December 1993, 9 January 1994.

to the "Land of the Malays," during the colonial and early postcolonial periods they often felt culturally alienated in the predominantly non-Malay urban centers. This sense of alienation fueled the racist sentiments that exploded in 1969.

During the colonial period most Malays lived in rural areas where they spoke Malay and observed Malay customs.[30] Except for the British and the small Malay elite, the urban areas were largely dominated by Chinese whose shops established the character of the cities and towns. Thus, it was understandable that ordinary Malays venturing into the towns felt that they had become strangers in their own land. The language of administration was English while the language of the marketplace was Chinese. As late as the 1960s, Dr. Mahathir recorded that even the subtitles of English films were in Chinese.[31]

More than language separated non-elite Malays from non-elite non-Malays. Popular stereotypes of racial characteristics are notoriously unreliable, but a stereotype cannot endure unless it bears some relationship to reality. In contrast to the stereotype of the energetic, aggressive, self-confident, and entrepreneurial Chinese, the Malay is usually portrayed as polite and self-effacing, avoiding open conflict wherever possible, and preferring to sit around chatting rather than work hard. As Mahathir said, "it is typical of the Malay to stand aside and let someone else pass"; but among Malays such behavior is reciprocal because "the Malay who avails himself of this courtesy shows his breeding by not completely taking the path proffered. He too gives way and inclines himself. Each expects these little courtesies from the other."[32] Difficulties arise when Malays come into contact with others who do not observe the same etiquette. I have often observed in supermarkets, banks, petrol stations and student enrollment lines that Malays tend to hang back while it is not uncommon for Chinese to push ahead, expecting that everyone else will be pushing as well.[33] While the Malays quietly fume, the Chinese seem unaware that they have done anything reprehensible.

While many Chinese and Indians remained poor, non-Malays made up a large part of the wealthy classes in the urban areas and therefore had

---

[30] Members of the Malay elite, however, while retaining much of their Malayness, were also expected to adapt themselves to the ways of the British. In 1905 the British established the Malay College at Kuala Kangsar—sometimes describing it as "the Eton of the East"—to train Malay aristocrats to become minor civil servants. In addition to acquiring "those qualities which corresponded with the British idea of a good Civil Servant," the boys at the college played soccer, rugby, cricket, golf, tennis, hockey, and even Eton's Fives and were instructed in the proper use of the spoon and fork. Khasnor 1984:39–40, 43, 49.

[31] Mahathir 1970:138.

[32] Ibid.:116.

[33] Let me emphasize that I am talking about tendencies. Of course, there are Malays who push and Chinese who wait their turn.

access to higher levels of education. As in all societies, the wealthy and better educated feel superior to the poor; but in Malaysia the well-off were mainly Chinese, and most Malays were among the poor. It was therefore not uncommon for well-off Chinese to treat poor Malays in a condescending manner.[34] Thus, "arrogance" became part of the Chinese stereotype in Malay eyes. There were also Chinese who made a point of trying to develop good relations with Malays but, lacking Malay finesse, often appeared patronizing.

Following the watershed events of 1969, the Malay-dominated government took measures to give the state an unambiguously Malay identity. It was now the turn of non-Malays, particularly the Chinese, to feel alienated in the land they regarded as home. By 1970, most non-Malays fully identified themselves with Malaysia. But they regarded themselves as Malaysian Chinese or Malaysian Indians and resisted pressures toward assimilation with the Malays. Proud of their own culture and identity, they saw no conflict between giving their full loyalty to Malaysia while retaining their cultural identity.

In 1971, the government sponsored a congress on national culture that adopted three principles to define the national culture:

1. National culture must be based on the indigenous culture of this region.
2. Suitable elements from other cultures can be accepted as part of the national culture.
3. Islam is an important component in the molding of the national culture.

Although most of the participants in the congress were Malay intellectuals (non-Malay cultural organizations were not represented), its decisions were later adopted by the government as the basis of its own cultural policy.[35]

The basic principles of the national cultural policy were not accepted by most non-Malays; and when the Ministry of Culture, Youth, and Sports called in 1981 for evaluations of the policy's implementation during the previous decade, major Chinese guilds and associations held a cultural congress that concluded that present policies were "heavily tainted with communalism and tend[ed] towards forced assimilation." In their own memorandum they called for cultural pluralism, the abolition of the distinction between bumiputeras and immigrants, and the adoption of a cul-

---

[34] Even not-so-poor Malays could be badly treated. For example, on one occasion in the 1970s, my Malay wife enquired about the price of a particular expensive fish at the market in the small town of Kajang and was told by the Chinese fishmonger, "No need to ask. You can't afford it!" Over the years many Malays have had similar experiences from which they tend to draw conclusions about Chinese attitudes in general.

[35] Kua 1985b:1–2.

tural policy based on "the fine elements of the culture of each ethnic community."[36]

During the 1970s and 80s, the government and its agencies regularly took action that seemed to disregard and downgrade aspects of non-Malay culture. Malay culture, however, was treated as if it were synonymous with Malaysian culture.[37] While many of these measures did not have enormous significance in themselves, they were a constant source of irritation that contributed to a massive sense of frustration and alienation among non-Malays. For example, a proposed 118-foot-high statue of Kuan Yin (the goddess of mercy) at Ayer Itam hill in Penang had to be reduced to eighty-three feet in response to Malay protests in 1980.[38] In Melaka the state government planned in 1984 to level a large part of Bukit China (China Hill), which was reputed to be the largest Chinese graveyard outside China and contained some twelve thousand graves dating back to the days of the Melaka sultanate in the fifteenth century.[39] In 1977 many Chinese graduates boycotted the installation of the sultan of Johore as chancellor of the Technological University of Malaysia when the university's vice chancellor required them to wear black Malay costumes.[40] Chinese in general were angered by state-government regulations that required Malay letters on shop signboards to be much larger than those in Chinese or other languages.[41] They also resented restrictions imposed on the performance of the Chinese lion dance to celebrate the Chinese new year. Responding to a government television program entitled "Today in History," Chinese organizations called on the government to portray non-Malay figures and historic events as well as those that emphasized the role of Malays. They also asked that more government buildings, roads, and new suburbs be named after non-Malays.[42] To the Chinese it seemed that the government regarded anything associated with Chinese culture and history as unimportant while great efforts were made to promote Malay culture and preserve historic monuments associated with the Malays.

[36] The memorandum is reproduced in ibid.:241–302.

[37] Horowitz notes that "short of eliminating ethnic diversity in the physical sense, exclusionary groups seek to impose a homogeneous identity on the state and to compel acknowledgment of their preeminence in it." In Assam, he points out, "the model of appropriate Bengali behaviour that was held up was nothing short of abandonment of Bengali identity." Horowitz 1985:199–200. While non-Malays were certainly subjected to pressures of this sort in Malaysia, they were nevertheless able to maintain much of their culture.

[38] *NST* 8 November 1980.

[39] *NST* 26 November 1984. In this case, Chinese protests supported by both the MCA and DAP were effective; and the plan was abandoned.

[40] I was present at the ceremony. The color of the costumes added insult to injury because black is associated with death and mourning among the Chinese. In 1978 the government instructed the vice chancellor to allow Chinese graduates to wear Western suits, but the convocation had to be postponed when Malay students demonstrated against the government's failure "to stand firm." *UM* 27 September, 6 October 1978.

[41] *UM* 14 April 1983, 23 February 1984.

[42] Kua 1985b:258–59.

Like education and language, culture was an extremely sensitive area for communal relations. But while the Chinese and Tamil communities undoubtedly suffered from cultural discrimination, their cultures were not dying, and the government did take their protests into account. After all, lion dances are still performed, and Bukit China remains intact. Although radio and television were heavily Malay-oriented, news services were provided in Mandarin and Tamil, while Cantonese and Hindi films seemed popular with more than Chinese and Indian television viewers. The position of the Chinese and Tamil primary schools seemed impregnable, and the various Chinese dialects and Tamil continued to be the normal medium of communication for non-Malays along with increased fluency in Malay. The main threat to Chinese and Indian cultures, in fact, came from Westernization. But the Malay-dominated government's attempts to make Malay culture the core of the national culture strongly reinforced the non-Malays' sense of second-class citizenship.

Religion

Religion constituted another key element in ethnic identity and was a source of communal suspicion. Virtually all Malays are Muslim, and a Malay who abandons Islam is no longer legally considered a Malay—the Federal Constitution defining a Malay as "a person who professes the religion of Islam, habitually speaks the Malay language [and] conforms to Malay custom."[43] Apart from Malays, a significant minority of Indians and a tiny number of Chinese are Muslims. But most Chinese are Taoist, Buddhist, Confucianist, or a combination of these religions; and the majority of Indians follow Hinduism. Small minorities of both the Chinese and Indian communities are Christian, either Catholic or Protestant. Not all bumiputeras are Muslim: the peninsular aborigines and many of the indigenous communities in Eastern Malaysia, such as the Kadazan in Sabah and the Iban in Sarawak, have resisted Islamization and in some cases have adopted Christianity.

At the time of independence in 1957, one of the symbols of the Malay nature of the state was the adoption of Islam as "the religion of the Federation."[44] In 1958, when a member of the legislative council raised the question of implementing *shariah* (Islamic) law, the prime minister, Tunku Abdul Rahman, explained that "this country is not an Islamic state as it is generally understood; we merely provide that Islam shall be the official

---

[43] Federal Constitution, article 160(2).
[44] Ibid., article 3(1).

religion of the State."[45] The Alliance party explained "that the intention in making Islam the official religion of the Federation was primarily for ceremonial purposes, for instance to enable prayers to be offered in the Islamic way on official occasions such as the installation of the Yang di-Pertuan Agong, Merdeka Day and similar occasions."[46] The constitution stated that "other religions may be practised in peace and harmony in any part of the Federation" and "every person has the right to profess and practise his religion and, subject to Clause (4), to propagate it."[47]

The constitution, therefore, guaranteed the freedom of non-Muslims to propagate their religion among non-Muslims, but clause 4 enabled laws to be passed to "control or restrict the propagation of any religious doctrine or belief among the persons professing the religion of Islam."[48] Laws based on this provision prevent non-Muslims from proselytizing among Muslims, but there is no obstacle to Muslims' seeking non-Muslim converts. Indeed, the government itself supported Perkim (Pertubuhan Kebajikan Islam Malaysia, or Malaysian Muslim Welfare Organization), which concerns itself with missionary activities among non-Malays, especially Chinese.

Apart from the restriction on missionary activities among Muslims, however, non-Muslim religious leaders pointed to other instances of discrimination. For example, Islamic programs were transmitted daily by government-owned radio and television stations whereas brief programs relating to other religions were permitted only during major festivals such as Christmas, Easter, Deepavali, or Wesak.[49] Non-Muslims also complained that while provision was made to allocate land for mosques in new housing areas, provision was not usually made for churches or temples or for non-Muslim burial grounds. Moreover, local officials sometimes applied their own interpretations of the rules—for example, by refusing to approve a plan for a church if a cross were placed on the top of the building.[50]

Another issue that disturbed non-Muslim parents was religious conversion. In 1989 the Selangor government adopted a revised Islamic Administration Enactment Act, which, among other things, permitted non-Muslim children to convert to Islam on reaching puberty.[51] Although the Supreme Court upheld an interpretation of the constitution that allowed parents or guardians to determine the religion of children up to the age of eighteen,

[45] Cited in Ahmad Ibrahim 1978:55.
[46] Ibid.:49.
[47] Federal Constitution, articles 3(1) and 11(1).
[48] Ibid., article 11(4).
[49] Tan 1986:115–16.
[50] Ibid.:109–14.
[51] *NST* 18 August 1989. The act was adopted on 19 July 1989.

non-Muslims viewed the Selangor legislation as a further move toward the assimilation of non-Malays.[52] Eventually, however, the MCA was able to persuade the government to change its position. Apparently the MCA had agreed not to conduct a public campaign on the issue on the understanding that the offending provision would be quietly withdrawn later. Eventually, in mid-1991, the Selangor Islamic Council gave its agreement to the amendment of the act.[53]

More threatening because of its broader implications was a demand that non-Muslims be subject to Muslim personal law in regard to certain sexual offenses. The constitution permitted state governments to make laws regarding the practice of Islam that applied only to Muslims. One such law related to punishment for *khalwat* (close proximity between unrelated members of the opposite sex).[54] Khalwat was not limited to actual sexual intercourse but also covered cases of young couples found together in isolated places such as a beach or a park. Many Muslims found the law unfair: in the rare cases where one partner was Muslim and the other not, only the Muslim partner was punished. In October 1982 the Islamic Consultative Body proposed new regulations that allowed religious courts to punish non-Muslims as well as Muslims in such cases. Non-Malays express strong opposition, and the regulations were never implemented.[55]

Non-Muslim anxiety increased in the 1980s when, after Dr. Mahathir became prime minister, the government launched its Islamization program. At the 1982 UMNO general assembly Mahathir declared that "UMNO's struggle has not ended. Today we face the biggest struggle—the struggle to change the attitude of the Malays in line with the requirements of Islam in this modern age. . . . UMNO's task now is to enhance the Islamic practices and ensure that the Malay community truly adheres to Islamic teachings."[56] Several minor steps were taken in this direction, such as banning the import of non-*halal* beef (from cattle not slaughtered according to Islamic ritual) and prohibiting Muslims from entering the Genting Highlands casino. In addition, two substantial projects were launched, the Islamic Bank and the International Islamic University, both of which opened in July 1983. Compulsory courses in Islamic civilization were introduced in the universities, and in 1984 an Islamic insurance company was established. While the bans and the establishment of the three institutions enhanced the Islamic image of the government, they did not consti-

---

[52] *NST* 22 April 1990. See Federal Constitution, article 12(4).

[53] *NST* 3 August 1991.

[54] The meaning of khalwat was transformed during its transition from Arabic to Malay. In Arabic it means "to isolate oneself in order to meditate."

[55] DAP 1988:56.

[56] *NST* 11 September 1982, cited in Mauzy and Milne 1986:97.

tute impositions on non-Malays; and the Islamic civilization course constituted only a tiny proportion of university course requirements.[57]

The Islamization program also involved a campaign to apply Islamic values in government administration. Thus, the government promoted values such as justice, honesty, dedication, diligence, and self-discipline. Non-Malays pointed out that such values were also found in religions other than Islam, and government spokespeople increasingly referred to the "universal human values" found in Islam. Once again the campaign to promote Islamic values in government may have strengthened the government's Islamic image, but it did not harm non-Malay interests. Indeed, non-Malays, like everyone else, would have been better off if some of the campaign's ideals had been effectively implemented; but there seemed to be no noticeable improvement in the behavior of civil servants.

While the government's Islamization campaign caused unease among non-Malays who feared that the government's ultimate aim was the establishment of some kind of Islamic state with the full implementation of Islamic law, in reality the campaign was launched partly to prevent such an outcome.[58] The Malay elite has, of course, always been Muslim; but explicitly Islamic ideas were not prominent in the political philosophy of most UMNO leaders and senior civil servants. In the 1970s, however, Islamic consciousness, perhaps partly reflecting international trends, became much stronger in the Malay community. The increased identification of Malays with Islam coincided with the implementation of the NEP. Rural Malays moved into the cities, including many students in tertiary educational institutions, with the result that a new type of Malay entered the urban world during a time of racial polarization and suspicion following the racial riots of 1969. Communal emotions were deeply felt, and ethnic identification became paramount among both Malays and non-Malays. In this atmosphere Malays tended to emphasize those characteristics that distinguished them from non-Malays. In addition to calling for economic benefits, Malays were mobilized in support of the Malay language, observance of Malay customs, and (quite naturally in the circumstances) Islam. The rise in Islamic consciousness, therefore, was part of a general strengthening of communal consciousness. Although many Indians and a few Chinese were also Muslim, Islam in effect became a rallying cry for Malays.[59]

The religious attitudes of many young Malays in the universities and other educational institutions were not simply a result of bringing village beliefs and practices to the cities.[60] Unlike their parents, whose practice of

---

[57] For further discussion see Hussin 1990:ch. 5.
[58] The following paragraphs are based in part on Crouch 1988 and 1990.
[59] See Chandra Muzaffar 1987; Nagata 1984; Hussin 1990.
[60] See Zainah Anwar 1987.

Islam was often ritualistic and traditional, the educated offspring came into contact with new religious ideas and interpretations through student organizations, visiting preachers, and Islamic literature, much of which was translated from Arabic or Urdu. Influenced by new Islamic ideas and inspired to some extent by events such as the Iranian revolution, the *dakwah* movement reflected a desire to overhaul Malay (and, indeed, Malaysian) society to bring it fully into accord with the tenets of Islam. However, the dakwah movement was by no means a united homogenous wave but consisted of a variety of groups with their own interests and emphases. One of the most prominent organizations was ABIM, led by Anwar Ibrahim until he joined UMNO in 1982.[61]

The increasingly self-conscious commitment of young urban Malays to Islam, in contrast to the more routine Islamic identification of the older generation, was naturally a development to which UMNO, facing the ever-present challenge from PAS, had to respond. In this context the new UMNO leadership, under Mahathir, launched its Islamization drive. UMNO's motives in embarking on a largely symbolic program were mixed. While the attitude of some leaders was cynical and opportunist, others, represented by new recruit Anwar Ibrahim, believed that the new policies did bring Malaysian society closer to Islamic ideals. Nevertheless, all acknowledged that progress would necessarily be slow in Malaysia's multicommunal and multireligious society. The Islamization program enabled UMNO, at least to some extent, to undercut the criticisms of its radical Muslim opponents while at the same time appeasing the consciences of its own increasingly self-conscious Muslim members. In 1992, when the PAS-dominated state government of Kelantan proposed Islamic criminal law, UMNO did not reject the concept of Islamic law but attempted to brand the Kelantan laws as a deviation from true Islam.[62]

Religious identity largely reinforced ethnicity, despite the presence of Muslim non-Malays. Probably more than any other element in ethnic identification, religion had the greatest potential for mobilizing ethnic groups against each other. Communal disputes over mundane issues could be transformed into campaigns with divine blessings. Malays, in particular, were inclined to talk of resorting to *jihad* (holy war) to settle communal issues. The Malay leadership of the government strongly identified itself with Islam but at the same time had an interest in curbing religious

---

[61] For discussion of ABIM and other dakwah organizations, see Funston 1981; Nagata 1984:ch. 4; Hussin 1990:ch. 3; Jomo and Ahmad Shabery 1992.

[62] According to Mahathir, "Pas' *hudud* law is the result of Pas' interpretation on the teaching of Islam. It is not the original Islamic law. . . . This does not mean that we reject the *hudud*. We only reject the interpretation and laws of Kelantan Pas which are not compatible with the *Syariah*" NST 12 May 1994. Nevertheless, the tone of Mahathir's comments indicated that UMNO had no plans of its own to introduce Islamic law.

zealots who challenged not only non-Muslims but also those Muslims whom they regarded as lax and insufficiently committed to religious goals. The government's religious policy attempted to reconcile identification of the state with Islam with the protection of non-Muslim rights.[63] The uneasy balance between the two was a constant source of tension.

Population Growth and Immigration

The nature of intercommunal relations is greatly influenced by the numerical strength of the various ethnic groups. Thus, the ethnic composition of the population becomes an issue in ethnic politics. When Malaya obtained independence in 1957, its Malay and non-Malay populations were almost evenly balanced. But the rate of population increase among bumiputeras was much higher than that of non-bumiputeras, with the result than in 1985 bumiputeras made up 56.5 percent of the peninsular population while the Chinese share fell to 32.8 percent and the Indian share to 10.1 percent.[64] By 1990 the bumiputera share was expected to reach 58.3 percent.[65] For Malaysia as a whole the bumiputera share in the total population increased from 55.5 percent in 1970 to 60 percent in 1985.[66]

Apart from a higher fertility rate, the bumiputera population increased as a result of immigration—mainly illegal. As the Malaysian economy expanded, large numbers of Indonesians and Muslims from the southern Philippines crossed over to Malaysia in search of work. Most of these workers lacked immigration papers and were considered illegal immigrants. Nevertheless, Malaysian authorities generally refrained from vigorous action to deport them, partly because they worked in palm-oil plantations and the construction industry, occupations that were unattractive to most Malaysians. The inflow of illegal migrants was also tolerated for political reasons because of their ethnic affinity with the Malays. Many illegal Indonesian migrants were able to obtain, for a small unofficial payment, red identity cards that permitted them to reside permanently in Malaysia and eventually blue cards that indicated citizenship.[67] Estimates of

[63] Classical Islam does, of course, provide elaborate rules for the protection of non-Muslim rights, although not all the rights that non-Muslims regard as important. But once religion is tied to ethnicity, such rights can easily be ignored.

[64] 5MP:129.

[65] MTR—5MP:83 (Here and elsewhere "MTR" refers to the midterm review of the plan). The results of the 1991 census had still not been published in early 1995, perhaps because of what they revealed about illegal immigrants.

[66] The 1970 figure appears in Milne and Mauzy 1978:3; the 1985 figure is calculated from 5MP:129.

[67] In the 1980s the payment amounted to about $300.

the number of illegal Indonesian immigrants varied, but it was no less than half a million and possibly even a million in the 1980s.[68]

In contrast, the government adopted an extremely strict policy toward refugees from Indochina (the boat people) who crossed the South China Sea in large numbers during the years after the fall of the anti-Communist government in South Vietnam in 1975. Culturally, Vietnamese refugees were closer to Malaysia's Chinese population than to the Malays; many, in fact, were of Chinese descent. These refugees were only accepted on the condition that they would be moved on to other countries. They were placed in internment camps where they waited, sometimes for many years.[69] The difference in the treatment given to Indonesians and Vietnamese was not lost on Malaysia's Chinese population. While the bumiputera population received a boost from illegal migration, the non-Malay population suffered a drain as middle-class non-Malays, especially those with professional qualifications, opted for migration to places such as the United States, Canada, and Australia.

Overall, these developments have brought about a significant change in the balance between the races. The growth of the bumiputera population has meant that, by early in the next century, bumiputeras can be expected to outnumber non-bumiputeras by almost two to one. Unlike the emotional issues of education, language, culture, and religion, the changing demographic balance has been greeted with satisfaction by Malays and accepted with resignation by non-Malays. As the changing composition of the population further strengthens the Malay side in communal politics, it may have the positive effect of reducing Malay insecurity and the Malay-dominated government's tendency to turn to authoritarian means to defend Malay preeminence.

In what ways did communal antagonisms affect the nature of the political system? In Malaysia the experience of ethnic rioting, culminating in the killings of 1969, lay behind the public's broad acceptance of the government's authoritarian powers. Emergency provisions, the ISA, the Sedition Act, and controls on the press are all partly directed toward ensuring that violent communal conflict does not recur. Some argue that the ease with which apparently small issues can turn into emotional communal confrontations means that the government cannot afford to permit the free and open competition that is characteristic of democracy. But controls intended to prevent communal violence can easily be used to restrict political freedoms more generally.

[68] See Hugo 1993:42–44. It was officially estimated that about one million foreign workers were in Malaysia by 1993. MTR—6MP:37. Not all, however, were Indonesian.

[69] In 1993 there were still fourteen thousand Vietnamese boat people in camps in Malaysia. *FEER* 29 April 1993.

Despite the government's authoritarian powers, the system could not be described as fully authoritarian. It provided for substantial representation of both Malays and non-Malays. Although the government was dominated by its Malay component and the consociational principle of proportionality was not observed, non-Malay representation could not be dismissed as token. After 1970 the government carried out policies that increasingly identified the state with the Malay community, but significant concessions were regularly given to non-Malay interests. Even though the symbols of domination in education, language, culture, and religion were overwhelmingly Malay, non-Malay primary schools were preserved, the quotas on non-Malay entrance to universities were raised, the lion dance continued to be performed, Bukit China was not leveled, the Selangor religious code was amended, and the khalwat laws were not extended to cover non-Muslims. In the next two chapters we will see that non-Malay interests in the economy were also to a considerable extent preserved and even in some cases advanced.

The combination of communal representation and authoritarian controls succeeded in preventing a repetition of the events of 1969, although communal tensions ran high on several occasions, most seriously in 1987. During the 1970s armed clashes between the military and police and Communists in the jungles had communal overtones: the military and police were predominantly Malay and the Communists almost entirely Chinese. But during the 1980s Communist guerilla activity declined and finally ended. In fact, the main outbreaks of political violence during the 1970s and 80s were intracommunal clashes among Malays. In 1980, for example, eight members of a Muslim sect who attacked a police station in Batu Pahat (Johor) were killed in a clash with police who were almost all Malays.[70] In January 1985 one PAS member was killed and several seriously injured in fighting that broke out between supporters of UMNO and PAS during a by-election campaign for the federal seat of Padang Terap in Kedah.[71] In the worst clash, four police and fourteen villagers were killed when police, and later military units, attempted to arrest Muslim dissidents at Memali, a village in the Baling district of Kedah, in November 1985.[72]

Insofar as communal passions did not boil over into violent conflict, one can argue that the presence of several major communities provided built-in checks and balances in the political system. The minority communities were so large that, in order to maintain political stability, the leaders of the majority community believed that it was necessary to ensure that the

[70] Kamal Amir 1980.
[71] *NST* 22 January 1985; Suhaimi Said 1985.
[72] *Peristiwa Memali* 1986; Means 1991:128–29.

minorities were given scope to express their demands and that their interests were taken into account. Moreover, what Horowitz calls the "incentive structure" of the electoral system encouraged UMNO leaders in their competition with PAS to ally themselves with non-Malay parties to attract non-Malay support for the government.

In these circumstances political stability could be more easily achieved by developing political institutions that ensured that the minority communities were represented in the government. The presence of large ethnic minority communities did not, of course, make the establishment of full authoritarian rule impossible; but it created pressures that favored political institutions that facilitated responsiveness to minority interests. The ethnic balance and the nature of ethnic conflict in Malaysia did not determine the nature of the state but were congruent with a system that combined authoritarian powers with genuine, although still limited, responsiveness.

IO *The Evolving Class Structure*

THE CHARACTER of any political system is always influenced by the class structure, although the exact nature of the relationship is much debated. In Western Europe, the political system evolved over many centuries from feudal monarchy to modern democracy as the holders of central power were challenged first by relatively independent feudal barons, then by the rising bourgeoisie and middle class, and finally by the urban working class. In a process that differed markedly from country to country, the successive political mobilization of new economic classes created by economic change eventually brought about a complex balance of power that prevented any single class from completely dominating the rest.[1] While such a balance between classes need not automatically produce a democratic political system, it provides a social structure that supports established democracies and gives rise to pressures toward democratization in nondemocracies.

In the Third World, economic change during the colonial era produced a different type of class structure.[2] Colonial regimes typically buttressed aristocratic-bureaucratic or landed elites while economic development was largely monopolized by Europeans primarily interested in plantation agriculture, mining, and international commerce. There was little scope for the development of an indigenous business class in economies where business was dominated by Europeans. Nevertheless, a small Western-educated middle class consisting of subordinate bureaucrats, clerical staff in European enterprises, and professionals appeared; and a small laboring

---

[1] The classic study along these lines is Moore 1969.

[2] The distinctive development of class structures under colonial and imperial capitalism has been analyzed at length by the writers of the dependency and world-system schools. See, for example, Frank 1971; Amin 1974; Cardoso and Faletto 1979.

class was employed in Western commercial enterprises, plantations, and mines. The majority of the population, however, usually remained engaged in small-scale subsistence agriculture.

Although such a class structure was not favorable for democracy, many colonies after independence adopted more or less democratic constitutions following the model of the former colonial power. In reality, however, these democratic governments were dominated by and reflected the interests of the old aristocratic-bureaucratic and landed classes. Postcolonial democracy was often short lived, replaced instead by authoritarian regimes that were better able to defend and further the interests of the dominant aristocratic-bureaucratic and landed classes.

New governments sooner or later launched programs of economic modernization involving industrialization, rural development, and increased educational opportunities. These programs were inevitably accompanied by significant changes in the social structure. Local businesspeople began to take up opportunities left by still-dominant foreign enterprises, the middle class of educated professional and white-collar workers expanded, and a fledgling industrial working class appeared. At the same time, the proportion of the population engaged in agrarian pursuits declined.

For the political system, what are the implications of the emergence of business, middle, and working classes as a result of post-independence economic development? In the short run, the rise of new classes can represent a serious challenge to the established elite, which might then rely on authoritarian means to preserve its power and position. In the long run, however, the expansion of the new urban classes will probably undermine the political power of the old bureaucratic and landed classes and create (in embryonic form, at least) the balance between classes that proved conducive to the development of democracy in the West.

In the West a rising business class or bourgeoisie often played a key role in overturning autocracy and laying the foundations for democracy, but in the ex-colonies the domestic bourgeoisie was usually either nonexistent or extremely weak. The attention of scholars therefore turned to the middle class—consisting of educated urban groups including professionals, managers, technicians, white-collar workers, small businesspeople, and so on. Lipset has linked democracy to the presence of a large middle class indicated by high levels of education, urbanization, and income.[3] Members of the middle class are believed to be attracted to democratic values. They want access to information and the opportunity to participate in politics. They are opposed to arbitrary government and value the rule of law. Further, because of their education and their well-to-do status, they can use democratic opportunities to advance their own interests.[4] But the middle

---

[3] Lipset 1960:ch. 2.
[4] See Cheng 1990; Crouch and Morley 1993:285–87.

class is by no means a homogeneous and coherent entity. While some elements might support democratization, others might find their interests better served by authoritarian rule, especially at times of social upheaval when it seems that the existing social order can only be preserved through strong government.[5] Huntington has argued that in the longer term, as the middle class grows stronger and the potential threat from the lower classes declines, the middle class is likely to be a major element supporting democracy.[6]

The working class is often seen as interested in democratization but has generally been weak compared with other classes. Through trade unions and labor-based political parties, the working class has generally supported other classes in pushing for democratization and the extension of the franchise. Moreover, compared to the rural lower classes, "it [is] more insulated from the hegemony of dominant classes."[7]

In contrast to the new urban classes, which are often seen as pro-democratic, the rural classes are mostly portrayed as obstacles to democratization. In countries where there is a substantial landed class, the big landlords tend to be allied with the state and opposed to the participation of the rural masses in politics except where the population can be effectively controlled by the landlords.[8] The peasantry and other rural workers are usually dismissed as tools of the rural upper class who are manipulated through patron-client ties and therefore easily mobilized against democracy.[9]

While individual classes may be inherently more or less sympathetic toward democracy, class members' attitudes will, in the final analysis, be strongly influenced by the particular circumstances in which they find themselves. The attitude of the business class and the middle class will be greatly affected by their perception of the working class and the rural masses. If the lower classes are seen as nonthreatening, the business and middle classes are more likely to be interested in democratization. But if the demands of the lower classes seem to threaten fundamental business and middle-class interests, these classes might well oppose democratiza-

[5] Robison and Goodman 1992:322–25.

[6] Huntington 1991:66–67. See also Rueschemeyer et al. who argue that in the absence of a strong domestic bourgeoisie in Latin America, the role of the middle class was decisive in the push towards democratization. Rueschemeyer, Stephens, and Stephens 1992:181–82.

[7] Rueschemeyer, Stephens, and Stephens 1992:8.

[8] Moore portrays the landed upper class as playing a major role in the "Revolution from Above and Fascism." Moore 1969:ch. 8. See also Rueschemeyer, Stephens, and Stephens 1992:270. In some circumstances, however, the existence of a landlord class can be favorable for democracy. See Crouch and Morley 1993:292.

[9] Moore even suggests that democracy is unlikely to succeed as long as there is a large class of subsistence peasants. He writes, "The English experience tempts one to say that getting rid of agriculture as a major social activity is one prerequisite for successful democracy." Moore 1969:429.

tion. Sometimes, however, a weak business class might be so closely tied to the state that it opposes democratization while the middle class, allied to the working class, supports it. Much, therefore, depends on balance and alliances between classes. As Rueschemeyer and associates say, "the posture of one class can never be understood in isolation from that of all other classes, states and international actors in the historical situation."[10]

Economic development not only changes the class structure but also, in the long run, reduces poverty. The presence of mass poverty can, of course, be a serious threat to political stability.[11] The poor sometimes organize themselves and express their own demands spontaneously, but the presence of a large pool of poor citizens also provides opportunities for opposition groups in general to mobilize antigovernment feeling.[12] When the poor are politically mobilized on a large scale, it is often difficult for democratic regimes to preserve stability. As a result, it is common for governments either to turn to increasingly authoritarian means of control or be replaced by unambiguously authoritarian regimes.

In the context of the increasing political mobilization of the poor, economic growth and poverty reduction programs are of major political significance for governments. By reducing the extent of extreme poverty, governments can both win the gratitude of the beneficiaries of antipoverty programs and reduce the pool of malcontents who can be mobilized by opposition groups for demonstrations, riots, and other anti-government activities that make it difficult to preserve a democratic system.[13] When rapid economic growth is accompanied by a successful antipoverty program, one might expect that the prospects for the maintenance of a democratic political system would improve.

While analysis of the evolution of the class structure undoubtedly provides important insights for the understanding of political systems, explaining political phenomena primarily in class terms can be misleading in ethnically divided societies. Ethnicity, as Horowitz has argued, is "so often a more compelling and preemptive affiliation than social class is."[14] Therefore, it is necessary to place the class structure in ethnic context; it is not simply a matter of choosing between ethnic and class affiliation but of determining how both interact in particular circumstances. While Malay

[10] Rueschemeyer, Stephens, and Stephens 1992:273.

[11] But as Lipset points out, "this does not mean that economic hardship or poverty *per se* is the main cause of radicalism. There is much evidence to sustain the argument that stable poverty in a situation in which individuals are not exposed to the possibilities of change breeds, if anything, conservatism." Lipset 1960:63.

[12] But it is not easy to mobilize the poor. See Huntington and Nelson 1976:ch. 5.

[13] According to Lipset, economic development permits "those in the lower strata to develop longer time perspectives and more complex and gradualist views of politics." Lipset 1960:61.

[14] Horowitz 1985:89. See also pp. 105–35.

bureaucrats, businessmen, and peasants may have identical attitudes toward the symbolic issues discussed in Chapter 9, their interests and attitudes can diverge on economic matters. Similarly, Malay and non-Malay members of the middle class can have completely different views on language policy but still have common interests on issues such as urban development, taxation policy, or restrictions on the mass media.

Within an ethnic context, this chapter examines the changing balance between classes as a result of rapid economic growth and the simultaneous reduction in poverty. The NEP, which was launched in 1970, had two stated goals—restructuring society to eliminate the identification of occupation with race, and reducing poverty. The Malay-dominated government played a major role in shaping socioeconomic change by increasing Malay representation in the modern sector of the economy. Without the NEP, rapid economic growth and industrialization would no doubt have resulted in the expansion of the business, middle, and working classes; but these classes would have continued to be overwhelmingly non-Malay in composition. The goal of reducing poverty was also aimed mainly at the Malay community because Malays constituted the largest element among the poor. Thus, the NEP, like the pro-Malay policies outlined in Chapter 9, served as a major symbol of the Malay nature of the state but also resulted in a significant redistribution of material benefits.

The Transformation of the Class Structure

Malaysia's rapid economic growth in the years since independence transformed its class structure. The most striking changes have been the rapid growth of the urban middle class and the decline in agricultural occupations. By 1990 Malaysia's class profile reflected its new status as an advanced middle-income country. At the same time the implementation of the NEP resulted in a sharp increase in Malay participation in both middle- and working-class occupations.

My analysis of the evolution of the class structure uses occupational categories as rough approximations of class position. Malaysian statistics, following international practice, use seven main occupational classifications. The top two classifications—"professional and technical" and "administrative and managerial"—represent the upper or solid middle class. "Clerical" and "sales" workers have been counted as lower middle class but not the ambiguous "services" category.[15] Finally, the "production,

---

[15] Both the sales and services categories contain middle-class and lower-class occupations. While most occupations in the sales category are clearly middle class, the category also includes, for example, street vendors, hawkers, and petrol-pump attendants. On the other hand, while most of the service occupations are lower class, the category also includes hotel

transport, and other" classification is treated as a proxy for the working class, while the "agricultural" category covers farmers, peasants, other agricultural workers, and fishermen. Although these approximations of class are by no means fully satisfactory, they are adequate to serve as a rough guide to social change.

At the time of Malaya's independence, more than half—56.4 percent—of the employed work force was engaged in agriculture while the urban middle class was very small. The upper-middle-class occupational categories made up only 4.0 percent of the employed work force while another 11.5 percent were employed in the lower-middle-class categories, making up a broad white-collar middle-class category of 15.5 percent. The working class was small and dispersed. The "production, transport, and others" category amounted to 18.9 percent, but many worked in very small or nonindustrial establishments. Finally, 8.6 percent were employed in the mainly lower-class service sector.

The steady economic growth of the 1960s resulted in significant changes in the occupational structure by 1970. The proportion of workers engaged in agriculture in peninsular Malaysia dropped by more than ten percentage points to 44.9 percent while the "production, transport, and others" category grew to 27.3 percent. The upper middle class expanded to 5.9 percent, and the lower-middle class grew to 14.1 percent—making a total middle-class group of 20 percent, an increase of nearly one-third compared to 1957. Meanwhile the difficult-to-categorize service sector declined slightly to 7.9 percent.

Unfortunately, statistics published in the five-year plans are not fully comparable because the data for 1990 refer to all of Malaysia, not just the peninsula. Nevertheless, because my purpose is to present a broad general picture, I use the Malaysia-wide estimates for 1990. The inclusion of the East Malaysian states tends to understate the major trends because agricultural employment is higher and the working and middle classes smaller than in peninsular Malaysia.

By the end of the NEP period in 1990, employment in agriculture in Malaysia as a whole had continued its sharp decline and fallen to only 28.3 percent. But the fall in the share of agricultural employment was not accompanied by an equivalent rise in working-class employment; the category of production, transport, and others rose to 33.1 percent in 1980 and then declined, partly because of the statistical inclusion of the East Malaysia states, to 27.6 percent. Instead the middle-class categories grew at a

---

and restaurant managers, police officers, and tourist guides. Thus, I have opted to count the sales category as lower middle class but not the services category. The agricultural category, although it includes plantation managers, overwhelmingly consists of peasants, smallholders, and agricultural laborers. Manpower Department, Ministry at Labour and Mainpower: 1980.

spectacular rate during the two decades since 1970. The upper-middle-class categories rose to 11.3 percent, and the lower-middle-class group reached 21.3 percent, making a total middle-class component of 32.6 percent. Some workers in the service category, which had grown to 11.6 percent, should also be considered middle class.

No less significant than the changes in the general class structure were changes in its communal composition. In 1957 Malays made up 48.2 percent of the employed work force but were underrepresented in all occupational categories except agriculture, where they constituted 62.1 percent. In the middle-class occupations, Malays were well represented in the professional and technical category, where the inclusion of schoolteachers, nurses, and higher-level civil servants boosted their share to 35.1 percent; but they were heavily outnumbered in the administrative and managerial, clerical, and sales categories. Malays made up slightly more than a quarter of the working-class category and two-fifths of the service category. In general, therefore, the class structure largely conformed to the common stereotype, which presented Malays as peasants and civil servants, while the non-Malays, especially the Chinese, dominated employment in the modern private sectors of the economy.

By 1970 the identification between race and economic role seemed to have strengthened, although the apparent trend might only reflect better statistical methods. In 1970, when Malays constituted 51.8 percent of the employed work force, they made up 72.0 percent of agricultural employment, an even larger majority than in 1957. Once again the only middle-class category where Malays were well represented—with 47.0 percent—was the professional and technical category, which included a high proportion of government employees. But there had been steady overall growth

Table 2. Occupational structure, 1957, 1970, and 1990 (percentages)

	1957	1970	1990
Middle class	15.5	20.0	32.6
Upper middle class	(4.0)	(5.9)	(11.3)
Lower middle class	(11.5)	(14.1)	(21.3)
Working class	18.9	27.3	27.6
Agriculture	56.4	44.9	28.3

Sources: Jomo 1990:82; 4MP:59; Second Outline Perspective Plan:118.
Notes: The 1957 and 1970 figures refer to peninsular Malaysia, while the 1990 figures cover all of Malaysia. The ambiguous service sector is not included. In 1990 teachers and nurses were taken out of the professional and technical category in the official statistics; however, I have included them here in calculating the upper middle class figure.

in both the middle and working classes, where Malay representation had expanded to about one-third in both.

Twenty years of the NEP's implementation, however, brought about substantial changes in the communal composition of the work force. According to the 1990 statistics, which refer to Malaysia as a whole and not just the peninsula, the bumiputera share in the total employed work force rose to 57.8 percent; they had also made substantial inroads into fields where previously they had constituted small minorities. Although bumiputeras still constituted minorities in the administrative and managerial and the sales categories, their participation in the other two middle-class categories more or less reflected their numbers in the total work force. In the middle-class categories as a whole, bumiputeras made up 48.1 percent while the bumiputera component among production and related workers rose to 48.5 percent and in services to 61.5 percent. Meanwhile, bumiputeras remained dominant in agriculture, making up 76.4 percent of the agricultural work force, a larger proportion than in the peninsula in 1970.

Increased Malay participation in almost all fields raises the question of what happened to the non-Malays. Part of the explanation of the rise in Malay participation between 1970 and 1990 lies in the inclusion of the East Malaysian states in the statistics, which slightly increases the bumiputera share in the work force. More rapid population growth when compared to non-Malays also brought about increased Malay participation in the work force. The other part of the explanation lies in the rapid expansion of sectors where non-Malays were heavily concentrated. Although the proportion of non-Malays in the middle- and working-class categories declined, those categories themselves grew rapidly in absolute terms and thus absorbed the growth in both bumiputera and non-bumiputera workers—but with the bumiputera component growing at a faster rate.

Table 3. Bumiputera participation in employment, 1957, 1970, and 1990 (percentages)

	1957	1970	1990
Middle class	22.0	33.6	48.1
Professional and technical	(35.1)	(47.0)	(60.3)
Administrative and managerial	(17.5)	(24.1)	(33.3)
Clerical	(27.1)	(35.4)	(54.9)
Sales	(15.9)	(26.7)	(36.0)
Working class	26.5	34.2	48.5
Agricultural	62.1	72.0	76.4
Service	39.7	44.3	61.5
Total	48.2	51.8	57.8

Sources: Jomo 1990:82; 4MP:59; Second Outline Perspective Plan:118.
Note: The 1957 and 1970 figures refer to peninsular Malaysia, while the 1990 figures refer to Malaysia as a whole.

The changing class structure and its changing communal composition also meant that the class structures within each community underwent considerable change, especially that of the Malay community. During the twenty years after 1970 the stereotyped image of the Malay community as predominantly composed of peasants had to be abandoned. That image may still have contained some truth in 1970 when 62.3 percent of Malays in peninsular Malaysia were engaged in agriculture, but by 1990 the proportion of bumiputeras throughout Malaysia who were employed in agriculture had fallen to 37.4 percent. On the other hand, there had been an extraordinary doubling of the percentage of bumiputeras employed in white-collar, middle-class occupations—from 12.9 percent in 1970 to 27.0 percent in 1990. At the same time, the percentage of Malays in working-class occupations had risen steadily from 18.0 to 23.2 percent and in the service sector, usually in low-level urban occupations, from 6.8 to 12.4 percent.

The class composition of the Chinese community also changed rapidly in response to economic growth. As in the Malay community, middle-class occupations grew fastest. By 1990 43.2 percent of Chinese were employed in middle-class occupations compared to 28.6 percent in 1970. On the other hand, the percentage of Chinese employed in working-class occupations declined from 41.6 to 33.8 percent and in agriculture from 21.2 to 13.5 percent, while there was a slight increase in those providing services from 8.6 to 9.5 percent.

Among Indians, change was less marked but still significant. The middle class grew from 23.4 percent in 1970 to 27.3 percent in 1990 and the working class from 24.7 to 34.8 percent while the percentage employed in agriculture declined sharply from 41.0 to 23.4 percent as the stereotyped image of the Indians as a race of rubber tappers faded. The services sector expanded slightly from 10.9 to 14.5 percent.

The extraordinary growth of the middle class was partly a product of the expansion of educational opportunities since the 1960s. Although almost 90 percent of children of primary-school age were going to school

Table 4. Class composition of communities, 1970 and 1990 (percentages)

	Bumiputera		Chinese		Indian	
	1970	1990	1970	1990	1970	1990
Middle class	12.9	27.0	28.6	43.2	23.4	27.3
Working class	18.0	23.2	41.6	33.8	24.7	34.8
Agriculture	62.3	37.4	21.2	13.5	41.0	23.4
Services	6.8	12.4	8.6	9.5	10.9	14.5

Sources: 4MP:59; Second Outline Perspective Plan:118.

by 1970, opportunities to attend secondary school were much more limited. While distance from a secondary school did not constitute an obstacle for children living in urban areas during the colonial period, rural children from poor families had limited prospects of acquiring a secondary education. In the years after independence the government devoted substantial resources to expanding the educational system and making it accessible to the rural majority.

As a result of a massive expansion program in peninsular Malaysia, the number of children attending government secondary schools increased by an extraordinary 72.8 percent during the five years before 1970, 86 percent during the 1970s, and another 56 percent in the 1980s.[16] In 1980, 75.3 percent of children of the appropriate age were attending lower secondary classes, and 41.1 percent were attending upper secondary school.[17]

This enormous expansion in secondary education created pressures to expand opportunities for tertiary education. In 1965, only 12,965 students were enrolled in tertiary education, of whom 2,835 were at Malaysia's only university, the University of Malaya. By 1970, enrollments in tertiary education had risen to 16,404, including 8,505 at university level; and two new universities had been founded.[18] During the next twenty years, opportunities for tertiary education grew enormously. In 1990 there were seven universities and dozens of colleges awarding certificates and diplomas in a wide range of fields. Altogether 193,910 students were enrolled in postsecondary courses at government or government-aided institutions, including 60,010 who were taking degree courses at local universities or colleges affiliated with foreign universities.[19] Another 35,600 were taking tertiary courses at private institutions.[20] In addition, in 1985, 34,535 Malaysian students were enrolled in overseas institutions, 22,684 of them in degree courses.[21]

The educational system was thus churning out recruits for the burgeoning middle class. Many of the new graduates came from relatively humble backgrounds, achieving in one generation a rise in social status of which their parents could not have even dreamed. Although a survey conducted in 1983 showed that access to university study was still heavily biased in favor of those from wealthy backgrounds, it also indicated that most students did not come from the higher reaches of society. Of the two-thirds of students at Malaysian universities receiving government scholarships,

---

[16] 2MP:223; 4MP:220; 6MP:160. In addition to 1,385,430 students in government secondary schools in 1990, another 153,000 were enrolled in private secondary schools. 6MP:167.

[17] 4MT:220.

[18] 2MP:223–224.

[19] 6MP:160, 164.

[20] 6MP:166.

[21] 5MP:490–91.

only 12 percent were from families with monthly household incomes of less than $300 while 25 percent came from families with incomes over $1,000. Although Mehmet stresses this bias against the very poor, for our purposes it is important to note that 75 percent came from families with incomes less than $1,000 and 43 percent from families earning less than $500.[22] Government scholarships did not open the universities in a big way to the very poor, but Mehmet's figures clearly show that access to university education was available for students who would have had little prospect of tertiary, let alone university, education fifteen years earlier.

A major goal of the NEP was to provide increased opportunities for Malays to get higher education and thus move into the middle class. In 1957 only about 16,000 Malay children were enrolled in secondary schools, compared to 57,000 Chinese.[23] During the colonial period rural Malay children had normally gone to Malay-medium primary schools, but virtually all the government secondary schools used English as the medium of instruction. Thus, the children of urban Malays (especially government employees), whose primary education had been in English schools, had much better prospects of moving successfully to secondary school. After independence the government opened Malay-medium secondary schools, especially in the smaller towns; and by 1969 29 percent of secondary students were attending Malay-medium schools compared to 3 percent in 1957.[24] At the same time, the number of Malay children attending English schools also increased. By 1967, as a result of raising the level of Malay education, the number of Malays at high school, both English- and Malay-medium, had already exceeded the number of Chinese—the number of Malays having risen to 219,000 and the Chinese to 178,000.[25]

Although language was no obstacle for Malay graduates of English-medium secondary schools who planned to move on to the country's sole university, the English-medium University of Malaya, most Malays went to Malay-medium high schools. Thus, many had great difficulty bridging the gap between secondary and tertiary education. In 1963, Malays, who represented 53 percent of the peninsular population, made up only 20.6 percent of the undergraduates at the University of Malaya.[26] By 1970, with the opening of two new local universities, including the Malay-medium Universiti Kebangsaan Malaysia (National University of Malaysia), the proportion of Malays increased to 39.7 percent while that of Chinese students declined to 49.2 percent.[27]

[22] Mehmet 1988:122–23.
[23] Tan 1982:2.
[24] Lee 1972:18.
[25] Tan 1982:2.
[26] Hussin 1990:58.
[27] Tan 1982:3.

During the 1970s an enormous effort was made to increase the number of Malays studying at university level. Malay increasingly replaced English as the medium of instruction, quotas that heavily favored bumiputeras (reaching a peak of 74.9 percent of the 1977 intake) were imposed on entrance to the universities, and government scholarships of one sort or another were provided for virtually all bumiputera students.[28] At the same time, the government also provided scholarships for a large number of Malays to study at overseas universities. By 1980 bumiputera enrollment in degree courses in local universities had increased to 67 percent of the total while the number of bumiputera students in absolute terms had increased fourfold from 3,084 in 1970 to 13,857 in 1980 with another 5,194 studying at universities overseas.[29] By 1988 the number of bumiputera students in degree courses had more than doubled since 1980 to 30,085, while the number studying overseas had almost trebled to 14,531.[30] Similar preference was given to Malays at diploma-level and other professional and semiprofessional courses at government institutions, and in 1988 bumiputeras made up 92.8 percent of students enrolled in diploma courses at government institutions and 70.2 percent in certificate courses.[31]

The emphasis on providing higher education for Malays was reflected in sharply increasing Malay participation in the professions. Between 1970 and 1990 the proportion of bumiputeras among doctors rose from 4 to 28 percent; among dentists, from 3 to 24 percent; among architects, from 4 to 24 percent; among engineers, from 7 to 35 percent; and among accountants, from 7 to 11 percent.[32]

Therefore, the rapid economic growth of the 1970s and 80s brought about a major transformation of the Malaysian class structure while the NEP transformed its communal composition. In contrast to a population predominantly occupied with agricultural pursuits at the time of independence in 1957 and still largely so occupied in 1970, by 1990 the white-collar middle class made up one-third of the work force and outnumbered those involved in agriculture while the working class constituted a quarter of the work force. At the same time, old communal stereotypes were losing their validity. By 1990 less than two in five Malays were involved in agriculture while one in four was employed in a white-collar middle-class occupation. Among the Chinese, the proportion in the working class had fallen to only one-third while the proportion in middle-class occupations had risen to more than two-fifths. Among Indians, estate laborers had lost

[28] *UM* 12 July 1977.
[29] 4MP:352.
[30] MTR—5MP:277–78.
[31] MTR—5MP:274.
[32] 4MP:60; *Second Outline Perspective Plan*:120.

their previous predominance as employment in both working-class and middle-class occupations expanded.

The Reduction of Poverty

Economic growth trickled down and contributed to progress in implementing the NEP's second prong—the reduction of poverty. From 1970 to 1990, real per-capita income more than doubled.[33] While significant areas of poverty remained, the economic position of most of the population improved. As a result, the likelihood was diminished that the poor might be mobilized as a political threat to the regime. The government's measures to reduce poverty were directed mainly at the Malay community, where poverty was more widespread, and thus helped to strengthen the government's base of support.

In 1970 the government estimated that almost half the peninsular population was living in poverty; it assumed that the incidence of poverty in Sabah and Sarawak was even higher. According to a survey held in conjunction with the 1970 population census, the incomes of 49.3 percent of the peninsula population (792,000 out of 1.6 million households) fell below the poverty line. Of these, some 706,000 or 89 percent were in the largely Malay rural areas, although a substantial number, 86,000, were urban. In the rural areas 59 percent were considered poor, with rubber smallholders, *padi* (rice) cultivators, agricultural laborers, and estate workers making up more than two-thirds of the group. The urban poor constituted about 21 percent of the urban population.[34] Given the high incidence of poverty in rural occupations, it is not surprising that Malays made up 74 percent of the poor group while Chinese made up 17 percent, Indians 8 percent, and others 1 percent. Sixty-five percent of Malay households were considered poor compared to 26 percent of Chinese and 39 percent of Indian.[35]

The rapid economic growth of the 1970s and 80s resulted in a reduction of the proportion of families living below the poverty line (as shown by official estimates). The proportion of households below the poverty line in the peninsula fell steadily from 49.3 percent in 1970 to 30.3 percent in 1983, 18.4 percent in 1984, and 15.0 percent in 1990. Statistics on poverty are, of course, sensitive to different definitions of the poverty line and different methods of estimation. Thus, on the basis of the 1984 household-income survey, the estimate dropped drastically between 1983 and 1984.

[33] Per capita income in constant 1978 prices rose from $1937 in 1970 to $4268 in 1990. Second Outline Perspective Plan:37.
[34] 5MP:86.
[35] 3MP:179.

In the rural areas the incidence of poverty fell from 58.7 percent in 1970 to 41.6 percent in 1983 and then drastically (partly as a result of "improved" methods of estimation) to 24.7 percent in 1984 and 19.3 percent in 1990. In the urban areas it fell from 21.3 percent in 1970 to 11.1 percent in 1983, 8.2 percent in 1984, and 7.3 percent in 1990.[36] In terms of ethnic groups the poverty rate in the peninsula had fallen by 1990 to 20.8 percent among bumiputeras, 5.7 percent among Chinese, and 8.0 percent among Indians.[37]

The government's estimates of the level of poverty may, of course, be questioned. But there is little doubt that the trend was significantly downward. The decline of severe poverty was supported by other social indicators for Malaysia as a whole, such as the fall in the infant-mortality rate from 39.4 per 1,000 in 1970 to 13.5 in 1990, the rise in primary-school enrollment from 88.2 percent of children between ages six and eleven to 98.9 percent, and the rise in life expectancy from 61.6 to 69.0 for men and 65.6 to 73.5 for women.[38] By 1987, 88 percent of rural households in the peninsula were supplied with electricity compared to 29 percent in 1970, and 73 percent had access to piped or potable water compared to 39 percent. From 1971 to 1980 the number of rural health centers and clinics increased by 55 percent, and by 1987 63 percent of the rural population lived within five kilometers of a village clinic.[39] These statistics show that a substantial minority of the rural population still did not have access to basic amenities, but they also indicate that real benefits had been provided for the majority.

Despite the sharp fall in the proportion of poor families, significant numbers of people continued to live in poverty. In the urban areas the total number declined by only 10 percent from 85,900 in 1970 to 77,500 in 1990. In the predominantly Malay rural areas, the decline was much larger, especially after the revised post-1984 figures were used. The number of rural poor households was estimated to have declined from 706,000 in 1970 to 619,700 on the basis of the 1983 estimate and 402,000 according to the 1984 figure and then to 371,400 in 1990.[40] The largest concentrations of rural poverty continued to be found among predominantly Malay rubber smallholders, padi farmers, and rural laborers as well as estate workers, about half of whom were Indian.[41]

[36] MTR—4MP:80; 5MP:86; *Second Outline Perspective Plan*:46. For an official explanation of the discrepancy between the 1983 and 1984 estimates, see 5MP:89.

[37] *Second Outline Perspective Plan*:46.

[38] *Second Outline Perspective Plan*:44.

[39] MTR—5MP:58–59; 4MP:43. For a description of accelerated socioeconomic development in a village in Johor, see Rogers 1992:ch. 6.

[40] MTR—4MP:80; 5MP:86; 6MP:32.

[41] According to 1984 statistics, 83 percent of the poor were rural, making up about one-quarter of the rural population. Rubber smallholders made up 14 percent and padi farmers

The government carried out many rural-development programs to bene-
fit smallholders and peasants, such as a rubber-replanting scheme for
smallholders and the encouragement of intensive cultivation in special rice-
growing areas, such as the Muda Scheme in Kedah. The government also
implemented land-settlement schemes, the largest of which was FELDA.
Under FELDA some 116,293 families, involving something like half a million people who were almost all Malays, were settled by 1990 on 315
schemes.[42] Perhaps the most important means of escaping rural poverty,
however, was through migration to urban areas. Demand for labor was so
strong during most of the period after 1970 that the government permitted
illegal Indonesian immigrants to take jobs, especially in the plantation and
construction industries, with the effect that the wage rates for unskilled
labor in general were held down. During the 1970s unemployment declined from 7.8 percent of the work force in 1970 to 5.3 percent in 1980.
As a result of the recession in the mid-1980s, however, it rose to 8.3 percent in 1986. Malaysia's extraordinary economic growth since the late
1980s brought unemployment down to only 3.0 percent in 1993.[43]

During the early years after independence the Malaysian government
could be considered an alliance between Malay aristocrat-bureaucrats and
Chinese business in the context of an economy dominated by foreign capital.[44] UMNO, the party of the Malay aristocrat-bureaucrats, derived its
legitimacy from the political support of the Malay rural classes, which
were linked to the dominant party by ties of ethnic solidarity and patronage. The Malay rural population consisted of small landlords and peasants
who were in no position to challenge the leadership of the aristocrat-bureaucrats.[45] Although less successful than UMNO, the Chinese business
elite in the MCA aspired to win the loyalty of the Chinese lower class by
playing the role of patron and protector. The cooperation of the Malay
and non-Malay elites was the key to political stability.

To what extent did the emergence of the new urban classes, a result of
economic development, create a balance between classes that favor democ-

---

another 14 percent while estate workers constituted only 3 percent. The largest percentage,
amounting to 34 percent, was found in the catch-all "other agricultural" category, including
nonrubber smallholders and agricultural laborers (to which I have added the small category
of coconut smallholders). Another 16 percent were placed under "other rural industrial."
The urban poor made up 17 percent of the total and 8 percent of total urban households.
5MP:86.

[42] *UM* 2 April 1990.

[43] Ho 1994:191.

[44] See, for example, Brown 1994:ch. 6.

[45] There were no large Malay landlords. During the colonial era, large-scale agriculture
was dominated by foreign-owned plantations. As we will see in Chapter 11, the foreign
plantation-owning companies were bought out by state-affiliated companies in the late 1970s
and early 1980s.

racy? Rapid economic growth brought about a substantial transformation of the class structure and led to a significant reduction in poverty. The most striking change was the growth of the middle class, which could be increasingly expected to pressure the government to respond to society's demands. At the same time, the reduction in both rural and urban poverty made the mobilization of mass resentment against the political system less likely and may have allowed the government to be more relaxed in facing opposition. On the surface, therefore, the evolution of the Malaysian class structure seems to have progressed to a point where it could have been expected to strengthen the democratic characteristics of the political system.

This assessment, however, needs to be qualified in two important ways. First, my discussion so far has largely ignored the central significance in class theory of the business class or bourgeoisie, an omission that will be rectified in Chapter 11. Second, the evolution of the class structure took place in an ethnic context where different communities were affected differently and ethnic loyalties were often paramount.

The impact of the rapid expansion of the middle class was weaker than might have been expected because the class remained sharply divided along ethnic lines. While Malay members of the middle class were the main beneficiaries of government programs, Chinese and Indians continued to resent discrimination. Although members of the middle class might have reacted in similar ways to a wide range of issues (tax policy, educational facilities, housing and urban development, corruption, and bureaucratic inefficiency, restrictions on the press and mass media, and so on), they remained irreconcilably divided on the symbolic ethnic issues discussed in Chapter 9. The middle class, therefore, did not constitute a cohesive force and must be examined within ethnic communities.

The Malay middle class had limited influence during the early years after independence when the aristocratic-bureaucratic leadership of UMNO enjoyed the overwhelming support of rural Malays, who regarded the party as the defender of the Malays against the Chinese. But rapid urbanization among the Malays, especially after the launching of the NEP in 1971, transformed the Malay class structure as the proportion of people engaged in agriculture declined drastically. This represented a serious challenge to UMNO, which could no longer rely on its largely passive rural base to ensure electoral victory but had to pay attention to other sections of the Malay community. In contrast to the peasantry, these other sections were more inclined to make substantial demands on the government in return for votes.

As the profile of the Malay community changed, so did UMNO's. On the whole, the growing Malay middle class, a major beneficiary of the NEP, continued to support the party; but the influx of members from the new educated middle class led to changes in its character. Unlike the rural-based party of the past in which ordinary members usually respected the right of established leaders to lead, the new middle-class members of UMNO had their own political aspirations. Competition for party posts became increasingly intense, and the resulting factionalism contributed to the party split in the late 1980s and the formation of Semangat '46. The rise of the Malay middle class also affected the main Malay opposition party, PAS, which in the 1980s was taken over by well-educated leaders who downplayed the party's rural-Malay ethos and stressed its Islamic foundations, which they hoped would appeal to educated Malays in the cities. Thus, the political fragmentation and increased competitiveness in the 1980s took place against the background of the growth of the Malay middle class.

The growing middle class was also important in non-Malay politics. Despite the discriminatory policies in education, employment, and business, the proportion of non-Malays in middle-class occupations continued to grow, especially in the Chinese community. However alienated many Chinese felt over the government's discriminatory policies, a substantial number were improving their economic and social position, which made it easier for them to tolerate discrimination. Among Indians there was also an expansion of the middle class, although at a markedly less rapid rate than among Malays and Chinese.

While a large part of the Chinese middle class protested against discrimination by voting for the DAP, a substantial minority supported the MCA. As in UMNO, the influx of educated middle-class Chinese into the MCA contributed to factionalism and challenges to the party leadership, which in the 1960s was still dominated by wealthy towkays. Members of the growing Chinese middle class demanded more influence in the party and also played a major role in setting up Gerakan. Although a major split in UMNO did not take place until the late 1980s, the MCA was riven by sharp internal conflict in the early 1970s, the late 1970s, and again in the mid-1980s. Gerakan also had its share of internal factionalism. While the factionalism in the Chinese parties had several causes, the increased participation of independent-minded and ambitious members of the educated middle class was one of them. In the case of the MIC, however, it is difficult to attribute factionalism to the influence of the new middle class because severe factionalism had always been rife in that party.

Thus, the expanding role of members of the middle class in the government parties led to increased intraparty rivalry and factionalism. In the struggle for votes in party elections, incumbent and aspiring leaders were forced to appeal to popular sentiments within their respective communities in a way that had been less necessary in the past. Rivalries within the BN component parties, therefore, checked the power of government leaders and made them more responsive to pressures from below.

The political significance of the working class and the trade-union movement remained limited partly because it was communally divided with little sense of class solidarity. In general, Malay workers gave their votes to either UMNO or PAS, while Chinese and Indian workers in urban areas tended to support opposition parties—the Labour Party in the 1960s and the DAP in the 1970s and 80s. The bargaining position of labor was also undermined by the government's unofficial toleration of illegal immigration.

As I have shown, rapid economic growth during most of the 1970s and 80s had a substantial impact in reducing poverty in general, while specific programs particularly benefited the Malay poor. Although reduced significantly, however, especially in the predominantly Malay rural areas, extreme poverty was by no means eliminated; according to the government's own statistics, one in six Malaysians was still poor in 1990. Nevertheless, the potential impact of poverty as a destabilizing factor had declined. First, the unambiguous reduction in the level of poverty meant that the poor, while still numerous, were heavily outnumbered by the rest of the population. Second, the fact that many of the poor experienced substantial improvements during the previous two decades might give hope to those still in the poor category, especially among Malays: they, too, might be beneficiaries in the future. Third, the poor are not overwhelmingly concentrated in particular areas or occupations but tend to be scattered and isolated from each other. The incidence of poverty is quite high among rubber smallholders and padi farmers, for example, but there are also many well-off and moderately well-off rubber smallholders and padi farmers. Thus, there is no sharp gap between a rich rural elite and the masses in these areas. Moreover, the fact that most of the rural poor are placed in the "other agricultural" and "other industrial" categories shows that they are spread throughout a range of economic activities and not heavily concentrated anywhere. Fourth, while the government has continued to stress policies designed to reduce poverty among rural Malays, less attention has been given to other areas, such as the predominantly Indian and Indonesian estate workers or the largely non-Malay urban poor, because these groups, in normal circumstances, have lacked political influence and do not constitute a threat to the government. UMNO, after all, has not been challenged by PAS in constituencies where Indian estate workers are numerous or in Chinese-dominated areas that normally support opposition parties in elections anyway; and illegal Indonesian immigrants cannot vote.

Therefore, the persistence of poverty in the context of general economic growth has not led to the threat of serious political upheaval or necessitated the introduction of severely authoritarian measures to preserve the government and the social order. On the contrary, the presence of a substantial poor segment, especially among rural Malays, may have strengthened the government. In normal times it is often the poorest Malays who are most dependent on government patronage and therefore most reluctant to risk alienating the government party by supporting the opposition in elections.

Overall, the changes in the Malaysian class structure and its communal composition, especially during the two decades after 1970, had ambiguous consequences for the political system. Rapid economic growth had strengthened the foundations of political stability by facilitating the growth of a middle class with a material stake in the established social order, while poverty was substantially reduced among the poorer classes. Although non-Malays deeply resented discrimination, this feeling was balanced, for many, by material improvements. Thus, it was easier for them to accept, however reluctantly, the basic character of the political order. The growth of the middle class, both Malay and non-Malay, also meant that the government was subjected to more demands from society to which it had to be more willing to respond. At the same time, however, the ethnic segmentation of the middle class meant that its members were sharply divided on many crucial political issues. As the middle class grew, political rivalries within ethnic communities increased: members of the middle class aspired to gain access to political influence and economic opportunity. The resulting competitiveness forced leaders to become more responsive to popular pressures and sentiments. The growth of the middle class was a force pushing the system in a democratic direction. But the middle class was by no means committed to full democracy; its members usually welcomed authoritarian measures intended to preserve the system from the threat of political instability, while most of the Malay middle class had no objection to authoritarian controls imposed on non-Malay dissidents and "troublemakers."

I I *The Fragmented*
Business Class

IN THE CLASSIC West European model, the bourgeoisie made a crucial contribution to the evolution of political democracy.[1] The expansion of commerce and the industrial revolution produced a business class whose growing economic strength enabled it to challenge and eventually displace the ruling aristocracies with their economic base in agriculture.[2] The rise of the bourgeoisie, however, did not lead automatically to democracy. As Moore shows, it sometimes allied itself with the state and the landed classes to produce what he calls fascism.[3] Others, beginning with Marx, have argued that the bourgeoisie has often been satisfied with a form of parliamentarism that protects bourgeois interests but falls well short of full democracy based on universal franchise.[4] The business class can, therefore, be a major force in undermining authoritarian power and furthering democratization, although it does not necessarily play that role.

In most of the Third World a strong and independent national bourgeoisie did not develop along classic European lines. While one scholarly tradition attributes the weakness of indigenous bourgeois classes to the lack of entrepreneurial spirit in traditional cultures, another argues that nascent bourgeoisies were crushed by colonialism and competition from European imports and European business.[5] Whatever the explanation, the result was

---

[1] In this chapter I am distinguishing between the bourgeoisie or business class and the middle class in general, which was discussed in the previous chapter. Members of the business class make the crucial decisions about investment in capitalist economies. The class, however, is by no means homogeneous and includes industrialists, bankers, real estate investors, and directors of mining and plantation companies, among others.

[2] Moore 1969:ch. 7.

[3] Ibid.:ch. 8.

[4] Rueschemeyer, Stephens, and Stephens 1992:ch. 4.

[5] See, for example, McClelland 1961 and Frank 1971.

that business in the colonies was dominated by Europeans, although it was common for subordinate domestic trade to be controlled by ethnic, often immigrant, minorities. Members of the indigenous elite were usually recruited to junior positions in the colonial bureaucracy or entered urban professions while indigenous involvement in commercial activity was limited to small-scale petty trading.

In the absence of a strong indigenous bourgeoisie, new national governments often increased the national share in commerce and industry after independence by expanding the state sector (dominated by the indigenous ethnic majority), rather than encouraging the transformation of the old subordinate domestic trading class (made up predominantly of members of ethnic minorities) into a strong national bourgeoisie. In this context the state tended to acquire the characteristics of the bureaucratic polity.[6] Unchecked by extrabureaucratic forces, the controllers of the state were free to pursue personal and group interests without giving much consideration to anyone else. Politics revolved around intrabureaucratic struggles to control the major sources of patronage. Private businesspeople could not succeed without tying themselves to bureaucratic patrons with whom they were obliged to share the profits of their enterprise. Economic growth, therefore, turned politicians and bureaucrats into millionaires but did not result in the development of a strong and independent bourgeoisie capable of pursuing its own interests as a class.

In bureaucratic polities, businesspeople did not constitute a class that shared a set of common interests but behaved more like individual clients of politicians and bureaucrats, especially when the businesspeople were members of an ethnic minority that lacked political legitimacy and the capacity to mobilize widespread political support. These "pariah entrepreneurs," as Riggs calls them, had no wish to prejudice links with their bureaucratic patrons by asserting political independence.[7] Instead, they joined together with politically connected indigenous partners who could provide them with favors from the state such as licenses, concessions, contracts, and credit as well as protect them against claims made by rival groups of politicians and bureaucrats. Rent seeking, in such circumstances, took precedence over productive investment.[8] Ethnic-minority businesspeople were in no position to oppose the state, and their politically connected indigenous partners had no interest in doing so. The bureaucratic-polity model thus seemed to offer little prospect of political transformation and democratization under the leadership of the bourgeoisie.

[6] The term comes from Riggs's study of Thailand in the 1950s. See Riggs 1966; Girling 1981.

[7] Riggs 1964:139–49.

[8] On rent seeking in Southeast Asia see "Rent-seekers and Speculators" in Yoshihara 1988:ch. 4.

One could argue, however, that in the long run economic development will generate pressures leading to the internal transformation of bureaucratic polities. Although a politically assertive bourgeoisie is unlikely to emerge from a business class consisting of members of an ethnic minority, and there seems to be little prospect of an indigenous bourgeoisie's developing along European lines, Robison suggested in the Indonesian case that a national bourgeoisie might eventually arise from within the state itself.[9] One might expect that eventually "political-bureaucratic power-holders [will] believe that their interests would be better served by promoting rather than squeezing business."[10] In the bureaucratic polity the controllers of the state often set up their own state-favored enterprises, which, despite their initial heavy dependence on state patronage, sometimes develop into large corporations capable of standing on their own feet. Although the original politico-bureaucrats normally do not transform themselves into self-reliant businesspeople, the enterprises that they establish eventually become like any other capitalist enterprise with interests distinct from those of the state.

At this stage, one might argue, the bourgeoisie can begin to play its classic role. The growth of an indigenous business class as a result of economic growth can reach a stage where businesspeople are no longer mere clients of politicians and bureaucrats but constitute a political force in their own right. Businesspeople begin to rely less on individual favors from political and bureaucratic patrons and more on pressure exerted by business as a whole. Increasingly, indigenous business can be expected to seek to influence policy by forming business associations and channeling support to political parties on behalf of business in general. As business pressure results in a more predictable business environment and reduced individual dependence on state favors, ethnic-minority businesspeople might also feel confident enough to become more assertive. The growing strength of the bourgeoisie then enables it to check and limit the power of the state. But, although this can be an important step toward democracy, business is not necessarily committed to full democratization.

How far has economic growth and industrialization resulted in the emergence of a self-reliant bourgeoisie in Malaysia?[11] The Malaysian experience was broadly similar to that of other Third World countries, but there were also significant differences. As in many colonies, business in Malaya was dominated by Europeans while domestic trade was largely in the hands of an ethnic minority—in this case, the Chinese. In Malaya the Chinese immigrant minority was very large and, together with the Indians,

[9] Robison 1986.
[10] McVey 1992:30.
[11] For a survey of Malaysian business groups, see Sieh 1992.

made up half the population at the time of independence in 1957. Thus, the business minority was not in the extremely vulnerable political position of business minorities in other Southeast Asian countries because it was able to offer political leadership to a substantial part of the population.[12] After independence, it seemed possible that the Chinese business class, backed by the broader Chinese community, might to some extent play the classic role of the bourgeoisie in countervailing the power of the predominantly Malay state.

The Malay-dominated state, however, eventually moved to strengthen itself. Like other ex-colonies, although rather later than most, the Malaysian government embarked on a program of economic nationalism in the 1970s that encouraged the transfer of substantial foreign holdings into the hands of the Malaysian state. The adoption of economic nationalist measures was motivated as much (if not more) by anti-Chinese sentiments as antiforeign ones and was designed to strengthen an essentially Malay state against non-Malay domestic rivals. The huge expansion of the state role in the economy in the 1970s and first half of the 1980s strengthened the state side of the state-business balance with the result that the political weight of the Chinese bourgeoisie was greatly reduced. Meanwhile, the government committed itself to a program of creating a Malay bourgeoisie, which, if successful, could conceivably create a new class capable of checking state power. But in the short run, the new Malay business class was tied to its political and bureaucratic patrons and did not constitute a check on state power. Therefore, the Malay politico-bureaucrats who controlled the state enjoyed a substantial degree of autonomy from business pressures, although such pressures could not be completely ignored.

As we saw in Chapter 9, broad social changes in the 1970s and 80s created a social structure that was somewhat more supportive of democratization. Nevertheless, a key element was missing—a strong bourgeoisie. In this chapter we will examine how the huge expansion of the state sector outweighed the political influence of the Chinese bourgeoisie while the new Malay bourgeoisie remained tied to the state through patronage links.

Business before 1970

During the first dozen years of independence the Malaysian government adopted a primarily laissez-faire approach.[13] Not only did it make no attempt to reduce foreign domination of the economy but it actively sought

---

[12] For a comparison of the position of Chinese business in Malaysia with other Southeast Asian countries, see Mackie 1992.

[13] See Jesudason 1989:ch. 3.

new foreign investment. The position of Chinese business was also undisturbed. In the informal agreement between UMNO and the MCA reached just before independence, it was understood that the Chinese would not challenge Malay control of the government while the Malays would not undermine the Chinese economic position. Nevertheless, some measures were taken to facilitate the entry of Malays into modern economic activities. The government set up the Bank Bumiputera in 1965 and the Majlis Amanah Rakyat (MARA, or People's Trust Council) in 1966 specifically to assist Malays in business.

Despite these steps, Malay participation in business was still extremely limited at the beginning of the 1970s. In 1970 official estimates showed that 63.3 percent of share capital in limited companies in peninsular Malaysia was held by foreigners, 34.3 percent by "other Malaysians," and only 2.4 percent by Malays. The Malay share was subdivided into holdings of individuals, which amounted to only 1.6 percent, and Malay interests (meaning government-sponsored agencies said to be holding shares on behalf of Malays), which held 0.8 percent.[14] The estimate of shares held by other Malaysians appears to be quite rough: it included nominee companies and third-company minority holdings, some of which may in fact have been foreign-owned. It was clear, however, that other Malaysians were predominantly Chinese. An earlier calculation made at the end of 1969 had estimated that Chinese held 22.8 percent compared to 1.5 percent held by Malays and Malay interests and 0.9 percent by Indians. These figures presumably underestimate the Chinese share because nominee companies were listed separately and a further category of "other individuals and locally controlled companies" was estimated to hold 10.1 percent.[15]

The Expansion of the State Sector

The major goal of the NEP was to increase Malay participation in the modern sector of the economy. But the Malay leaders of the government realized that Malays could not simply set up businesses and compete successfully with established Chinese and foreign corporations. According to the NEP, by 1990 30 percent of share capital should be in Malay hands; but it was obvious that this goal could not be achieved by private Malay capitalists acting alone. The government therefore established state corporations and trust agencies said to be acting on behalf of bumiputeras. Of the 30 percent that the NEP projected for the bumiputeras, 22.6 percent was to be achieved by the trust agencies.

[14] 3MP:86.
[15] 2MP:40.

In addition to MARA and Bank Bumiputra, the government formed a number of new state enterprises to help bumiputeras go into business or engage in business activities themselves "on behalf of" bumiputeras. Bank Bumiputra was expected to make banking services more accessible to bumiputeras while MARA provided loans and technical advice to small businesspeople; set up bus companies that were eventually transferred to bumiputera businesspeople; established a major financial corporation, Komplek Kewangan, which among other things managed a unit trust fund—Amanah Saham MARA—through which Malays could acquire interests in companies; and established technical and commercial training institutions. One of the new bodies, the Urban Development Authority (UDA), set up in 1971, provided business premises and assistance to Malays in predominantly Chinese commercial areas.[16] In addition, all the state governments set up their own State Economic Development Corporations (SEDCs), which became involved in hundreds of joint ventures with both Chinese and foreign companies in agriculture, manufacturing, housing, and other areas.

The most important of the new 1970s enterprises was the Perbadanan Nasional (Pernas or National Corporation), which was incorporated in late 1969 and set up numerous subsidiaries and other associated companies covering a wide range of activities. Beginning in insurance and construction, it soon expanded with substantial government assistance into trading, engineering, real estate, mining, and securities and by the end of the 1970s became one of Malaysia's largest conglomerates.[17] In the 1980s Pernas's leading role was taken over by a new body, Permodalan Nasional Berhad (PNB, or National Equity Corporation), which was set up in 1978. One of the PNB's purposes was to guarantee greater direct participation for individual Malays in the agencies ostensibly acting on their behalf. In 1981 the PNB established a unit trust fund, Amanah Saham Nasional (ASN, or National Trust Fund), through which bumiputeras could acquire stakes in PNB's holdings. Pernas and other agencies such as the SEDCs and MARA were required to transfer their most profitable shares to the PNB, which also embarked on a share-purchasing program of its own with an enormous amount of government funds. At the same time, heavy pressure was placed on foreign companies to restructure by making shares for Malaysian interests available through the Ministry of Trade and Industry, which then allocated a substantial portion of them to the PNB. By the end of 1985 the PNB had interests in 159 companies and was Malaysia's largest business conglomerate.[18] Two other public sector corporations also

---

[16] For details on MARA and UDA in the 1970s, see Gale 1981b:chs. 3 and 5.
[17] Ibid.:ch. 4.
[18] 5MP:111; Cheong 1990b:161–75.

played a major role in the expansion of the state sector. In 1974 the government established Petronas as the national petroleum corporation after the discovery of extensive new oil reserves, and in 1980 the Heavy Industries Corporation of Malaysia (Hicom) was founded to oversee Malaysia's proposed heavy industrialization program.

One consequence of the huge expansion of the public sector was a decline in accountability and increased scope for the misuse of public funds. Many of the new enterprises set up by the state sector proved unsuccessful. For example, of 314 companies set up by the thirteen SEDCs, only 103 made profits in 1982 while 125 showed losses and 86 did not even submit reports.[19] According to a newspaper report "most SEDC officials were inexperienced negotiators and were thus given a raw deal by the multi-nationals and big local companies who had their pool of experts to lead the negotiations."[20] Part of the problem arose from the use of the SEDC subsidiaries to reward political supporters with appointments as board members of state corporations and their many subsidiary companies. Reportedly, some individuals sat on as many as twenty boards.[21] Evidence of waste of public funds was presented annually in the reports of the auditor-general, who regularly pointed to huge losses by government departments and agencies.

The most spectacular loss involved a Hongkong-based subsidiary of Bank Bumiputra, Bumiputera Malaysia Finance Ltd. (BMF), which lost about $2.5 billion on loans to three Hongkong property developers who went bankrupt in the wake of the 1982 collapse of the Hongkong property market. An official committee of inquiry revealed that many of the loans were not properly secured and in fact often lacked documentation, while members of BMF's management enjoyed extremely warm relations with the chairman of the largest defaulting property developer. The enormity of the BMF affair naturally raised questions about the close links between BMF officials and top UMNO leaders. Although Prime Minister Mahathir had been briefed by the governor of the reserve bank in late 1982 and early 1983 on the seriousness of the losses, BMF officials were only asked to resign in October 1983 and the committee of inquiry only set up in January 1984. As a result of these losses, Bank Bumiputra suffered a pre-tax loss of $969 million in 1983, virtually wiping out its shareholders' funds.[22]

The expansion of the state economic role after 1970 was justified as a

[19] *NST* 4 March 1984.
[20] *NST* 13 February 1982.
[21] *NST* 8 April 1981.
[22] Two critical accounts of the BMF affair are provided in Insan 1986 and Lim 1986. See also *AWSJ* 17 March 1983 (R. Pura and M. Miller, "Bank Bumiputra's Ills Begin to Shake Malaysia").

means to increase Malay participation in the modern sector of the economy, but it also greatly strengthened the state vis-à-vis private business. The mainly Malay politicians and bureaucrats who controlled the state were able to ensure that many key areas of the economy fell under effective state control.[23] The rapid expansion of the state's role in business also placed vastly enhanced patronage resources in the hands of government leaders who were able to consolidate their political power through the distribution of business opportunities to political supporters. Established non-Malay businesspeople became increasingly dependent on government patronage while a new class of dependent Malay businesspeople was created. The growth of the state sector thus undermined the capacity of the ethnically divided business class to check the power of the state and create a balance favorable for democratization.

The Changing Role of Foreign Investment

The expansion of the state sector was largely at the expense of foreign capital. To increase the Malay share in the corporate sector, the government aimed to reduce the share of foreign ownership from an estimated 63.3 percent in 1970 to 30 percent by 1990. During that period the foreign share in fact fell to 25.1 percent. Despite its decline in relative terms, however, foreign capital grew in absolute terms, rising at an average annual rate of 13.3 percent during the 1970s and at a slower pace in the 1980s.[24]

The government's policy toward foreign investment was the product of a delicate balancing act. On the one hand, it needed to reduce the foreign share in the economy to achieve its domestic restructuring aims—in particular, to increase the share for bumiputeras without imposing unbearable strains on Chinese business. On the other hand, the dynamism of the economy depended on continuing foreign investment. The government's industrialization plans required foreign technology and expertise while its program to increase manufactured exports benefited from foreign companies' access to markets. Further, foreign investment helped to make up a shortfall in domestic investment due to the reluctance of Chinese business to invest during the NEP. In its approach to foreign capital, therefore, the Malaysian government was careful to avoid any suggestion of nationalization. Rather, it emphasized local participation through the purchase of shares and the establishment of joint ventures.

In the 1970s the government set out on a program to gain control of the

[23] Jomo refers to these politicians and bureaucrats as "statist capitalists." Jomo 1986:ch. 10.

[24] 4MP:62; *Second Outline Perspective Plan*:103.

major resource-based industries—oil, tin mining, and plantations—as well as banking. At the same time it wanted to ensure that Malaysian interests were represented in the growing manufacturing sector. The main industries targeted were the "commanding heights" of the Malaysian economy at that time. Unlike manufacturing investment, the established resource-based industries were immobile and therefore especially vulnerable to political pressures.

The first major step was taken in 1974 with the formation of Petronas, headed by Tengku Razaleigh, which was given exclusive rights to oil exploration and exploitation in Malaysia. In place of the old system, under which foreign oil companies obtained concessions on easy terms from state governments, all oil companies had to enter production-sharing agreements with Petronas based on the Indonesian model. Initial terms were so strict that several companies, including Exxon, threatened to withdraw from oil exploration in Malaysia. In addition to supervising the foreign oil companies, Petronas itself entered the fields of oil exploration and refining and set up retail petrol stations in competition with foreign companies.[25]

Steps were also taken to increase the national stake in tin mining, 64.1 percent of which was estimated to be foreign-owned in 1969.[26] The main target was the British-controlled London Tin Corporation—not only the largest tin company in Malaysia but the largest in the world, with mines in Britain, Thailand, and Nigeria as well as Malaysia. After an initial takeover maneuver failed in 1975, Pernas Securities succeeded in 1976 in cooperation with Charter Consolidated Ltd., the second largest tin group in Malaysia, which also transferred its mines to the new Pernas-controlled company.[27] By the early 1980s, the Malaysian Mining Corporation, as it was then known, produced about one-quarter of Malaysia's tin. Meanwhile, state governments pressured other foreign tin companies by using powers over land matters entrusted to them under the Malaysian constitution. They made renewal of mining leases conditional on the company's restructuring its equity to give Malaysian interests a majority of shares.

A similar process took place in the plantation sector where both Malaysian government and private interests gradually bought into and gained control of the major British plantation companies. Sime Darby was taken over in 1976 by a group that included both Pernas and private Malaysian interests.[28] The Guthrie Corporation narrowly defeated a government-backed attempted acquisition by Sime Darby in 1979 but fell when the PNB bought up a majority of Guthrie shares on the London stock ex-

[25] See Gale 1981a.
[26] 2MP:173.
[27] Gale 1981b:116–26; Tan 1982:155–58.
[28] Gale 1981b:126–29.

change one morning in 1981.[29] A year later, the PNB reached an agreement with a third large plantation company, Harrisons and Crosfield, to take majority control of its plantation subsidiary, Harrisons Malaysian Estates.[30] Thus, by 1982 the three largest plantation groups, holding about one-third of plantation land, had been brought under effective government control. Meanwhile, most of the remaining big foreign plantation groups succumbed to government pressure and were taken over by Malaysian companies, both public and private—although foreign capital continued to retain minority holdings in many companies. By 1984 the government claimed that some 32 percent of the hectarage of the corporate plantation sector was owned by bumiputera companies, but the real percentage was higher because the gigantic Sime Darby group appears to have been excluded.[31]

The state also expanded into the banking and financial sector. It established Bank Bumiputra in 1965 and then in 1966 took over the Chinese-owned Malayan Banking Bhd following a run on its deposits. By 1975 government patronage enabled Malayan Banking and Bank Bumiputra to replace previously dominant British institutions as the top two banks while another local bank, the private United Malayan Banking Corporation (UMBC), moved into fourth position.[32] Allegations of malpractice against the directors of UMBC in 1976 allowed the central bank to intervene and restructure its ownership. Pernas took 30 percent of equity, which by 1988 had risen to 85 percent.[33] Other government agencies also acquired substantial shareholdings in private banks.

In the case of manufacturing industry, the government continued to welcome foreign investment; but in contrast to the open-door approach of the 1960s, guidelines were laid down in the 1970s. Under the Industrial Coordination Act of 1975, foreign companies producing for the domestic market were expected to restructure their equity by reducing their own holdings to 30 percent so that Malaysian interests would hold 70 percent, including a minimum of 30 percent in Malay hands. These guidelines, however, were liberalized on several occasions to stimulate foreign investment. Eventually they permitted 100 percent foreign ownership in export-oriented projects.[34] Despite the liberalization, most foreign firms were in the form of joint ventures in which Malaysian interests held substantial stakes but normally exercised little control over production. In many cases, equity was shared between the foreign investor, one or another of

[29] Jesudason 1989:89–91.
[30] Cheong 1990b:170.
[31] 5MP:110.
[32] Tan 1982:159–62.
[33] Jesudason 1989:93; *NST* 14 September 1988.
[34] Jesudason 1989:188–89; *NST* 23 July 1988.

the state agencies, and private Malaysian businesspeople (either Chinese, Malay, or both). Nevertheless, foreign investment continued to flow into the manufacturing sector and regularly exceeded domestic investment.

The expansion of Malaysian ownership was largely at the expense of the British who, as the former colonial power, had dominated the colonial economy. Although long-established British capital continued to play an important role, the government succeeded in diversifying its sources of foreign investment so that it was no longer overly dependent on any one country. In the 1970s Japan overtook Britain as the main source of new investment, but no single country was dominant.[35]

Thus, in the 1970s and early 1980s the Malaysian state made a concerted effort to achieve a dominant role in key sectors of the economy that had hitherto been controlled by foreign interests. The government did not adopt a radical-nationalist stance but continued to welcome and depend upon foreign capital that could provide modern technology, access to export markets, management skills, and employment opportunities, particularly in the manufacturing sector. When extending its ownership over the established export industries, the government moved indirectly. In some cases it adopted the normal business practice of quietly purchasing shares on the stock market and then followed with a sudden takeover bid. In other cases it pressured foreign companies to reorganize their equity structures "voluntarily" and thus avoid being subjected to a later takeover bid or face difficulties in acquiring licenses and other necessary facilities. In effect, the state reduced the previously dominant role of foreign capital and tied it to the state. In this way the Malay-dominated state was able to face domestic Chinese capital from a position of vastly enhanced strength.

Chinese Business: Bourgeoisie or Pariah Entrepreneurs?

Since the early colonial era, Chinese traders dominated domestic trade, later branching into tin mining and plantation agriculture and establishing their own banks. Therefore, at the time of independence a substantial Chinese bourgeoisie already existed, although it was largely nonindustrial and subordinate to British capital. Unlike the national bourgeoisie of Marxist theory, which is seen as providing crucial support for national independence movements, much of the Chinese bourgeoisie, whose economic interests often intermeshed with those of British business, was loyal or not actively opposed to the colonial regime.[36] The Chinese bourgeoisie was

[35] The largest sources of investment in 1989 were Japan (31.3 percent), Taiwan (24.7 percent), Singapore (10.6 percent), and Britain (8.9 percent). The U.S. share was only 3.7 percent. *FEER* 1 February 1990.
[36] See Jomo 1986:ch. 8; Jesudason 1989:ch. 2.

also no doubt aware that it could never lead an independent Malaya, which would inevitably be largely under Malay control.

Chinese business prospered and expanded during the 1960s.[37] Although foreign capital remained dominant, a number of large Chinese enterprises emerged, while middle-level and small-scale business in manufacturing, construction, transport, wholesaling, and retailing continued to be firmly in Chinese hands.[38] Despite the prominence of some big Chinese companies, most businesses were medium-sized or small. The interests of Chinese business, both large and small, were represented by various Chinese chambers of commerce as well as the MCA, whose leaders occupied key economic ministries, including Finance, and Trade and Industry. Undoubtedly the MCA acted as a patronage machine providing individual benefits to its supporters, but it also represented the broad interests of the Chinese bourgeoisie whose wishes were always taken into account when government policy was formulated.

The new atmosphere after 1969 and the implementation of the NEP brought about a drastic change in the position of the Chinese community in general and Chinese business in particular. The government always asserted that in a growing economy there would be no need to rob Peter to pay Paul and that the relative and absolute growth of the Malay sector would mean only a relative and *not* absolute decline in the Chinese sector. In practice, however, the NEP hurt many Chinese enterprises and restricted opportunities for others. Enterprises with Malay partners received advantages in gaining licenses, permits, leases, credit, contracts, and concessions that were often denied to purely Chinese enterprises. Chinese businesspeople were therefore under pressure to take in Malay partners who often had no business skills and no capital despite their good political connections.

In 1975 the government introduced a major new policy instrument, the Industrial Coordination Act, which required all manufacturers to obtain a license except those with capital of less than $100,000 and fewer than twenty-five employees. Under regulations issued in 1976 the minister was given wide powers to grant or refuse a license in "the national interest," a term that was not defined in the regulations. To obtain a license manufacturers had to take steps toward ensuring that 30 percent of equity was owned by Malay interests and, in the case of foreign enterprises, 70 percent was in Malaysian hands (except in the case of export-oriented indus-

[37] Jesudason 1989:60–64; Tan 1982:171–77.

[38] According to Mahathir, "this greatly increased share in the nation's commercial activities which were opened to Malaysians meant simply that greater wealth accrued to the Chinese. . . . Indeed Malaysian anxiety to Malayanize and Malaysianize meant complete Sinocization of the economy of the country." Mahathir 1970:51. In fact, the Chinese role continued to be dwarfed by the British.

tries). Manufacturers were also obliged to seek Malay distributors so that at least 30 percent of distribution would be in Malay hands and to recruit and train Malay workers so that their work force at all levels reflected the communal composition of the population.[39]

The legislation was strongly opposed by both Chinese and foreign business; but the government remained fully committed to the act in principle, although it was flexible on some matters of detail. Initially all existing manufacturers were automatically licensed, and in 1977 the act was amended in minor ways to take into account some of the objections raised by foreign business and remove some of the grievances of small Chinese manufacturers.[40] Later, in response to the recession of 1985, the exemption limit was raised to $1 million and the number of workers to fifty while enterprises with shareholders' funds of less than $2.5 million no longer needed approval to expand or diversify products.[41]

The NEP and the Industrial Coordination Act had a generally negative impact on Chinese investment, as indicated by signs of significant capital flight. Between 1976 and 1985 more than $3 billion per year appears to have been sent out of Malaysia while the finance minister announced that some $10 billion had been transferred overseas between 1983 and 1985.[42] Nevertheless, economic conditions were generally buoyant until the early 1980s; and Chinese participation in business continued to grow, although at a slower pace than might have been the case without the NEP.[43] According to the NEP's projections, the non-Malay share in the equity of limited companies was expected to grow from 34.3 percent in 1970 to 40 percent in 1990. But by 1980 the non-Malay share had already reached 40.1 percent, slightly above the target for 1990.[44] By 1990, the Chinese share had risen to 44.9 percent out of a total non-Malay share of 46.2 percent.[45] It is possible, however, that part of the increase in the Chinese share in the corporate sector was due to a trend among small enterprises to incorporate themselves.[46]

In adjusting to the circumstances of the 1970s and 80s, Chinese business pursued three different types of strategy. For most Chinese businesspeople, whatever political influence they had was mainly exercised collectively as part of the Chinese bourgeoisie. Although it was common for Chinese businesspeople with small and medium-sized business to seek links with

[39] Jesudason 1989:137.
[40] Ibid.:141.
[41] Ho 1988:236.
[42] Khor 1987:57–58.
[43] See Jesudason 1989:159; Tan 1982:190.
[44] 4MP:62.
[45] *Second Outline Perspective Plan*:103.
[46] Gale 1985:212. For example, a small business might incorporate itself to gain better access to credit or reduce taxes.

local Malay politicians, they were usually too small and insignificant to be able to pursue their interests individually. Therefore, they looked to the various Chinese chambers of commerce and industry as well as the MCA to make demands on behalf of Chinese business in general. At this level, the Chinese business class was not able to prevent the change in the balance of political power that had adverse consequences for Chinese business. Nevertheless, the sheer weight of the Chinese bourgeoisie meant that the government had to ensure that circumstances were not so bad that people could not go on with their businesses.

A second strategy was adopted by some of the bigger businesspeople who were strong enough to approach the government directly. In control of giant enterprises, they found it easier to make room for Malay partners and worked closely with them. For example, Robert Kuok, whose fortune was based on sugar, had developed close ties with Malay politicians and was already involved in joint ventures with the government before 1970.[47] Property developer Tan Sri Lim Goh Tong also had Malay partners— among them Tan Sri Mohd Noah Omar, not only a former speaker of the national Parliament but also father-in-law of two successive prime ministers, Tun Razak and Datuk Hussein. Another example was Datuk Lee Loy Seng, whose group controlled the Kuala Lumpur-Kepong plantation and included Tengku Razaleigh Hamzah and later his brother, Tengku Robert Hamzah, on its board.[48] In the 1990s the close association of the Quek family's Hong Leong group with UMNO-affiliated companies also fits this pattern.[49] These businesspeople did not simply rely on the collective influence of the Chinese business community but developed special relationships with particular members of the Malay elite. But they could not be dismissed as mere pariah entrepreneurs. Although they received favors from their Malay partners, their business success was not derived primarily from government patronage; and they were already well established before the expansion of the state sector in the 1970s. Moreover, many had strong international connections with substantial investments in other countries.[50]

Another subcategory of Chinese businesspeople also had close ties to UMNO leaders, but in this case their ties seem to have preceded their success in the business world.[51] For example, Tan Sri Khoo Kay Peng, who transformed Malayan United Industries from a small manufacturing com-

---

[47] *FEER* 30 October 1986 (R. Cottrell, "The Silent Empire of the Kuok Family").
[48] Lim 1981:109–10; Tan 1982:286.
[49] Searle 1994:ch. 9.
[50] Heng, however, notes with irony that some of these tycoons, "nearly all of whom were themselves immigrants or the sons of immigrants, are poised on the brink of emigration at the very moment of their maximum success in integrating themselves into contemporary Malaysian society." Heng 1992:144.
[51] See Searle 1994:ch. 9.

pany in the mid-1970s to a major conglomerate in the early 1980s with interests in property, hotels, finance, and trading, was an associate of Tengku Razaleigh, then minister of finance. Later, Tan Sri Vincent Tan Chee Yioun, an associate of Razleigh's successor at the ministry, Datuk Paduka Daim Zainuddin, achieved spectacular business success. A car salesman and insurance agent in the 1970s, Tan was allocated the Malaysian franchise for McDonald's in 1982 and then in 1985 gained the newly privatized lottery, Sports Toto, from the government. Both enterprises were extremely lucrative and provided quick access to huge amounts of money, enabling Tan to build up his main company, the Berjaya Corporation. Berjaya proved adept at taking over other companies and by the end of the 1980s had become one of Malaysia's bigger conglomerates. While Chinese businesspeople in this category conformed more closely to the pariah entrepreneur image, Khoo at least was able to transform himself into a businessman who could stand on his own feet: he survived his patron's loss of position in UMNO and the government and supported the assertiveness of his friend, Tan Koon Swan. Such businesspeople did not build up small industries into large conglomerates but gained their wealth through stock-market maneuvers, corporate acquisitions, and takeovers that needed close links with Malay politicians and bureaucrats to ensure success.

A third response to the post-1970 environment was more assertive. Despite its position in the government, the MCA was unable to resist the post-1969 changes, which seriously undermined its credibility as representative of the Chinese community; government adoption of the Industrial Coordination Act was a particularly severe blow. Responding to the rapid expansion of the state sector, the new MCA leadership under Datuk Lee San Choon set up a company, Multi-Purpose Holdings Berhad (MPH), to compete with the new bumiputera corporations. The company's sponsors argued that Chinese businesses, almost all of which consisted of family-based enterprises, could not compete with the new state corporations unless they established their own large-scale modern corporations. MPH, which was established in 1975, attracted funds from the Chinese community in general, especially small-scale investors who were reluctant to place their savings with the established family-based enterprises. In the early 1980s it had more than two hundred thousand shareholders.

Like the state corporations, MPH was not interested in building up its own industries from scratch but specialized in taking over established enterprises and purchasing property such as agricultural land that, with political connections, MPH hoped to convert to housing estates.[52] Under its

---

[52] The most complete study of MPH is Gale 1985. His study, however, was completed in 1984 when MPH was at the height of its influence. MPH's fall is discussed in Gomez 1994:ch. 4; and Searle 1994:ch. 9.

dynamic managing director, Tan Koon Swan, MPH financed itself through loans. As a result, much of its income had to be devoted to debt servicing while shareholders received no return on their investments. Its highly unfavorable debt-equity ratio made it vulnerable to the recession of the mid-1980s, and its loss of $192 million in 1985 was the largest ever made by a private Malaysian company. Although MPH survived, its attempt to find an assertive role for the Chinese business community failed dismally. Eventually it was taken over by a Chinese company, Kamunting Corporation, which seemed to have good links with some UMNO leaders, especially Minister of Finance Daim Zainuddin.[53] Meanwhile, as I noted in Chapter 3, Tan Koon Swan, who had been elected president of the MCA, was convicted and imprisoned for commercial crimes in both Singapore and Malaysia.

Chinese business was in a somewhat ambiguous position. Chinese businesspeople in general could not be simply dismissed as pariah entrepreneurs, although some, such as Tan Sri Khoo Kay Peng and Tan Sri Vincent Tan, at the beginning of their careers at least, seemed to owe much to Malay patrons and more or less fitted that category. But the Chinese business class as a whole had strong commercial foundations and continued to make a substantial contribution to industry and commerce. It was not, however, able to play the classic political role of the bourgeoisie. Precisely because it was Chinese, it was unable to convert its economic strength into political power. After 1970, as the Malay elite tightened its grip on the state and fostered the growth of a Malay business class, Chinese business—as part of the Chinese community—was forced onto the defensive. Nevertheless, its business influence was not negligible. While Chinese business could not prevent the implementation of NEP policies favoring the state and Malay business, it was successful in maintaining, and even increasing, its own large share in the economy.

Malay Business: Entrepreneurs or Rentiers?

Before 1970 Malay involvement in business was very limited. Certainly some foreign and Chinese enterprises understood the benefits of appointing a prominent Malay—a retired politician or bureaucrat or a member of a royal family—to their boards to facilitate dealings with the government, but such Malays virtually never played an active part in the management of the enterprise. As Dr. Mahathir put it, "everyone knows that more often than not these Malays have neither a single cent invested, nor probably

---

[53] These links are outlined in *AWSJ* 31 May 1988 (R. Pura, "Malaysia's Daim Tied to Contract Award").

have they the personal capacity to contribute to the all-important job of making profits for the company. Everyone knows that some of these Malays are merely selling their names and taking advantage of the policies of a government which wants to see a more equitable distribution of wealth."[54] As we have seen, medium-and small-scale enterprise was primarily in Chinese hands, although Malays sometimes engaged in small businesses, especially in the Malay regions of the north and northeast. Therefore, restructuring the society after 1969 required an increase in bumiputera participation in business. In the words of the Second Malaysia Plan, "an essential part of the racial balance objective is the creation of a Malay entrepreneurial community."[55]

The NEP also aimed to increase Malay participation in business more generally. One of the main indicators of Malay progress was to be measured in terms of ownership of shares in the corporate sector, which the government hoped would grow to 30 percent by 1990. As we have seen, in 1970 Malay holdings amounted to only 2.4 percent, of which 0.8 percent was in the hands of government agencies acting on behalf of bumiputeras. Only 1.6 percent was owned directly by Malay individuals. In its plans to achieve the 30-percent goal the government adopted a cautious approach, believing that it would take a long time before private Malay businesspeople could effectively compete with the Chinese and foreigners. It therefore placed high priority on developing the state sector, which was to act "on behalf of" the bumiputera community. By 1990 Malay individuals were expected to own only 7.4 percent of the corporate sector compared to 22.6 percent owned by so-called Malay interests.[56] This goal, however, was not achieved; in 1990 the Malay share reached only 20.3 percent. Ownership by Malay individuals, on the other hand, seemed higher than expected at 14.0 percent; but this consisted of only 8.2 percent directly owned by individuals and enterprises while 5.8 percent was invested in "institutions channeling bumiputera funds" such as ASN. The remaining 6.3 percent was owned by state-sector trust agencies on behalf of Malay interests.[57] Although the post-1990 Second Outline Perspective

[54] Mahathir, however, also noted some benefits from this situation. "Most of them are not entirely stupid," he said. Thus, "their mere presence on the boards prevents the bias against the Malays in general, and employing Malays in particular, from being as absolute as it was in the past." Mahathir 1970:43.

[55] 2MP:47.

[56] 3MP:86.

[57] *Second Outline Perspective Plan*:103–4. These statistics, however, have been subject to criticism. First, they do not take account of nominee companies that held 8.4 percent of shares in 1990. It is quite likely that Malays held shares in these companies. Second, the statistics are calculated on the basis of par values rather than current values. There is some evidence to suggest that the market value of Malay-owned shares might have been higher than average. Faarland, Parkinson, and Saniman 1990:141–43; Jomo 1990:160–61. The case that "restructuring of the economy as a whole has more than fulfilled the corporate target aspirations of the NEP" can be found in Fong 1990. Professor Fong later became a member of Parliament representing the MCA and was appointed deputy minister for education.

Plan no longer set communal targets for ownership, the goal of expanding bumiputera business continued to be central.

Under the NEP the government introduced a variety of programs to facilitate the entry of Malays into business. Special training courses were run, loans were provided, business premises were made available, and government bodies were instructed to give special preference to Malays in the allocation of contracts, licenses, and distribution agencies. But these measures met with only mixed success. Many Malay entrepreneurs defaulted on loans.[58] In addition, so-called Ali-Baba arrangements were common: Malays (Ali) surreptitiously transferred licenses and other privileges to non-Malays (Baba). For example, official estimates in 1981 showed that some 75 percent of timber licenses granted to bumiputeras were in practice used by non-Malays, while about two-thirds of bumiputeras with rice wholesale licenses were described as inactive largely because of Ali-Baba deals.[59]

Bumiputeras were also given special opportunities to buy shares. The government pressured major companies to make special issues of shares to Malays at discounted prices through the Ministry of Trade and Industry, which maintained a register of bumiputera applicants for shares. By 1980 the number of registered bumiputera applicants had grown from 1,819 in 1976 to more than seventeen thousand, including twelve thousand individuals.[60] Unfortunately, however, virtually all the shares acquired cheaply by individuals and private companies were resold almost immediately to non-bumiputeras at the market rate, thereby bringing about increased wealth for a tiny minority of politically well connected bumiputeras but little addition to bumiputera share ownership.[61] Among the identified recipients of shares were members of royal families and local UMNO leaders.[62] By 1980, when the scheme was abandoned, the share of individual bumiputeras in ownership of the corporate sector had risen to only 4.3 percent.[63] In 1983, however, the Ministry of Trade and Industry revived the register; and individuals once again became eligible for share allocations.[64]

In 1981 the government turned to the PNB to increase individual share ownership. Unlike the earlier bumiputera trust agencies, the PNB set up a

[58] For example, 40 percent of loans made by MARA were outstanding in 1982. *NST* 29 January 1983.

[59] *NST* 27 January 1980, 1 December 1981.

[60] *UM* 10 September 1978; *Business Times* 28 May 1980.

[61] Minister for Trade and Industry Mahathir claimed that 90 percent of shares allocated to bumiputera groups and 100 percent allocated to bumiputera individuals were resold to non-bumiputeras. *UM* 13 January 1981.

[62] *FEER* 6 October 1978 (G. Sacerdoti and P. Wilson, "Stockmarket Spoils for Sons of the Soil").

[63] 4MP:62.

[64] See Horowitz 1989:266–67.

unit trust company, ASN, through which individual bumiputeras could acquire a stake in the PNB's holdings. ASN units could only be resold to ASN itself, not to non-bumiputeras on the open market. Following ASN's establishment in 1981, a campaign was launched to encourage individual bumiputeras to buy ASN units. By 1989 45 percent of about 5.3 million eligible bumiputeras had done so; but most investments were small, 83.9 percent being worth less than $500 in 1985.[65] Although individual bumiputera ownership in the corporate sector increased considerably, control remained with the government through the PNB.

The expansion of share ownership was not the same as the growth of entrepreneurship in the Malay community. During the 1970s and 80s a number of Malays emerged as big businesspeople; but their wealth was rarely, if ever, acquired by building up a small enterprise until it became large in the way that many Chinese businesspeople had done. Rather, the successful Malay businessperson typically had close connections with government leaders that were used to acquire land for housing development, timber or mining concessions, shares in newly restructured companies, special access to credit and licenses, and so on. Many gained great wealth through property speculation and maneuvers on the share market. After 1983 they were among the principal beneficiaries of the government's privatization policy. The main bumiputera businesspeople were from three groups: UMNO supporters, retired civil servants, and royalty.

Perhaps the most successful bumiputera tycoon was Datuk Paduka (raised to Tun in 1991) Daim Zainuddin, who was born in the same Kedah village as Dr. Mahathir and was appointed Mahathir's finance minister in 1984.[66] Daim's first business success came in 1973 when the state government of Selangor, then led by Datuk Harun Idris, provided him with a one hundred-hectare block of land in Kuala Lumpur, which he developed into the Taman Maluri housing estate. But it was only in the early 1980s that his personal business empire grew at a spectacular rate, often intertwined with state and party corporations. In 1979 he was appointed chairman of Peremba, the property development subsidiary of UDA, and in 1982 became chairman of Fleet Holdings, UMNO's own investment arm, both of which had stakes in various companies in which Daim had personal interests. According to Daim, this situation led to "commonness" rather than "conflict" of interest.[67]

[65] *NST* 5 July 1989.

[66] See Searle 1994:ch. 6; *AWSJ* 24–25 August 1984 (Raphael Pura, "Malaysia's Daim Charts Path to Power"); *AWSJ* 30 April 1986 (Raphael Pura, "Malaysia's Daim Tied to Private Bank Deal").

[67] *NST* 21 July 1984 (Hardev Kaur, "Daim: Person Behind the Name").

UMNO itself sponsored two of the largest bumiputera conglomerates.[68] In 1972 party treasurer Razaleigh, acting on behalf of UMNO, set up Fleet Holdings for the purpose of taking over the Malaysian edition of the Singapore-based *Straits Times* (renamed the *New Straits Times* and reconstituted as a completely separate newspaper). During the 1970s Fleet Holdings expanded into other areas, mainly those related to publishing, printing, and book retailing. But after the appointment of Daim as head of the Fleet Group in 1982 (following Razaleigh's unsuccessful challenge to Musa Hitam for the deputy presidency of the party), the group grew into a huge conglomerate with interests in a wide range of fields including hotels, television, retailing, and banking. Like other companies, however, the Fleet Group was not able to escape the effects of the recession of the mid-1980s and was particularly hurt by heavy losses from its venture into property.

While the Fleet Group was facing substantial losses, a new enterprise, Hatibudi Sendirian Berhad, was established.[69] Legally, Hatibudi was completely separate from the Fleet Group; but its personnel were largely linked to Fleet, Peremba (UDA's property subsidiary managed by Daim's proteges), and Daim's personal companies. In 1985 Hatibudi took over a heavily indebted Singapore-based company, United Engineers (M) Berhad (UEM), which in 1986 was selected from several tendering companies for a $3.4 billion contract to complete the construction of and collect tolls from the new North-South Highway. That Hatibudi was an UMNO-controlled company did not become public knowledge until July 1987 when MIC president and minister for works, Samy Vellu, apparently inadvertently revealed that its trustees included Mahathir, Ghafar Baba, Daim Zainuddin, and UMNO general-secretary Sanusi Junid. The following month the Minister for Youth and Sports, Datuk Najib, explained that "in the case of the North-South Highway project, it is a means of UMNO solving its problems by repaying loans taken for the new UMNO headquarters building." In reply to critics who questioned the propriety of the case, Dr. Mahathir said, "We agree . . . but who is going to pay the $360 million for the UMNO complex?"[70] As DAP leader Lim Kit Siang pointed out, however, the total toll to be collected by UEM over its thirty-year contract would amount to some $54 billion, far in excess of the cost of the UMNO building.[71] The final signing of the highway contract was delayed when the High Court upheld an injunction filed by DAP leaders that was later lifted by a 3-2 majority of the Supreme Court in January 1988.

[68] For a detailed examination of UMNO's business activities, see Gomez 1990, 1994:ch. 3; Searle 1994:ch. 5.

[69] See Gomez 1990:ch. 4; Cheong 1990a:93–106; Searle 1994:ch. 5.

[70] Gomez 1990:129.

[71] Ibid.:130.

Meanwhile, Lim Kit Siang and other DAP leaders were detained under the ISA in Operasi Lalang in October 1987.

The administration of UMNO's business empire became more complicated in 1988 when the party was declared illegal and its assets, the most important being Fleet Holdings and Hatibudi, were placed under the control of the Official Assignee's Office. A new entity, Hatibudi Nominees, was quickly formed and received the Official Assignee's permission to purchase the original Hatibudi's assets. Then in 1990 a minor publicly listed company, Renong Berhad, purchased the assets of both Fleet Holdings and Hatibudi Nominees in exchange for Renong shares. The $1.23 billion purchase was the biggest takeover deal ever in Malaysian history. As a result, many of UMNO's assets were freed from the control of the official assignee (permission perhaps being facilitated by the fact that the Official Assignee's Office was part of the Ministry for Home Affairs under Mahathir) and consolidated into a single corporation. Fleet Holdings was also able to raise about $440 million by selling some of its newly acquired Renong shares and thus retire a substantial part of its debts. The Renong shares were sold by Fleet Holdings at about one-quarter of their market value, giving the lucky purchasers huge windfall profits that may have helped to finance UMNO's campaign in the 1990 election. UMNO claimed that it had divested itself of its business holdings; but Renong's directors were basically proxies for the party, and Fleet Holdings continued to hold 28.5 percent of Renong's equity.[72] Meanwhile, Hatibudi's prize subsidiary, UEM, continued to win big government contracts, such as the contract for the first phase of a second causeway linking Johor with Singapore, which was awarded in December 1990 without open tendering.[73]

UMNO's business activities were not limited to Fleet, Hatibudi, and Renong, which were managed at the national level. State and local branches were also heavily involved in commercial ventures ostensibly designed to raise funds for the party, although weak lines of accountability undoubtedly provided opportunities for private profiteering.

Malay participation in business, therefore, increased substantially during the NEP period. Although a small number of new Malay businesspeople seemed to have genuine entrepreneurial abilities, virtually all the big Malay tycoons depended heavily on their connections with politicians and bureaucrats.[74] Indeed, the largest "private" Malay conglomerate was actually owned by UMNO and received extremely favorable treatment from the government. The rise of the Malay business class introduced an impor-

[72] See Gomez 1991:8–22; Cheong 1990a:106–8.
[73] *NST* 13 December 1990.
[74] See Searle 1994:ch. 9.

tant element into Malay politics. Nevertheless, the nascent Malay bourgeoisie was tied too closely to the state to constitute a significant check on government power.

Rapid economic growth undoubtedly boosted the strength of the Malaysian business class, but its rising economic power was not matched by an equivalent rise in political power. Despite its growth, the bourgeoisie's capacity to counteract the power of the state was impaired by the presence of the large state sector and the conflicting interests of its Malay and non-Malay components.

There was a huge expansion of the state-controlled sector after 1970 as state corporations took over the commanding heights of the economy, which since independence had been dominated by British and other foreign capital. This expansion represented a formidable barrier to the exercise of political influence by the business class. Not only did the large size of the state sector reduce the political weight of the private sector but many private businesspeople, both Malay and Chinese, were dependent on government (that is, UMNO) patronage and closely associated with the state sector in joint-venture and other arrangements.

The NEP succeeded in bringing Malays into business, but it failed to create an independent Malay entrepreneurial class. Although a handful of Malay businesspeople seemed to be developing enterprises with potential to prosper without undue government assistance, the most prominent were those who used their political and bureaucratic contacts to obtain special privileges and were mainly concerned with buying and selling shares rather than establishing productive enterprises. Such businesspeople did not constitute a class determined to further its common interests but were preoccupied with maintaining individual links to political patrons. Unlike the classic role of the bourgeoisie, which at a certain stage of its development can be expected to press for broad policies favorable to business, including the reduction of government controls on business activity, most Malay businesspeople wanted to preserve a system where the government intervened to provide them with special privileges.

The new Malay businesspeople nevertheless had a significant impact on the political process. They were virtually united in their support for UMNO but were also competitors for its favors. When the economy was booming in the 1970s and early 1980s, they received substantial benefits. But once austerity measures were adopted in the mid-1980s, patrons were no longer in a position to distribute the same amount of largesse to all their clients. As a result, many of the new businesspeople faced the prospect of bankruptcy. This life-or-death struggle between endangered businesspeople fueled the UMNO split in the late 1980s. To the extent that the split increased democratic competitiveness, it could be said that Malay businesspeople contributed in an indirect way to democratization. They acted, however, not as a class pursing common interests but as individuals fighting for survival. When the economy embarked on a new phase of rapid economic growth after 1988, intra-UMNO tensions subsided.

The Chinese business class was still the leading component of the domestic bourgeoisie, but its potential to exercise independent political power was limited. Chinese businesspeople were disqualified from playing a dominant role in politics because of their ethnic origin, and the growth of the state role in the economy put them increasingly at the mercy of a Malay-dominated government committed to expanding Malay participation in business. Dependent on licenses, permits, and approvals, Chinese businesspeople were forced to seek Malay partners. Some even became clients of Malay politicians in much the same way that Malay businesspeople had. Nevertheless, the government could not simply ignore the demands of Chinese business because it still constituted a large part of economic activity in general. The commercial climate became much less favorable for Chinese business after 1970; but even weakened, the Chinese bourgeoisie could still protect its interests by preserving an environment that allowed it to continue to make profits. As the economy grew rapidly after the mid-1980s recession, Chinese businesspeople benefited no less than Malays.

The balance between the state and private business swung substantially in favor of the state during the 1970s and early 1980s. Although the class structure in general had evolved in a way that could be expected to facilitate the emergence of checks and balances on government power (see Chapter 10), an important ingredient was missing. The Chinese business class was on the defensive and wanted to preserve what it had, while Malay businesspeople were still mainly individual clients rather than a class pursuing the interests of business as a whole. Like other classes, the business community lacked political cohesion because it was divided along racial lines.

12 *Economic Growth, Industrialization, and Recession*

Lipset associates stable democracy with a high level of economic development, while authoritarian and unstable democratic government is common in less-developed countries.[1] Compared to many Third World countries, the Malaysian economy is relatively advanced, although it cannot be considered fully developed. In terms of per-capita income the World Bank ranked Malaysia in 1988 at the upper end of its lower-middle-income category, in twenty-third place out of ninety-six low- and middle-income economies. With a per-capita income of U.S. $1,940, Malaysia was much better off than other Southeast Asian countries such as Thailand (U.S. $1,000), the Philippines (U.S. $630), and Indonesia (U.S. $440) and far ahead of Pakistan (U.S. $350), India (U.S. $340), and China (U.S. $330). It lagged behind South Korea (U.S. $3,600) and was far below Singapore (U.S. $9,070), however.[2] If it is true that prosperity helps a country practice democracy, we would expect Malaysia to be more democratic than most Third World countries but not as democratic as the high-income industrialized countries.

While Lipset's scheme helps to explain the relationship between levels of economic development and the political system at the extreme ends of the scale, it is less illuminating in the case of countries such as Malaysia that are in the midst of the industrialization process. Lipset himself acknowledged that while economic development tends to produce democracy in the long run, rapid economic growth and industrialization can have a disruptive impact on society in the short run. It is now common to argue that the social changes (social mobilization) that inevitably accompany

[1] Lipset 1960:ch. 2.
[2] World Bank 1990:178–79.

economic growth and industrialization often lead to growing tensions and conflict. Urbanization, education, and exposure to the mass media often create a greater awareness of deprivation among the poor and disaffection among the middle classes as well as higher expectations. When economic growth fails to meet these expectations, the socially mobilized part of the population is more inclined to participate in political organizations to further their demands and protest when their hopes are dashed. According to this argument, the social mobilization that inevitably accompanies rapid growth and industrialization is likely to produce conflicts and tensions too severe for democracy to handle. As a result, governments are likely to be authoritarian rather than democratic.[3] One could expect, therefore, that the strains of the industrialization process would be felt in Malaysia where economic growth has been rapid, industrialization has wrought drastic changes in the country's social structure, and class tensions are inextricably linked to communal tensions.

The argument that the industrialization process might be associated with authoritarian rule rather than democracy has been taken further by O'Donnell.[4] According to him, Latin-American experience suggested an association between the early import-substitution stage of industrialization and relatively democratic government. But the easy stage of consumer-goods import-substitution industrialization ended when domestic markets became saturated. The way forward was through industrial "deepening"—the establishment of domestic intermediate and capital-goods industries—a strategy that imposed substantial political costs. Living standards had to be held down to provide resources for the new heavy industrialization program. Workers were forced to accept low wages and tight controls on trade unions. Domestic capitalists, who had neither the capital nor the technology to embark on heavy industrialization, felt discriminated against as the state looked increasingly to foreign capital while expanding its own role. An essential condition for foreign participation in heavy industry was the government's capacity to guarantee a favorable ideological atmosphere and political stability. Thus, repressive "bureaucratic-authoritarian" regimes were installed in countries such as Brazil and Argentina as they embarked on industrial deepening.

The experience of the East Asian newly industrializing countries (NICs) provides a variant on this theme.[5] Like the Latin-American countries, several East Asian countries found that the early stage of consumer-goods import-substitution industrialization was compatible with fairly open, semi-democratic or semi-authoritarian political systems. Import-substitu-

---

[3] Huntington 1968.
[4] O'Donnell 1973, 1978; Collier 1979.
[5] Deyo 1987.

tion industrialization provided profits for a growing business class and employment for workers without imposing major sacrifices on other sectors. But sooner or later domestic markets became saturated with locally produced consumer goods, and the scope for further industrialization was limited. Rather than opting for industrial deepening as a way out, East Asia turned to manufactured exports. The new strategy was based on producing cheap manufactured goods for the world market. Efficiency required new capital and technology that could best be provided by the state and foreign investment. The key to the success of the strategy lay in maintaining low wage rates. Many of the inefficient manufacturers who sprang up during the import-substitution phase faced bankruptcy. To the extent that members of the business class could not adapt to the new conditions, it could be expected that they would become a source of political opposition, while strong controls had to be imposed on the working class to ensure that labor remained disciplined and cheap. Thus, in East Asia, too, the post-import-substitution phase of industrial development has been associated with authoritarian political systems.[6]

There is a case, therefore, for expecting that the early and middle stages of industrialization in Third World countries might be associated with a trend toward authoritarian rule. In Malaysia, economic growth was rapid; as we have seen, the political system acquired more authoritarian characteristics during the 1970s and 80s. The communal riot of 1969 marks the obvious turning point, but the move toward increasingly authoritarian rule also coincided with the end of the easy import-substitution phase and the implementation of an export-oriented strategy in the 1970s. In the early 1980s Malaysia embarked on industrial deepening through heavy industrialization, which might also have been expected to reinforce pressures toward authoritarian rule. But the link between rapid economic growth and industrialization on the one hand and political change on the other was by no means straightforward. As I outlined in Part 1, the political system continued to exhibit important democratic characteristics alongside its authoritarian features.

Short-term economic ups and downs must also be taken into account. Long-term economic growth is usually interrupted from time to time by periods of slowdown and even recession that create special strains in a society that has become used to rapid growth. Malaysia quickly recovered from a brief period of slow growth in 1974–75 but experienced a more severe economic crisis in the mid-1980s as a result of a prolonged worldwide recession. That recession was accompanied by increased political tensions, including the split in UMNO, which were partly overcome by recourse to authoritarian measures. But the consequences of the recession

---

[6] See Haggard 1990:ch. 10; Wade 1990:370–75.

did not last long, and by the late 1980s the Malaysian economy was growing faster than ever while the political system continued to balance between its democratic and authoritarian characteristics.

Diversification and Industrialization

The Malaysian economy experienced remarkably rapid long-term growth. After growing at an average rate of more than 6 percent during the initial post-independence phase (1957 to 1970), the Gross Domestic Product (GDP) grew slightly faster under the NEP from 1970 to 1990 when average growth rose to 6.7 percent.[7] Growth was particularly impressive during the first fourteen years of the NEP, averaging 7.8 percent during the 1970s[8] and 6.9 percent between 1980 and 1984. But the effects of a severe world recession, which began in 1982, hit Malaysia in 1985 when the economy actually contracted—by 1 percent—for the first time since independence.[9] Recovery, however, was fairly quick; and by 1988 growth had already surpassed the pre-1985 level. Overall, the economy almost doubled in size during the 1960s and more than tripled between 1970 and 1990.[10]

Economic growth was accompanied by significant structural change. The economy of Malaya under British colonialism was a classic example of an economy organized around the export of raw materials—in this case rubber and tin. Before 1957, exports made up about 45 percent of GDP while tin and rubber contributed about 85 percent of export earnings.[11] During the 1960s efforts were made to diversify, particularly by encouraging the expansion of palm oil as an estate crop, while a program of industrialization through import substitution was launched. Still, rubber and tin made up more than half of Malaysia's exports in 1970.[12] Although exports continued to contribute about half the GDP during the 1970s and 80s, dependence on rubber and tin declined drastically; rubber's contribution to total exports fell from 33.4 in 1970 to only 3.8 percent in 1990, while tin dropped from 19.6 to 1.1 percent.[13] Among commodity exports, petroleum, large reserves of which had been discovered in the mid-1970s, made the largest contribution to total exports (23.5 percent in 1985), although this figure had fallen to 13.4 percent in 1990 after the collapse in oil prices.

[7] 3MP:3; *Second Outline Perspective Plan*:36.
[8] 4MP:9.
[9] MTR—5MP:13.
[10] 3MP:3; *Second Outline Perspective Plan*:37.
[11] Lim 1973:7.
[12] Calculated from 3MP:20–21.
[13] Calculated from 4MP:18; 6MP:23.

LNG (liquefied natural gas), which began to be exported in 1983, contributed 6.1 percent in 1985 and 2.8 percent in 1990.[14] Rubber and tin were also overtaken by palm oil and timber in the form of sawlogs and sawed timber. But the most extraordinary growth was experienced by manufactured exports, which rose from 11.1 percent in 1970 to 60.4 percent in 1990.[15] The diversification of the 1970s and 80s was reflected in the contributions made by major sectors to GDP. The contribution of agriculture and forestry declined from 29.0 percent in 1970 to 18.7 percent in 1990, while the share of manufacturing rose during the same period from 13.9 percent to 27.0 percent.[16]

Industrialization in Malaysia moved through several phases. During the colonial period, Malaya provided a market for imported manufactured consumer goods, mainly from Britain. The absence of protective tariffs and other incentives meant that domestic manufacturing could not develop. Manufacturing contributed only 8.5 percent of the GDP in 1960 and employed only 6.4 percent of the work force in 1957.[17] The only substantial industries were those producing consumer goods that enjoyed some degree of natural protection (such as food, beverages, cigarettes) or involving the preparation of raw materials for export (such as rubber processing and tin smelting). The manufacturing sector consisted mainly of small family enterprises.

After independence, the government promoted industrialization through import substitution. Pioneer enterprises were granted tax concessions; and despite low nominal rates of protection, high effective rates in terms of value added provided a major incentive for manufacturers.[18] Between 1960 and 1970 the share of manufacturing in the GDP of peninsular Malaysia rose from 8.5 percent to 13.1 percent while employment rose to 11.1 percent of the work force.[19] The import-substitution strategy diversified manufacturing: the share of agricultural processing declined sharply while relatively new industries grew (chemicals, nonmetallic mineral products, metal products, printing, and so on). As a consequence of manufacturing growth, the share of consumption goods in total imports dropped from 47 percent in 1961 to 27 percent in 1970 while imports of intermediate and capital goods increased.[20]

But the limits of import substitution imposed by Malaysia's small domestic market were soon reached. Import substitution had created new

[14] Calculated from 5MP:47–48; 6MP:23.
[15] Calculated from 4MP:19 and 6MP:23.
[16] *Second Outline Perspective Plan*:41.
[17] Lim 1973:109; Jomo 1990:80.
[18] Jomo and Edwards 1993:19–20.
[19] Lim 1973:109; Jomo 1990:80.
[20] Osman-Rani 1982:263.

industries that in many cases were not internationally competitive. Of the small quantity of manufactured exports, traditional resource-based commodities such as food, beverages and tobacco, petroleum products, and wood products made up about 60 percent.[21] Therefore Malaysia's fairly rapid industrial growth through import substitution seemed to have reached its limits by the end of the 1960s, leaving the country with an economy that was still essentially nonindustrial.

Influenced by the examples of South Korea, Taiwan, and Singapore, the Malaysian government gave increasing attention to manufactured exports in the late 1960s. Special incentives were provided for export industries, and efforts were made to attract foreign capital that was expected to bring both new technology and access to export markets. The new approach was apparent in the Investment Incentives Act of 1968.[22] The act continued to offer tax concessions to pioneer enterprises but also introduced special taxation concessions to encourage export-oriented manufacturing. Special export-processing zones were also established. The search for export markets, however, did not lead to a complete reorientation of economic strategy. Although the main emphasis shifted to the stimulation of exports, existing industries oriented toward the domestic market continued to be protected; and new import-substitution industries were still encouraged.

The new industrialization strategy was backed by restrictions on trade-union activity, including severe limitations on the right to strike. In 1965, during the confrontation emergency, the government promulgated regulations that allowed the minister of labor to refer industrial disputes to compulsory arbitration. But despite the end of confrontation in 1966, these emergency regulations were embodied in 1967 in a new Industrial Relations Act, under which strikes became illegal once a dispute was referred by the minister to the industrial court.[23] Strikes were also discouraged because of the cumbersome procedures required from unions under the Trade Unions Act. In public utility services such as railways; posts and telegraph; public health; and power, light, and water establishments, two-weeks' notice of strikes had been required since the Trade Disputes Ordinance of 1949. But in the new Industrial Relations Act of 1967 and amendments under the 1969 emergency regulations the concept of public utility service was greatly expanded and included any "businesses and industries which are connected with the defence and security of Malaysia."[24]

Control over unions was further strengthened in 1980 following a strike by employees of the national airline, MAS.[25] As amended in 1980, the

[21] Ibid.:280.

[22] Lim 1973:265–68.

[23] Ali Raza 1969.

[24] Arudsothy 1989.

[25] The MAS strike, which began in December 1988, was finally broken when twenty-three unionists were detained under the ISA in February 1979. *NST* 15 April 1979. See Jomo and Todd 1994:142–43.

Trade Unions Act now required that a strike be approved in a secret ballot by two-thirds of those entitled to vote. In the ballot, the resolution had to state clearly the reasons for the strike and the exact nature of what was to be done or not done during the strike, which could not begin until seven days after the secret ballot. Illegal strikes were punished with heavy fines and imprisonment of up to one year. Further, in the Industrial Relations Act, the concept of public utility services was replaced by "essential services," which covered sixteen fields ranging from banking to transport, electricity, and postal services; and the period of strike notice was increased from fourteen to twenty-one days. Finally, the minister was given power to suspend the registration of a union for six months if he or she believed, at the minister's absolute discretion, that the union was engaged in activities "prejudicial to or incompatible with security or public order."[26]

The restrictions imposed on unions were part of the government's drive to attract foreign capital in manufacturing. This was particularly clear in the case of the most important of the new export-oriented industries, electronics, which grew rapidly after the establishment of the first plants in 1974 and employed some eighty thousand workers in the 1980s—about 80 percent of whom were female. Apparently the government reached an understanding with foreign electronics companies not to allow the unionization of workers. In 1976, when the Electrical Industry Workers Union attempted to enroll workers employed in the electronics industry, the registrar of trade unions ruled that the electrical and electronics industries were not similar so that electronics workers could not join the union.[27] Attempts by the Malaysian Trade Unions Congress (MTUC) and electronics workers themselves to form a union were regularly rejected by the government until 1988 when the minister of labour, Lee Kim Sai, suddenly announced that "workers can no longer be deprived of their basic rights."[28] The MTUC immediately encouraged electronics workers to set up a national union, but this was strongly opposed by the foreign electronics companies. The government then announced that it would only permit in-house unions limited to individual plants.[29] In the textile and garment industries, the government also prevented the formation of a national union to unite five state and regional unions.[30]

---

[26] See Wu 1982:chs. 4 and 5; Koh 1980; Chew 1980.

[27] Wu 1982:14.

[28] *NST* 23, 25 September 1988. The government's decision coincided with an American congressional hearing into complaints that Malaysian antilabor practices had given Malaysia an unfair advantage in trade with the United States. The hearing was held to consider the withdrawal of privileges for Malaysia under the Generalized System of Preferences.

[29] *NST* 20 October 1988. See Grace 1990, who emphasizes the aspect of gender in the suppression of the unions because the work force was overwhelmingly female.

[30] Jomo 1990:122.

The strengthening of industrial-relations legislation in 1967, followed by the introduction of emergency rule in 1969 and further amendments during the 1970s and 80s, helped bring about a substantial reduction in industrial unrest. Between 1962 and 1968 the number of mandays lost each year in strikes ranged from a low of 152,660 in 1967 to a high of 458,720 in 1962, but the number dropped to 76,779 in 1969 and 1,867 in 1970. During the 1970s the number of mandays lost exceeded one hundred thousand in only two years (1974 and 1976), while in seven years the number was less than fifty thousand. Between 1980 and 1991, the number of mandays lost never exceeded twenty-five thousand, except in 1990 when 301,978 mandays were lost, almost all due to a short nationwide strike of plantation workers.[31]

The manufacturing sector grew rapidly during the 1970s and 80s at an average annual rate of 10.3 percent, its share in the GDP (for Malaysia, not just the peninsula) rising from 13.9 percent in 1970 to 27 percent in 1990.[32] The increase was partly due to further import substitution, but most was in export-oriented industries. Part of the expansion was re-source-based, such as in wood and rubber products; but the most rapid increases were in the labor-intensive industries of electronics and textiles, which both made only modest contributions to total value added but achieved spectacular progress in exports. Electronics exports grew annually during the 1970s by 69 percent and textiles by 26 percent.[33] By 1990 electronics and textiles together made up almost two-thirds of manufactured exports.[34] At the same time, manufactured exports rose from 11.1 percent of exports in 1970 to 60.4 percent in 1990.[35] The rapid growth of manufacturing industries resulted in a rise in employment in manufacturing from 11.4 percent of the work force in 1970 to 19.5 percent in 1990.[36]

Nevertheless, the future of Malaysia's new export-oriented industries was by no means assured. In the 1980s, industries such as textiles and footwear faced growing protectionism in the advanced countries while labor-intensive industries, including electronics as well as textiles and footwear, were confronted by the prospect of rising labor costs as industrialization absorbed unemployment and created a tighter labor market. There was always the possibility that rising wages might push the electronics industry away from Malaysia to poorer neighbors.

The government continued to encourage the growth of manufactured

---

[31] Hua Wu Yin 1983:163; Ministry of Labour 1985:55; Ministry of Human Resources 1992:27.
[32] *Second Outline Perspective Plan*:40.
[33] 4MP:294–95.
[34] 6MP:128.
[35] Calculated from 4MP:19 and 6MP:23.
[36] 4MP:295; 6MP:28.

exports, but in the early 1980s it also launched a second round of import substitution to take advantage of the growth in the size and prosperity of the domestic market during the 1970s. After a decade of export orientation, Malaysia turned toward industrial deepening.[37] The government hoped that the second round would not be limited to consumer goods but would also cover some intermediate and capital-goods industries. By the end of the 1970s, the capital-goods sector was still small and concentrated on transport equipment and light machinery; but in the 1980s the government, now headed by Dr. Mahathir, cited the examples of Japan and South Korea in what it called its Look East Policy.[38] It argued that "heavy industries are needed to create new engines of growth and to provide strong forward and backward linkages for the development of industries.[39] Moreover, the expansion of the petroleum industry and the rising price of oil during the 1970s provided the government with the funds to launch new heavy industries.[40] Because the investment outlay in such projects was so large and the gestation period so long, the government established Hicom to implement projects, normally in joint ventures with foreign corporations. Among the heavy industrial projects were several cement plants, sponge-iron plants, a cold rolling mill, a methanol plant, an ammonia-urea plant, a pulp and paper plant, a petrochemical complex, and the prime minister's Malaysian car project which was produced in a joint venture with Japan's Mitsubishi Corporation. The heavy-industry program was extremely expensive and required large government subsidies and substantial tariff protection. Unfortunately, the program, which was launched when the economy was growing rapidly and oil prices were rising, soon faced difficulties due to economic slowdown and the collapse in oil prices. Moreover, management problems meant that several projects were turned over to new managers from overseas or the private sector.[41] The mid-1980s recession forced the restriction of the heavy industrialization program. By the 1990s, however, car production was increasing; and in 1993

[37] Bowie, however, argues that the move toward heavy industrialization was driven by political rather than economic logic. According to him, the Malay-dominated state had to expand its economic role at the end of the 1970s to compensate for the Chinese reluctance to invest. The choice of heavy industrialization was also influenced by the personal preferences of Dr. Mahathir who became prime minister in 1981. Bowie 1991:ch. 7.

[38] Mahathir announced the Look East Policy in late 1981. He called on Malaysians to emulate the examples of countries such as Japan and South Korea rather than the old examples of the West, which he no longer regarded as suitable. The policy was also intended to encourage the acceptance of a new work ethic among Malays by emphasizing discipline, commitment, punctuality, and so on. For a critical discussion of the Look East Policy see Jomo 1985.

[39] MTR—4MP:271.

[40] Government revenue from petroleum increased from $400 million in 1975 to $2.8 billion in 1980 and $5.4 billion in 1985, its share in total government revenue rising from 8 percent to 20 percent and then 26 percent. Jomo 1990:175.

[41] See Machado 1989–90 for a discussion of some of these problems.

the government announced that a second car project would be launched in association with the Japanese car producer Daihatsu.

During the thirty years after 1960, the Malaysian economy was substantially transformed from one based on the export of raw materials to one in which the industrial sector played a constantly expanding role. After an initial period of import substitution in the 1960s, emphasis turned to exports in the 1970s and limited heavy industrialization in the 1980s. The adoption of a new strategy, however, did not mean the abandonment of old strategies. Despite the conflicting policy requirements of import substitution and export orientation, import substitution continued to be encouraged during the export-oriented 1970s, while the launching of heavy industries, which inevitably pushed up domestic prices, did not imply an abandonment of the stress on manufactured exports.

The Mid-Eighties Recession

Rapid growth and industrialization had not made the Malaysian economy less dependent on the world economy.[42] In the 1980s its growth was still connected to the continued expansion of world trade, which in turn depended on the continued expansion of markets in the United States, Western Europe, and Japan. When world trade stagnated in the early 1980s, the Malaysian government adopted countercyclical policies. Assuming that its revenues from petroleum would continue to grow, the government increased its borrowings and expanded public investment, which almost doubled its share of GNP from 14.3 percent in 1976–80 to more than 27 percent in 1981 and again in 1982.[43] Malaysia's foreign debt (both public and private) rose from a miniscule $11.6 billion in 1980 to almost M$51 billion in 1986.[44] Countercyclical measures softened the effects but in the end only postponed the recession's impact until 1985. The consequences of the mid-1980s recession were severe for Malaysia and lasted until 1987.

In 1985 prices for all of Malaysia's main exports—petroleum, palm oil, rubber, sawlogs, tin, and cocoa—collapsed. In nominal terms the total value of major commodity exports fell by about one-quarter between 1984 and 1986 while manufactured exports also declined.[45] Growth halted; and, for the first time since independence, the economy contracted. In 1985 the GDP declined by 1 percent and grew by only 1.2 percent in

[42] For a dependency interpretation of the Malaysian economy, see Khor 1983.
[43] World Bank 1989:6.
[44] Ministry of Finance 1988–89:93–94; Khor 1987:50.
[45] World Bank 1989:16–17.

1986.[46] Unemployment, which was only 5.1 percent in 1982, rose to 9.1 percent.[47] More than half the reported retrenchments were in manufacturing.[48] Real national income per capita fell by 6.5 percent in 1985 and 11.2 percent in 1986.[49] Many businesses were bankrupted, and loans could not be repaid.[50] As a result of bad debts, the central bank had to take over the country's sixth- and seventh-largest banks, and a massive influx of funds had to be provided for the state-owned Bank Bumiputra. Construction projects remained unfinished, and hundreds of housing estates throughout the country were abandoned.

But the recession was short-lived. The government responded by adopting relatively liberal policies in 1986. The heavy industrialization program was cut back, and the implementation of the privatization policy was accelerated. In particular, measures were taken to provide additional incentives to foreign investment, including relaxation of requirements for Malaysian participation in foreign-investment projects. At the same time, the ringgit was allowed to depreciate sharply.[51] Within a short time, foreign investment, especially from East Asian countries, was flowing into the country; and the prices of Malaysia's exports had began to recover. By 1988 the economy was expanding rapidly, and by 1995 Malaysia had experienced eight successive years of annual growth of more than 8 percent.

The Economy and the Political System

In what ways have rapid economic growth and industrialization affected the political system?[52] Has economic change pushed the political system toward authoritarianism, or has it contributed to conditions that have checked authoritarian tendencies? In particular, what have been the political consequences of the progression of industrial development strategies from import substitution to export orientation and then to the promotion of heavy industries? To what extent have successive development strategies led to political tensions that required authoritarian means for their resolution? And what were the political consequences of the mid-1980s recession?

In the 1960s Malaysia launched its industrialization program based on a strategy of import substitution. As in Latin America, import-substitution

[46] MTR—5MP:13.
[47] World Bank 1989:10, 22. According to the official figure, however, unemployment reached its peak of 8.3 percent in 1986. 6MP:10.
[48] Jomo 1990:85; Khor 1987:63–66.
[49] World Bank 1989:15.
[50] See Khor 1987:42–49.
[51] See Jomo and Edwards 1993:33–34; Bowie 1994:178–87.
[52] The argument here follows Crouch 1994.

policies may have tended to strengthen the relatively democratic features of the political system because they provided benefits to key political groups without imposing excessive sacrifices on others. Not only did the expansion of the manufacturing sector provide jobs for urban workers and new migrants from the rural areas but it enabled the government to distribute patronage to political supporters in the elite. Much of the new manufacturing investment was in fact foreign; but granting pioneer status, issuing various licenses, and approving applications for tariff protection allowed the government to distribute benefits within the domestic business community, especially to Chinese businesspeople, in a way that strengthened support for the government while foreign investment did not seriously undermine local enterprise. Members of the Malay elite who helped Chinese and foreign businesspeople get their licenses also benefited. The establishment of new industries, therefore, did not harm any sectional interests or require large increases in government expenditure and taxation. Meanwhile, the economy continued to depend heavily on tin and rubber exports.

To what extent did the transition from import substitution to export orientation bring about a political crisis by forcing the government to reorient its policies in ways that harmed the interests of the beneficiaries of import substitution? Although import substitution and export orientation theoretically contradict each other, in the Malaysian case both policies were selectively pursued simultaneously.[53] Export promotion was not accompanied by the reduction of tariff protection in general. Old import-substitution industries continued to be protected, and some new ones were established as the domestic market expanded. The turn to export orientation, therefore, did not cause the government to lose support among the small industrial class that had benefited from import substitution. Relatively few established domestic enterprises suffered from competition due to the influx of foreign capital in manufacturing while many domestic capitalists became joint-venture partners in the new enterprises. In any case, any potential political threat from the domestic business class was blunted by the fact that virtually all of them were Chinese. On the other hand, the expansion of employment opportunities benefited the urban lower class, which was being augmented by the increasing migration of Malays from the rural areas. Finally, Malaysia's move beyond easy import substitution to export orientation did not lead to the imposition of excessive tax burdens to finance the program.

The export-oriented strategy, however, was dependent on the continued

[53] Tariffs imposed on imports to protect local industries have the effect of pushing up domestic costs in general, including the costs of export industries, and thus make exports less competitive.

availability of cheap, disciplined labor. The Labour Party, which had links to radical trade unions, was suppressed; and measures were taken to ensure that wage rates did not rise and labor remained passive. Industrial-relations legislation in 1967 and later amendments limited the right to strike, the government refused to permit unions to be formed in the crucial electronics industry, and the ISA was used to detain "subversive" trade unionists. Moreover, many factory workers were young women from the rural areas who were not likely to be attracted to militant unionism. The main cause of low wages, however, lay in the abundant supply of unskilled labor, partly from Malaysia's rural areas but also due to the government's unofficial tolerance of illegal immigration from Indonesia. By the mid-1980s several hundred thousand, perhaps as many as a million, Indonesians were living in Malaysia, many of them joining the work force as unskilled laborers.[54] Despite illegal immigration, indications of labor shortages were appearing in some areas in the late 1970s. While draconian industrial relations powers may not have been necessary as long as labor was abundant, one could argue that the export-oriented strategy would need authoritarian powers to control wage demands during a labor shortage. The full impact of this pressure, however, was postponed as a result of the recession in the mid-1980s, which contracted employment opportunities and increased unemployment. But by the 1990s labor shortages were reappearing, and wage levels were rising.

The transition to export-oriented industrialization in the 1970s, therefore, was not a seriously disruptive experience for Malaysian society. The new manufacturers of the 1960s did not suffer; their industries continued, on the whole, to be protected while the establishment of new export-oriented industries using foreign capital provided opportunities for joint-venture partners. Wage rates remained low largely because of a surplus of available labor rather than the use of repressive labor legislation—although the government was in a position to fall back on antilabor legislation if necessary, and the political party claiming to represent the interests of labor was effectively banned. In other words, export-oriented industrialization in the 1970s did not require the relatively severe authoritarianism with which it has often been associated in other countries, although authoritarian means were available to ensure that the work force remained disciplined and cheap.

The move toward heavy industrialization in the 1980s, however, might have made greater demands on limited resources and thus contributed to a rise in political tensions that could only be controlled by authoritarian means. But the heavy industrialization program was not extensive so that needed resources, while certainly substantial, did not require the imposi-

---

[54] Hugo 1993:45.

tion of a huge new tax burden on the population. In any case the program was launched in an economy that had experienced very rapid growth over two decades. Of great importance was the rapid expansion of the petroleum industry and the leaps in the oil price during the 1970s, which provided substantial windfall funds for the government.

Both the export-oriented industrialization strategy and the heavy industrialization program proved vulnerable to the world recession of the 1980s. The export-oriented manufacturing industries were faced with restricted markets and declining foreign investment, while government funds were no longer easily available to subsidize heavy industrialization. As a result, the government had to seek increased loans abroad while cutting back the program. The contraction of export-oriented manufacturing and the government's burden (due to its financing of heavy industrial projects and a much higher external debt) undoubtedly imposed strains on the economy as a whole, leading to many bankruptcies and increased unemployment. As we have seen, the recession, which was felt most severely in 1986 and 1987, coincided with increased communal tensions and sharp conflict within the ruling political party. It did not last long, however, and was succeeded by strong growth into the 1990s.

What was the impact of foreign investment? Unlike the expectations of theory based on Latin-American experience, foreign investment did not appear to have contributed much to political tensions in Malaysia during the period of rapid industrialization. Overall, the share of foreign investment in the economy, as we saw in Chapter 11, was declining quite rapidly during the 1970s and 80s despite the investment of new capital in manufacturing. In Latin America foreign investment seemed to restrict the scope for domestic business, but in Malaysia foreign investors normally had to seek domestic partners who were amply rewarded. Moreover, the political consequences of foreign investment were complicated by the peculiarities of Malaysia's plural society: the established domestic business class was overwhelmingly Chinese while the dominant policymakers in the government were Malay. From the point of view of Malay policymakers, restriction of the Chinese role in the economy was not unwelcome. That Chinese business felt frustrated during this period is obviously true; but that frustration had its roots, as we have seen, in matters far broader than the question of foreign investment.

The process of rapid economic development and industrialization in Malaysia undoubtedly created social and political tensions, but they were not severe enough to push the political system decisively in an authoritarian direction. Certainly, the adoption of strategies for export-oriented industrialization and heavy industrialization required measures to prevent an upsurge of labor militancy and pressure to push up wages. The effective ban on the Labour Party and the adoption of restrictive industrial relations and trade-union legislation were consistent with this requirement, although it is not obvious, in the context of surplus labor, that they were necessary for its achievement. On the other hand, the government's industrialization policy did not appear to damage domestic business seriously and in fact provided new opportunities. To the extent that one believes that the severe effects of the 1985–86 recession followed inevitably from the industrialization strategy, one could argue that political tensions arising from the recession had their roots in growth and industrialization. But in any case, the recession did not last long, and by 1988 the economy was growing again while political tensions subsided.

Economic growth and industrialization in Malaysia did not give rise to severe political conflict requiring bureaucratic-authoritarian rule for its control. But the transition to export-oriented industrialization and then heavy industrialization required the government to ensure that labor remained disciplined and wages low. Moreover, the government's dependence on foreign capital made it especially sensitive to the need to maintain a stable political environment that might have been undermined by unrestricted domestic political competition. Limited authoritarian measures were used to control labor and underwrite political stability more generally, but the industrialization process did not push the system toward full authoritarianism. The pressures generated by the industrialization process were roughly congruent with the mixed democratic-authoritarian nature of the political system.

PART FOUR

CONCLUSION

13 A Repressive-Responsive Regime

MALAYSIA IS AMONG the Third World countries that have experienced extraordinary economic and social changes during the last twenty or thirty years. Sustained high-economic growth not only made the country wealthier but modernized its class structure as the urban middle class expanded and the agrarian sector declined. Despite socioeconomic transformation, however, the 1990s political system was not in essence so very different from that of the 1960s. The government continued to consist of a Malay-dominated multicommunal coalition that ruled through a mixture of repression, manipulation, and responsiveness. Certainly important political changes had taken place over three decades, but an unambiguous general trend was difficult to discern. In some respects the political system had become more authoritarian, but in other ways it retained significant democratic characteristics. As in the 1960s, the government at the beginning of the 1990s continued to react to popular pressures in both repressive and responsive ways. The great economic and social changes over three decades undoubtedly affected important aspects of the political system, but they did not bring about its transformation. On the contrary, the political consequences of socioeconomic change tended to be mutually compensating, with the result that the political system did not undergo drastic change.

In the 1960s Malaysia exhibited many of the characteristics of the typical Third World country. The economy was heavily dependent on commodity exports; the manufacturing sector was very small; the "commanding heights" were dominated by foreigners; most of the population lived in rural areas; and a large part of it was poor. In addition, like many other Third World countries, although more sharply than most, Malaysian society was riven by ethnic rivalries in which racial, linguistic, cultural, religious, and class divisions largely reinforced each other. By the 1990s the ethnic divisions were still strong, but the economy and the social structure had been transformed.

From independence in 1957 until 1990, the economy grew steadily at an average annual rate of more than 6 percent. As the economy expanded, its composition changed. Industrialization through import substitution in the 1960s was followed by an emphasis on manufactured exports in the 1970s and the launching of heavy industries in the 1980s. The contribution of manufacturing to GDP rose to more than one-quarter in 1990—double its share in 1970—while the contribution of manufactures to total exports rose from slightly more than one-tenth in 1970 to more than 60 percent in 1990. Commodity exports (oil having become the largest during the 1980s) were still important in 1990, but the economy had long left its earlier neocolonial dependence on two export commodities.

Rapid economic growth was accompanied by a steady rise in per-capita income. The rate of population increase, which declined from 2.8 percent during the 1970s to 2.6 percent in the 1980s was far below the rate of economic growth.[1] There was no question that the general level of welfare had improved despite persistent pockets of poverty. Rapid growth and industrialization also led to fundamental changes in the social structure. By the 1990s Malaysia was no longer a predominantly rural and agrarian society. The decline in agricultural employment had been accompanied by a huge expansion in the middle class, defined here as those employed in white-collar occupations. Statistics presented in Chapter 10 show that the proportion so employed amounted to almost one-third of the work force, more than doubling since 1957. The growth of the middle class also reflected an enormous expansion of opportunities for education. At the same time, those employed in working-class occupations increased to about one-quarter of the work force.

The changes in the class structure involved changes in the distribution of ethnic communities between classes. Following the upheaval of 1969, the Malay-dominated government launched its NEP, which aimed to restructure society in such a way as to reduce the identification of economic function with race. The Malay leaders of the government believed that communal harmony could not be achieved if most Malays remained in low-income occupations while non-Malays, particularly Chinese, predominated in high-income areas. The NEP envisaged that Malays would enter the modern sector of the economy at all levels and that eventually the old stereotypes—Malay bureaucrats and peasants, Chinese business- and tradespeople, and Indian professionals and estate laborers—would fade away. The government embarked on a massive program to raise the educa-

[1] 4MP:71; *Second Outline Perspective Plan*:158–59.

tional levels of the Malay community and pressured private employers to employ Malays. As a result, by 1990 Malays and other bumiputeras made up almost half of both the white-collar and working-class employment categories, compared to only about one-third in each category in 1970 (although Malays still lagged well behind non-Malays in the administrative/managerial and sales subcategories). Nevertheless, progress toward the government's goal of creating a Malay business community capable of competing with the Chinese was ambiguous. The NEP envisaged that Malay ownership of shares in the corporate sector would be raised to 30 percent by 1990. Although this target was not met, significant progress was made: Malay holdings rose from 2.4 percent in 1970 to 20.3 percent in 1990. But the growth in Malay share ownership did not indicate the emergence of a strong and vigorous Malay entrepreneurial class. Significant proportions of shares were held by government agencies ostensibly on behalf of Malays and by the giant unit trust fund, PNB. Moreover, most Malay businesspeople relied heavily on their links with Malay politicians and bureaucrats for privileged access to business opportunities.

Part 3 focused on how socioeconomic factors can influence political development. According to one broad viewpoint, Malaysia's rapid economic and social change should have built a solid foundation for the strengthening of democratic political institutions. Rising prosperity and the evolution of a more complex class structure could be expected to favor a process of democratization. According to another view, however, in the short run the political system could be expected to become more authoritarian in order to control the political tensions arising from the social disruption that always accompanies rapid development. One could also argue that authoritarian controls were particularly needed to ensure labor discipline during the process of industrialization. Moreover, political tensions were likely to be especially severe in an ethnically divided society.

Both views, as it happens, were correct. Initially, it seemed that the latter interpretation was closer to the truth. The steady economic growth of the first dozen years of independence did not lay the foundations for communal harmony and democratization but culminated in the racial riots of 1969 and the imposition of authoritarian emergency rule. Growth during the 1960s had brought more benefits to foreign and Chinese business and the mainly non-Malay middle class than it had to the Malays in the rural areas. Moreover, economic growth had attracted increasing numbers of Malay migrants to urban areas where they were employed in low-income occupations or sometimes not employed at all. Although the majority of urban non-Malays also had low-income jobs, they were usually more skilled than the Malays. Against this background of Malay "backwardness" and festering resentment against Chinese "wealth" the 1969 racial clash took place and the NEP was formulated.

The NEP was designed to create the foundations for intercommunal harmony in the long term, but it inevitably aggravated tensions in the short term. It discriminated in favor of Malays and against non-Malays, with the result that non-Malays believed they were treated as second-class citizens. Non-Malay business faced increasing competition from the growing state sector and regularly experienced difficulties in obtaining licenses, permits, and contracts. Often Chinese businesspeople were forced to accept Malay partners who made little contribution to management but whose contacts with UMNO facilitated dealings with the government. Non-Malays were also disaffected by the government's push to prepare Malays for modern-sector employment, particularly the change to Malay as the language of secondary and tertiary education and the establishment of racial quotas that deprived qualified non-Malay students of places in universities. When great pressure was put on the private sector to employ Malays, non-Malays resented the government's unwillingness to give more opportunities to non-Malays in the public sector.

The NEP was accompanied by cultural policies that symbolized the ascendancy of the Malays. Malay replaced English as the language of administration and education (except at the primary level where Chinese and Tamil continued to be used). Malay culture was given increased prominence in official ceremonies and television programs, and Islam became more fully identified with the state. In practice, non-Malays continued to speak Chinese and Tamil, there was still plenty of scope for non-Malay cultural expression, and religious freedom continued to be respected. But many non-Malays felt alienated from a state that they perceived as being identified with Malay values. Some wealthy and well-qualified non-Malays reacted by migrating abroad.

Political tensions were also exacerbated by the industrialization process. In other countries, the adoption of an export-oriented strategy had been accompanied by strict policies to control labor in order to hold down wage costs while authoritarian measures were often implemented to guarantee the political stability necessary to attract foreign investment. In Malaysia, restrictive industrial-relations legislation and other measures brought about a sharp reduction in industrial unrest while other security laws ensured that working-class discontent did not manifest itself in ways that could destabilize the political system.

The state responded to political tensions by strengthening its authoritarian controls. Even before 1969 the government had exercised authoritarian powers, particularly through the emergency provisions of the constitution and the ISA. Following the 1969 rioting, existing controls were tightened and new measures introduced. Powers derived from the 1969 emergency continued in force long after emergency conditions had passed. The ISA's scope was extended; political debate was limited by the

Sedition Act and the Official Secrets Act; the mass media were subjected to more stringent controls; the mainstream media fell under the ownership of business groups connected to BN parties; and the government moved to reduce the independence of potential opposition groups in the universities, the trade unions, and middle-class nongovernmental organizations. At the same time, the electoral system was amended and manipulated to ensure that the ruling coalition retained a huge majority of seats in each election.

Despite the state's acquisition of enhanced authoritarian powers, the system was far from fully authoritarian. Although the ruling coalition routinely manipulated the electoral process to ensure its own victories, it was faced with strong opposition parties that regularly mobilized about 40 percent of the voters and, after the UMNO split in the late 1980s, 47 percent in the 1990 election. At the state level, since its formation in 1974, BN has been out of office twice in Sabah; and in 1990 a BN state government was defeated for the first time in a peninsula state. Moreover, the ruling coalition was not a rigidly controlled monolith but consisted of parties representing all ethnic communities. Despite the domination of the Malay UMNO, considerable competition took place between and within the BN parties.

The BN's grip on the government was not a matter of authoritarian controls and electoral manipulation alone. UMNO in particular, but also the other BN parties, had strong social roots that gave them solid bases of electoral support. Many Malays felt proud of UMNO's achievement in asserting Malay control over the state and benefited from the government's pro-Malay policies. On the other hand, many non-Malay supporters of the MCA, MIC, and other BN parties acknowledged, although often reluctantly, that the non-Malay communities needed strong representation in the ruling coalition. Dependent on continued electoral support, the BN parties were conscious of the need to pursue policies that could attract votes and were by no means insensitive to criticism. They also had a crucial advantage over the opposition parties because they could offer access to special favors and opportunities. In contrast, identification with the opposition meant denial of the benefits associated with the patronage network.

The Malaysian political system, then, was neither unambiguously democratic nor authoritarian. The constitutional structure was democratic in form but could not be described as democratic in practice because it was combined with repressive controls. The structure of power was authoritarian; but democratic political institutions, especially parties that contested regular elections, forced the government to respond to pressures from society. As I suggested in Part 3, the ambiguous nature of the political system reflected the complexities of Malaysia's communal composition and its evolving class structure at a time of rapid economic change.

Malaysian society was sharply divided along communal lines. While Malays always dominated the government, the opposition—whether the underground CPM or the opposition parties in Parliament—tended to attract the support of non-Malays. Political rivalry, therefore, often (although not always) took the form of a struggle over communal issues between a Malay-dominated government and non-Malay opposition. Almost all significant issues (for example, the economy, education, culture, religion, population policy, and security) had communal ramifications when government policies advantaged one community and disadvantaged others. From time to time, racial antagonisms boiled over into open conflict. The conflagration at the end of World War II remained fresh in the minds of both Malays and Chinese and was followed by a series of incidents in the 1950s and 60s culminating in the Kuala Lumpur rioting of 1969. Government leaders and many ordinary Malaysians concluded that the government needed special authoritarian powers to prevent the outbreak of further intercommunal violence, while many Malays believed that authoritarian measures were needed to preserve Malay predominance.

But the communal divisions in Malaysian society also encouraged consultation and compromise. Although Malays dominated the government, they could not disregard the interests of the other communities. First, the non-Malay communities were too large to be repressed continuously. Second, the severe repression of non-Malays would have had disastrous economic consequences because of the large role played by the Chinese in domestic business and the irreplaceable (at least in the short run) skills possessed by members of the non-Malay communities. Therefore, the strength of the non-Malay communities meant that it was far easier and indeed mutually beneficial for the representatives of the main communities to work together in the government.

Interethnic cooperation was also encouraged by the political system itself. In its electoral competition with PAS for the Malay vote, UMNO could not be assured of winning parliamentary majorities if it stood alone. Because the main threat to its electoral base of support in the Malay community came from the Malay PAS, it made electoral sense for UMNO to maintain its electoral alliance with non-Malay allies initially in the form of the Alliance and later the BN. By mobilizing non-Malay votes to support a Malay-dominated coalition, UMNO was able to ensure regular electoral victories.[2] But its partial dependence on non-Malay votes made it responsive to at least some non-Malay concerns. Thus, despite UMNO's preemi-

---

[2] Horowitz stresses the importance of what he calls "formal electoral incentives." Discussing the early period of UMNO-MCA cooperation, he writes: "By splitting both the Malay and the Chinese vote, the flank parties insured that neither UMNO nor MCA could govern alone; they drove the Alliance partners together and committed each to the survival of the other." Horowitz 1985:415.

nence, the multicommunal government lacked the internal cohesion of a truly authoritarian regime and worked out compromises that, while undoubtedly favoring the Malays, were at least tolerable for many non-Malays.

The evolving class structure also had implications for the political system. The economic growth of the 1970s and 80s transformed Malaysian society. A modern class structure was evolving in which the business, middle, and working classes became more prominent while the rural classes declined. These modern classes represented potential checks on government power and contributed to the kind of balance between classes that could provide a foundation for a democratic political system. But all three suffered from deficiencies as countervailing forces, in large part because they were communally divided.

The urban, white-collar middle class emerged as a new social base for political power during the 1970s and 80s. In the 1950s and 60s, UMNO's social base lay in the predominantly Malay rural areas where peasants and smallholders were closely tied to the party by the strings of patronage. Although UMNO's hold on rural loyalties was challenged by PAS in the north and northeast, support for UMNO elsewhere was virtually unwavering. As long as the party looked after the immediate interests of its rural supporters, they would not question what it did in other areas. But the extraordinary spread of education among Malays and the rapid expansion of the urban Malay middle class made it necessary for UMNO to respond to the expectations of more sophisticated voters. The entry into UMNO of young, well-educated Malays produced by the NEP resulted in increased competition within the party and contributed to the party split in the late 1980s. In a more competitive environment UMNO could no longer rely on semi-automatic Malay support but had to respond to the demands of increasingly independent-minded voters.

The non-Malay middle class also expanded as a result of rapid economic growth. Although most Chinese and Indians felt alienated by NEP's discriminatory policies and the government's elevation of Malay cultural symbols, rapid growth had made social mobility possible for an increasing number of non-Malays. While disaffected at one level, much of the non-Malay middle class also had reason to be satisfied; and a substantial proportion supported the non-Malay parties in the government. The Malay-dominated government usually, but not always, ignored the cultural aspirations of the non-Malay middle class; but as the largest component of the middle class, the group's interests could not be disregarded entirely.

Despite its rapid expansion, however, the political strength of the Malaysian middle class was attenuated because of its communal composition. Although members shared many values, they remained fundamentally divided on many key political issues.

Another crucial element in the modern class structure was even less able to play its classic democratizing role. Rapid economic growth had failed to produce a strong and politically assertive bourgeoisie. The 1970s and 80s had seen a large expansion of the state sector of the economy, which was ultimately under the control of Malay politicians and bureaucrats. Although an embryonic class of private Malay businesspeople was emerging, they were too heavily dependent on patronage links with UMNO to act as a check on government power. The Chinese business class was large and expanding, but political changes since 1969 had put it on the defensive. Chinese business interests represented a check on government power in the sense that they had to be taken into account, but Chinese businesspeople were also forced to cultivate good ties with the government and were usually unwilling to risk supporting the opposition.

The working class had also grown as a result of industrialization, but its political influence remained limited. Malaysia's export-oriented strategy required a high level of labor discipline and a low level of wages in order to attract domestic and foreign investment. The government adopted measures to weaken trade unionism. Further, the Labour Party was effectively banned; and several of its leading trade unionists were detained for long periods under the ISA. Apart from government restrictions, the political influence of the labor movement was undermined by a lack of cohesion due to communal divisions.

Meanwhile, economic growth had brought about a steady rise in living standards. A favorable world economic environment and the discovery of oil in large quantities contributed to Malaysia's rapid growth during the 1970s, which had allowed living standards to rise gradually. Many families remained poor, but a significant proportion experienced real improvements and were therefore less likely to be attracted to radical political movements. In any case, the poor were divided along ethnic grounds and had little sense of crossethnic class solidarity. Except for controls over the manufacturing work force and a low-level war until 1989 against remnants of the CPM, drastic authoritarian measures were not needed to protect political stability from lower-class discontent.

Economic and social development, therefore, had an ambiguous impact on the political system. The process of rapid economic growth led to the imposition of some authoritarian controls particularly directed at the working class. Continuing communal tensions also led to authoritarian controls aimed at preserving both communal harmony and Malay domination. But the government's power was potentially checked by the presence of large communal minorities and the growing middle class. Business as a countervailing power, however, remained less developed; Chinese business was on the defensive, and the new Malay business class was still largely clientelist.

The Malaysian political system was subjected to pressures that pushed simultaneously in authoritarian and democratic directions. On one hand, the state exercised strong authoritarian powers to preserve political stability and the continued domination of the Malay elite. On the other hand, it was faced with countervailing forces in society that limited its power while regular competitive elections, although loaded against the opposition, forced the government to be sensitive to popular pressures. The authoritarian and democratic characteristics of the political system were not necessarily in contradiction but often mutually supporting.

The government frequently responded to challenges with a combination of repressive and responsive measures, reflecting its combined authoritarian and democratic character. When confronted with the race riots of 1969, it reacted immediately in an authoritarian way with repressive measures—the emergency declaration, the suspension of Parliament, and arrests of opposition activists. But it also responded to popular grievances within the Malay community that lay behind the rioting—introducing the NEP, changing to Malay in education, and formulating other pro-Malay policies. In the late 1970s and 80s, the government was faced with the growing dakwah movement, which threatened to undermine the government's base of support in the Malay community. The government reacted by using the ISA to detain those it branded as extremist or fanatic but it also responded to pressure from below by launching an Islamization policy that affirmed the government's commitment to Islamic values. When rubber smallholders at Baling in 1974 protested against declining rubber prices, the government arrested protest leaders as well as student sympathizers in Kuala Lumpur and Penang but also immediately introduced a price-support scheme to alleviate the smallholders' hardships. Similarly, when a huge demonstration of rice farmers occurred in Alor Setar in 1980, protest leaders and PAS activists were detained while the government quickly amended the coupon system of payment to farmers that had been the focus of the peasant protests. While the government often took repressive measures to deal with protests, it was always alert to the need to maintain its electoral base of support in the Malay community.

The government was less responsive to pressures from the non-Malay communities. Indeed, much of its armory of authoritarian powers was directed at non-Malay dissent. Non-Malays were the main targets of the ISA, the Sedition Act, restrictions on the press, and controls over trade unions, while the DAP was the most affected political party (apart from the banned CPM and the effectively banned Labour Party). Nevertheless, Malay leaders in the government knew they needed their non-Malay coalition partners to maintain an adequate level of popular support in elections. The government, therefore, had to be responsive to non-Malay interests, although not as much as to Malay interests. Thus, despite the implementation of pro-Malay policies in response to the demands of the Malay community during the 1970s and 80s, Chinese business continued to obtain licenses, permits, and contracts from government agencies; non-Malays continued to be employed in the bureaucracy and state enterprises; non-Malay students continued to obtain places in universities; Chinese and Indian children continued to attend Chinese and Tamil primary schools; Chinese and Tamil programs continued to be aired on government radio and television; and non-Malays continued to follow their own religions. Although many Malays would have preferred to limit non-Malay rights in these areas, the government wanted to maintain a substantial level of electoral support among non-Malays and was therefore unwilling to pursue policies that would turn non-Malays overwhelmingly against the BN.

That the relationship between authoritarian and democratic trends was not necessarily inverse was especially apparent during the 1980s. In the middle of the decade, the government faced severe economic and political difficulties. As a result of the world recession, the Malaysian economy not only stopped growing but actually contracted in 1985; UMNO, the mainstay of the government since before independence, split in two; and racial tensions rose to a point where many people feared an outbreak of violent intercommunal conflict. The government responded to the developing crisis with a series of authoritarian measures. In 1987 more than one hundred opposition activists and government critics were detained under the ISA; in 1988 the head of the judiciary and two Supreme Court judges were dismissed; and a series of amendments strengthened restrictive laws such as the Printing Presses and Publications Act and the ISA by removing them from judicial review, while mandatory jail sentences were added to the Official Secrets Act. But the authoritarian trend was matched by (and, indeed, was partly in response to) a democratic trend as the party system became more competitive. During the same period, rivalries within UMNO finally resulted in the party split and the eventual formation of Semangat '46, which soon allied itself with the Malay opposition party, PAS, and later with the predominantly non-Malay DAP. As a result, the BN faced its strongest electoral challenge ever in 1990, winning only 53 percent of the votes compared with the combined opposition's 47 percent—a distribution not different from a typical result in a Western two-party democracy.

Despite the impressive performances of the opposition in 1990, the basic contours of the political system had not changed drastically during the 1960s, 70s, and 80s. The system had become unambiguously authoritarian for a short period after 1969 and continued to exhibit authoritarian characteristics during the next two decades. But as economic and social change strengthened the countervailing forces in society, democratic constitutional structures remained largely in place and provided the framework for increased electoral competition in the late 1980s. The Malaysian political system did not, of course, conform to democratic norms and was heavily weighted in favor of the ruling coalition; but it continued to provide scope for political opposition and the expression of popular demands to which the government often, although certainly not always, felt compelled to respond. The government, therefore, maintained itself in power through a combination of repression, manipulation, and responsiveness to popular demands.

Is Malaysia's repressive-responsive political system likely to undergo significant change in the foreseeable future? In recent years political scientists have stressed the importance of the decisions of political leaders in shaping the development of political system.[3] In this book I have argued that in general the present political system has suited the interests of leadership groups well. The Malay elite clearly benefits from the status quo while non-Malay elites are substantially represented in the system, which, if by no means entirely satisfactory from their point of view, is reasonably tolerable. Moreover, in a society in which the possibility of racial violence is ever-present, both the Malay and non-Malay elites, as well as much of the population, tend to value stability more than further democratization. The depth of the government's commitment to Malaysia's democratic structures has never been fully tested because the ruling coalition has never faced the prospect of electoral defeat at the national level. Its willingness on several occasions to accept defeat at the state level suggested democratic commitment, although in a context where ultimate power under the federal constitution remained in the BN's (and previously the Alliance's) hands. But the facility with which the government was prepared to violate democratic procedures in dealing with potential threats to its power (illustrated in the cases discussed in Chapter 7) suggests that democratic structures were valued less for their own sake than for the way in which they provided a mechanism for keeping the government legitimately in power.

It is sometimes argued that the stability of Malaysia's politics has been dependent on the country's remarkable record of continuous economic growth, which has brought significant benefits to much of Malaysian society while providing resources for the government's patronage machine. As long as the economy continues to expand rapidly, one might expect that the political system will not face serious challenges. But during the one extended period of severe recession (the mid-1980s), the system showed signs of crisis. Although the BN won the 1986 election comfortably, UMNO soon split. Racial tensions also increased, leading to the ISA arrests of 1987 and the adoption of various other authoritarian measures. One consequence of these events was the formation of a multicommunal

---

[3] See, for example, Diamond 1989; O'Donnell and Schmitter 1986.

opposition coalition calling for further democratization, but at the same time the government acquired additional authoritarian powers. As it happened, the economic crisis did not last long; and the political system eventually reverted to its normal condition. After seven years of GDP growth of more than 8 percent, the BN won the 1995 election with a record vote of 65 percent.

In the long run, however, observers commonly assume that economic development in Third World countries will lead to fuller democratization. Economic development produces a modern social structure in which new social classes emerge and demand political influence. Thus, the power of authoritarian and semi-authoritarian governments is undermined by countervailing forces created by the process of economic development. In the Malaysian case, the development of the middle class, especially the Malay middle class, is particularly important and might be expected to stimulate political competition and make the government more responsive to pressures from society. Nevertheless, the communal division of Malaysian society represents an enduring obstacle to full democratization, making it likely that Malay-dominated governments will retain authoritarian powers to ensure the continuation of Malay preeminence and prevent political stability's being undermined by intercommunal violence. Whatever the eventual outcome, the Malaysian case shows that economic and social change can proceed for many decades without leading to fundamental change in the political system. In practice, authoritarian and democratic characteristics have coexisted within a coherent political order in which the government has been both repressive and responsive to pressures from society.

Bibliography

Books, Monographs, Articles, Papers

Abdul Rahman Putra (Tunku). 1977. *Looking Back*. Kuala Lumpur: Pustaka Antara.

——. 1987. "Opening Speech." In Aliran, 18–20.

Ackerman, Susan. 1986. "Ethnicity and Trade Unionism in Malaysia: A Case Study of a Shoe Workers' Union," 145–67. In *Ethnicity and Ethnic Relations in Malaysia*. Edited by Raymond Lee. De Kalb: Center for Southeast Asian Studies, Northern Illinois University.

Ahmad Ibrahim. 1978. "The Position of Islam in the Constitution of Malaysia." In Mohamed Suffian (Tun) et al., eds., 41–68.

Alias Muhammad. 1975. *Kelantan: Politik dan Dilemma Pembangunan*. Kuala Lumpur: Penerbitan Utusan Melayu (M) Berhad.

——. 1978. *Sejarah Perjuangan PAS: Satu Dilemma*. Kuala Lumpur: Utusan Publications.

Aliran. 1979. *Merdeka University: The Real Issues*. Penang: Aliran Publications.

——. 1987. *Reflections on the Malaysian Constitution*. Penang: Persatuan Aliran Kesedaran Negara.

Ali Raza, M. 1969. "Legislative and Public Policy Developments in Malaysia's Industrial Relations." *Journal of Developing Areas* 3: 355–72.

Amin, Samir. 1974. *Accumulation on a World Scale: A Critique of the Theory of Underdevelopment*. New York: Monthly Review Press.

Amnesty International. 1979. *Report of an Amnesty International Mission to the Federation of Malaysia, 18 November–30 November 1978*. London: Amnesty International.

Arudsothy, Ponniah. 1989. "The State and Industrial Relations in Developing Countries: The Malaysian Situation." Paper presented at Joint Asian Studies Association of Australia–Institute of Southeast Asian Studies Conference, 1–4 February 1989, Singapore.

Arudsothy, Ponniah, and Craig R. Littler. 1993. "State Regulation and Union Fragmentation in Malaysia," 107–30. In *Organized Labor in the Asia-Pacific Region: A Comparative Study of Trade Unionism in Nine Countries*. Edited by Stephen Frenkel. Ithaca, N.Y.: ILR Press.

Azlan Shah (Raja). 1986. "The Role of Constitutional Rulers in Malaysia." In F. A. Trinidade and H. P. Lee, eds., 76–91.

Barraclough, Simon. 1984. "Political Participation and Its Regulation in Malaysia: Opposition to the Societies (Amendment) Act 1981." *Pacific Affairs* 57: 450–61.

Bedlington, Stanley S. 1978. *Malaysia and Singapore: The Building of New States*. Ithaca: Cornell University Press.

Bowie, Alasdair. 1991. *Crossing the Industrial Divide: State, Society and the Politics of Economic Transformation in Malaysia*. New York: Columbia University Press.

——. 1994. "The Dynamics of Business-Government Relations in Industrialising Malaysia," 167–94. In *Business and Government in Industrialising Asia*. Edited by Andrew MacIntyre. St. Leonards, Sydney: Allen and Unwin.

Brass, Paul. 1985. "Ethnic Groups and the State." In *Ethnic Groups and the State*. Edited by Paul Brass. London: Croom Helm.

Brennan, Martin. 1985. "Class, Politics and Race in Modern Malaysia." In *Southeast Asia: Essays in the Political Economy of Structural Change*. Edited by Richard Higgott and Richard Robison. London: Routledge and Kegan Paul.

Brown, David. 1994. *The State and Ethnic Politics in Southeast Asia*. London: Routledge.

Cardoso, Fernando Henrique, and Enzo Faletto. 1979. *Dependency and Development in Latin America*. Berkeley: University of California Press.

CARPA. 1988. *Tangled Web: Dissent, Deterrence and the 27 October 1987 Crackdown in Malaysia*. Haymarket, Australia: Committee against Repression in the Pacific and Asia.

Case, William. 1993. "Semi-Democracy in Malaysia: Withstanding the Pressures for Regime Change." *Pacific Affairs* 66: 183–205.

Chandra Muzaffar. 1979. *Protector?* Penang: Aliran.

——. 1987. *Islamic Resurgence in Malaysia*. Kuala Lumpur: Penerbit Fajar Bakti.

Chandran Jeshurun. 1980. *Malaysia's Defence Policy*. Kuala Lumpur: Penerbit Universiti Malaya.

——. 1988. "Development and Civil-Military Relations in Malaysia: The Evolution of the Officer Corps," 255–78. In *Soldiers and Stability in Southeast Asia*. Edited by J. Soedjati Djiwandono and Yong Mun Cheong. Singapore: Institute of Southeast Asian Studies.

Cheah Boon Kheng. 1983. *Red Star over Malaya*. Singapore: Singapore University Press.

Chee, Stephen, and Khong Kim Hoong. 1978. "The Role of Rural Organisations in Peninsula Malaysia," 213–66. In *Rural Organisations and Rural Development: Some Asian Experiences*. Edited by Inayatullah. Kuala Lumpur: Asian and Pacific Administrative Development Center.

Cheng Tun-jen. 1990. "Is the Dog Barking? The Middle Class and Democratic Movements in the East Asian NICs." *International Study Notes* 15: 10–17.

Cheong, Sally. 1990a. *Bumiputera Controlled Companies in the KLSE*. Petaling Jaya: Modern Law Publishers and Distributors.

——. 1990b. *Corporate Groupings in the KLSE*. Petaling Jaya: Modern Law Publishers and Distributors.

Chew Kim Seng. 1980. "Amendments to the Trade Union Ordinance 1959." *Malaysian Management Review* 15: 31–36.

Chung Kek Yoon. 1987. *Mahathir Administration: Leadership and Change in a Multi-racial Society.* Kuala Lumpur: Pelanduk Publications.

Collier, David, ed. 1979. *The New Authoritarianism in Latin America.* Princeton: Princeton University Press.

Connor, Walker. 1972. "Nation-building or Nation-destroying?" *World Politics* 24: 319–55.

Crouch, Harold. 1980. "The UMNO Crisis: 1975–1977." In Crouch et al., eds., 11–36.

———. 1982. *Malaysia's 1982 General Election.* Singapore: Institute of Southeast Asian Studies.

———. 1988. "The Politics of Islam in the ASEAN Countries," 30–45. In *New Zealand and the ASEAN Countries: The Papers of the Twenty-third Foreign Policy School.* Edited by Ralph H. C. Hayburn. Dunedin: University Extension, University of Otago.

———. 1990. "The Politics of Islam in the ASEAN Countries," 184–99. In *ASEAN into the 1990s.* Edited by Alison Broinowski. Houndmills, Hampshire: Macmillan.

———. 1991. "The Military in Malaysia," 121–38. In *The Military, the State, and Development in Asia and the Pacific.* Edited by Viberto Selochan. Boulder: Westview Press.

———. 1992. "Authoritarian Trends, the UMNO Split and the Limits of State Power." In Kahn and Loh, eds., 21–43.

———. 1994. "Industrialization and Political Change," 14–34. In *Transformation with Industrialization in Peninsular Malaysia.* Edited by Harold Brookfield. Kuala Lumpur: Oxford University Press.

Crouch, Harold, Lee Kam Hing, and Michael Ong, eds. 1980. *Malaysian Politics and the 1978 Election.* Kuala Lumpur: Oxford University Press.

Crouch, Harold, and James W. Morley. 1993. "The Dynamics of Political Change," 277–309. In *Driven by Growth: Political Change in the Asia-Pacific Region.* Edited by James W. Morley. Armonk, N.Y.: Sharpe.

Dahl, Robert A. 1971. *Polyarchy: Participation and Opposition.* New Haven: Yale University Press.

DAP (Democratic Action Party). 1988. *The Real Reason.* Petaling Jaya: Democratic Action Party.

Das, K. 1987. *Malay Dominance? The Abdullah Rubric.* Kuala Lumpur: K. Das Ink.

Deyo, Frederic C., ed. 1987. *The Political Economy of the New Asian Industrialism.* Ithaca: Cornell University Press.

Diamond, Larry. 1989. "Introduction: Persistence, Erosion, Breakdown, and Renewal." In Diamond et al., eds., 1–25.

Diamond, Larry, Juan J. Linz, and Seymour Martin Lipset, eds. 1989. *Democracy in Developing Countries. Volume Three: Asia.* Boulder, Colo.: Lynne Rienner.

Enloe, Cynthia. 1978. "The Issue Saliency of the Military-Ethnic Connection: Some Thoughts on Malaysia." *Comparative Politics* 10: 267–85.

Faarland, Just, J. R. Parkinson, and Rais Saniman. 1990. *Growth and Ethnic Inequality: Malaysia's New Economic Policy.* Kuala Lumpur: Dewan Bahasa dan Pustaka.

Firdaus Haji Abdullah. 1980. "PAS and the 1978 Election." In Crouch et al., eds., 69–96.

Fong Chan Onn. 1990. "Malaysian Corporate Economy Restructuring: Progress Since 1970." Paper presented at the fourth conference of the Persatuan Sains Sosial Malaysia on "Dasar Ekonomi Baru dan Masa Depannya," July, Kuala Lumpur.

Frank, A. G. 1971. *Capitalism and Underdevelopment in Latin America.* Harmondsworth, Middlesex: Penguin.

Funston, John. 1980. *Malay Politics in Malaysia: A Study of the United Malays National Organisation and Party Islam.* Kuala Lumpur: Heinemann.

——. 1981. "Malaysia," 165–89. In *The Politics of Islamic Reassertion.* Edited by Mohammed Ayoob. London: Croom Helm.

Gale, Bruce. 1981a. "Petronas: Malaysia's National Oil Corporation." *Asian Survey* 21: 1129–44.

——. 1981b. *Politics and Public Enterprise in Malaysia.* Singapore: Eastern Universities Press Sdn Bhd.

——. 1982. *Musa Hitam: A Political Biography.* Petaling Jaya: Eastern Universities Press (M) Sdn Bhd.

——. 1985. *Politics and Business: A Study of Multi-Purpose Holdings Berhad.* Petaling Jaya: Eastern Universities Press (M) Sdn Bhd.

——, ed. 1986. *Readings in Malaysian Politics.* Kuala Lumpur: Pelanduk.

Geertz, Clifford. 1963. "The Integrative Revolution." In *Old Societies and New States.* Edited by Clifford Geertz. New York: Free Press.

Gibbons, D. S., and Zakaria Ahmad. 1971. "Politics and Selection for the High Civil Service in New States: The Malaysian Example." *Journal of Comparative Administration* 3: 330–48.

Gill, Ranjit. 1987. *Razaleigh: Cita-Cita dan Perjuangan.* Petaling Jaya: Pelanduk.

Girling, John L. S. 1981. *The Bureaucratic Polity in Modernizing Societies.* Singapore: Institute of Southeast Asian Studies.

Gomez, Edmund Terence. 1990. *Politics in Business: UMNO's Corporate Investments.* Kuala Lumpur: Forum.

——. 1991. *Money Politics in the Barisan National.* Kuala Lumpur: Forum.

——. 1994. *Political Business: Corporate Involvement of Malaysian Political Parties.* Townsville, Queensland, Australia: Center for South-East Asian Studies, James Cook University of North Queensland.

Grace, Elizabeth. 1990. *Shortcircuiting Labour: Unionising Electronic Workers in Malaysia.* Kuala Lumpur: Insan.

Gurmit Singh K. S. 1984. *Malaysian Societies: Friendly or Political?* Petaling Jaya: Environmental Protection Society Malaysia/Selangor Graduates Society.

Gurunathan, K. 1990. *The Cheras Toll Clash.* Petaling Jaya: Democratic Action Party.

Guyot, Dorothy. 1971. "The Politics of Land: Comparative Development in Two States of Malaysia." *Pacific Affairs* 44: 368–89.

Haggard, Stephan. 1990. *Pathways from the Periphery: The Politics of Growth in the Newly Industrializing Countries.* Ithaca: Cornell University Press.

Hanafiah A. Samad, M. 1989. *Kontroversil Kes Tun Salleh.* Kuala Lumpur: Syarikat S. Abdul Majeed.

Heng Pek Koon. 1988. *Chinese Politics in Malaysia: A History of the Malaysian Chinese Association.* Singapore: Oxford University Press.

——. 1992. "The Chinese Business Elite of Malaysia." In McVey, ed., 127–44.

Ho Khai Leong. 1988. "Indigenizing the State: The New Economic Policy and the Bumiputra State in Peninsular Malaysia." Ph.D. diss., Ohio State University, Columbus.

——. 1994. "Malaysia: The Emergence of a New Generation of UMNO Leadership," 179–93. In *Southeast Asian Affairs 1994*. Edited by Daljit Singh. Singapore: Institute of Southeast Asian Studies.

Ho Kin Chai. 1984. *Malaysian Chinese Association: Leadership under Siege*. Kuala Lumpur: Ho Kin Chai.

Horowitz, Donald. 1985. *Ethnic Groups in Conflict*. Berkeley: University of California Press.

——. 1989. "Cause and Consequence in Public Policy Theory: Ethnic Policy and System Transformation in Malaysia." *Policy Sciences* 22: 249–87.

Hua Wu Yin. 1983. *Class and Communalism in Malaysia: Politics in a Dependent Capitalist State*. London: Zed Books, with Marram Books.

Hugo, Graeme. 1993. "Indonesian Labour Migration to Malaysia: Trends and Policy Implications." *Southeast Asian Journal of Social Science* 21: 36–70.

Hunter, Ed. 1976. *Episodes in Sabah Politics*. Hong Kong. Ed Hunter Enterprises.

Huntington, Samuel P. 1968. *Political Order in Changing Societies*. New Haven: Yale University Press.

——. 1991. *The Third Wave: Democratization in the Late Twentieth Century*. Norman: University of Oklahoma Press.

Huntington, Samuel P., and Joan M. Nelson. 1976. *No Easy Choice: Political Participation in Developing Countries*. Cambridge: Harvard University Press.

Husin Ali, S. 1975. *Malay Peasant Society and Leadership*. Kuala Lumpur: Oxford University Press.

——. 1987. "A Genuine Nationalist," 46–51. In *A Samad Ismail: Journalism and Politics*. Edited by Cheah Boon Kheng. Kuala Lumpur: Singamal Publishing Bureau.

Hussin Mutalib. 1990. *Islam and Ethnicity in Malay Politics*. Singapore: Oxford University Press.

Information Malaysia, 1990–91 Yearbook. 1990. Kuala Lumpur: Berita Publishing Company.

Insan. 1986. *BMF: The People's Black Paper*. Petaling Jaya: Insan.

Ismail Kassim. 1979. *Race, Politics and Moderation: A Study of Malaysian Electoral Process*. Singapore: Times Books International.

Jayakumar, S. 1978. "Emergency Powers in Malaysia." In Mohamed Suffian (Tun) et al., eds., 328–68.

Jesudason, James V. 1989. *Ethnicity and the Economy: The State, Chinese Business, and Multinationals in Malaysia*. Singapore: Oxford University Press.

Jomo Kwame Sundaram, ed. 1985. *The Sun Also Sets*. 2d ed. Kuala Lumpur: Insan.

——. 1986. *A Question of Class: Capital, the State, and Uneven Development in Malaya*. Singapore: Oxford University Press.

——. 1990. *Growth and Structural Change in the Malaysian Economy*. Houndmills, Hampshire: Macmillan.

——. 1993. *Industrialising Malaysia: Policy, Performance, Prospects*. London: Routledge.

Jomo Kwame Sundaram and Ahmad Shabery Cheek. 1992. "Malaysia's Islamic Movements." In Kahn and Loh, eds., 79–106.

Jomo Kwame Sundaram and Chris Edwards. 1993. "Malaysian Industrialisation in Historical Perspective." In Jomo., ed., 14–39.

Jomo Kwame Sundaram and Patricia Todd. 1994. *Trade Unions and the State in Peninsular Malaysia*. Kuala Lumpur: Oxford University Press.

Kahin, Audrey. 1992. "Crisis on the Periphery: The Rift between Kuala Lumpur and Sabah." *Pacific Affairs* 65: 30–49.

Kahn, Joel S. 1992. "Class, Ethnicity and Diversity: Some Remarks on Malay Culture in Malaysia." In Kahn and Loh, eds., 158–78.

Kahn, Joel S., and Francis Loh Kok Wah, eds. 1992. *Fragmented Vision: Culture and Politics in Contemporary Malaysia*. North Sydney: Asian Studies Association of Australia, with Allen and Unwin.

Kamal Amir. 1980. *Tragedi Batu Pahat*. Kuala Lumpur: Utusan Publications and Distributors Sdn. Bhd.

Kamlin, Muhammad. 1980. "The Storm before the Deluge: The Kelantan Prelude to the 1978 General Election." In Crouch et al., eds., 37–68.

Kessler, Clive S. 1974. "Muslim Identity and Political Behaviour in Kelantan," 272–313. In *Kelantan: Religion, Society and Politics in a Malay State*. Edited by William R. Roff. Kuala Lumpur: Oxford University Press.

———. 1978. *Islam and Politics in a Malay State: Kelantan 1838–1969*. Ithaca: Cornell University Press.

Khasnor Johan. 1984. *The Emergence of the Modern Malay Administrative Elite*. Singapore: Oxford University Press.

Khong Kim Hoong. 1984. *Merdeka! British Rule and the Struggle for Independence in Malaya, 1945–1957*. Kuala Lumpur: Institute for Social Analysis (Insan).

———. 1991. *Malaysia's General Election 1990: Continuity, Change and Ethnic Politics*. Singapore: Institute of Southeast Asian Studies.

Khoo Kay Jin. 1992. "The Grand Vision: Mahathir and Modernisation." In Kahn and Loh, eds., 44–76.

Khor Kok Peng. 1983. *The Malaysian Economy: Structures and Dependence*. Kuala Lumpur: Maricans/Institut Masyarakat.

———. 1987. *Malaysia's Economy in Decline*. Penang: Consumers' Association of Penang.

Koh Thian Swee. 1980. "Amendments to the Industrial Relations Act, 1967." *Malaysian Management Review* 15: 20–24.

Kua Kia Soong. 1985a. *The Chinese Schools of Malaysia: A Protean Saga*. Kuala Lumpur: United Chinese School Committees of Malaysia.

———, ed. 1985b. *National Culture and Democracy*. Petaling Jaya: Kersani Penerbit-penerbit Sdn Bhd.

———. 1989. *445 Days Behind the Wire*. Kuala Lumpur: Resource and Research Center, Selangor Chinese Assembly Hall.

"Lao Zhong." 1984. *The Struggle for the MCA*. Petaling Jaya: Pelanduk.

Lee, Eddy. 1972. *Educational Planning in West Malaysia*. Kuala Lumpur: Oxford University Press.

Lee, H. P. 1986a. "Emergency Powers in Malaysia." In Trinidade and Lee, eds., 135–56.

———. 1986b. "The Malaysian Constitutional Crisis: Kings, Rulers and Royal Assent." In Trinidade and Lee, eds., 237–61.

Lee Kam Hing. 1977. *Politics in Perak, 1969–1974: Some Preliminary Observa-*

tions with Reference to the Non-Malay Political Parties. Kuala Lumpur: Jabatan Sejarah, Universiti Malaya.

——. 1980. "The Peninsular Non-Malay Parties in the Barisan Nasional." In Crouch et al., eds., 176–212.

Lee Kam Hing and Michael Ong. 1987. "Malaysia," 112–46. In *Competitive Elections in Developing Countries*. Edited by Myron Weiner and Ergun Ozbudun. Durham: Duke University Press.

Leigh, Michael B. 1974. *The Rising Moon: Political Change in Sarawak*. Sydney: Sydney University Press.

Lent, John. 1974. "Malaysia—Where News Media Are State Business." *International Press Institute Report* 23.

Lijphart, A. 1977. *Democracy in Plural Societies: A Comparative Exploration*. New Haven: Yale University Press.

Lim, David. 1973. *Economic Growth and Development in West Malaysia, 1947–1970*. Kuala Lumpur: Oxford University Press.

Lim Kit Siang. 1986. *BMF: The Scandal of Scandals*. Petaling Jaya: Democratic Action Party.

Lim Mah Hui. 1981. *Ownership and Control of the One Hundred Largest Corporations in Malaysia*. Kuala Lumpur: Oxford University Press.

Linz, Juan J. 1970. "An Authoritarian Regime: Spain." In *Mass Politics: Studies in Political Sociology*. Edited by Erik Allardt and Stein Rokkan. New York: Free Press.

——. 1975. "Totalitarian and Authoritarian Regimes." In *Handbook of Political Science. Volume 3: Macropolitical Theory*. Edited by Fred Greenstein and Nelson Polsby. Reading, Mass.: Addison Wesley.

Lipset, Seymour Martin. 1960. *Political Man*. New York: Doubleday.

Loh Kok Wah. 1982. *The Politics of Chinese Unity in Malaysia*. Singapore: Methuen Asia.

——. 1984. "The Socio-Economic Basis of Ethnic Consciousness: The Chinese in the 1970s," 93–112. In *Ethnicity, Class and Development in Malaysia*. Edited by S. Husin Ali. Kuala Lumpur: Persatuan Sains Sosial Malaysia.

—— [Francis]. 1992. "Modernisation, Cultural Revival and Counter-Hegemony: The Kadazans of Sabah in the 1980s." in Kahn and Loh, eds., 225–53.

Lustick, I. 1979. "Stability in Deeply Divided Societies: Consociationalism versus Control." *World Politics* 31: 325–44.

Machado, Kit G. 1989–90. "Japanese Transnational Corporations in Malaysia's State Sponsored Heavy Industrialization Drive: The HICOM Automobile and Steel Projects." *Pacific Affairs* 62: 504–31.

Mackie, Jamie. 1992. "Changing Patterns of Chinese Big Business in Southeast Asia." In McVey, ed., 161–90.

Mahathir Mohamad. 1970. *The Malay Dilemma*. Singapore: Federal Publications.

Mauzy, Diane K. 1983. *Barisan Nasional: Coalition Government in Malaysia*. Kuala Lumpur: Maricans.

Mauzy, Diane K., and R. S. Milne. 1986. "The Mahathir Administration: Discipline Through Islam." In Gale, ed., 75–112. Originally published in *Pacific Affairs* 56 (1983–84): 617–48.

MCA. 1990. *The Malaysian Challenges in the 1990's: Strategies and Development*. Kuala Lumpur: Malaysian Chinese Association.

——. 1982. *The Malaysian Chinese: Towards National Unity*. Kuala Lumpur: Malaysian Chinese Association Federal Territory Research and Service Center.

McClelland, D. 1961. *The Achieving Society*. Princeton: Van Nostrand.

McVey, Ruth. 1992a. "The Materialization of the Southeast Asian Entrepreneur." In McVey, ed., 7–33.

——, ed. 1992b. *Southeast Asian Capitalists*. Ithaca: Southeast Asia Program, Cornell University.

Mead, Richard. 1988. *Malaysia's National Language Policy and the Legal System*. New Haven: Monograph Series 30, Yale University Southeast Asian Studies, Yale Center for International and Area Studies.

Means, Gordon P. 1976. *Malaysian Politics*. 2d ed. London: Hodder and Stoughton.

——. 1991. *Malaysian Politics: The Second Generation*. Singapore: Oxford University Press.

Mehmet, Ozay. 1988. *Development in Malaysia: Poverty, Wealth and Trusteeship*. Kuala Lumpur: Insan.

Melson, R. and H. Wolpe. 1970. "Modernization and the Politics of Communalism: A Theoretical Perspective." *American Political Science Review* 64: 1112–30.

Milne, R. S., 1973. "Patrons, Clients and Ethnicity: The Case of Sarawak and Sabah in Malaysia." *Asian Survey* 13: 891–907.

Milne, R. S., and Diane K. Mauzy. 1978. *Politics and Government in Malaysia*. Singapore: Federal Publications.

Milne, R. S., and K. J. Ratnam. 1974. *Malaysia—New States in a New Nation: Political Development of Sarawak and Sabah in Malaysia*. London: Frank Cass.

Mohamed Abu Bakar. 1980. "Communal Parties and the Urban Malay Vote: Perspective from Damansara." In Crouch et al., eds., 113–36.

Mohamed Suffian (Tun). 1978. "The Judiciary—During the First Twenty Years of Independence." In Mohamed Suffian et al., eds., 231–62.

Mohamed Suffian (Tun), H. P. Lee, and F. A. Trinidade, eds. 1978. *The Constitution of Malaysia: Its Development, 1957–1977*. Kuala Lumpur: Oxford University Press.

Moore, Barrington. 1969. *Social Origins of Dictatorship and Democracy*. Harmondsworth, Middlesex: Penguin.

Morais, J. Victor, ed. 1980. *Who's Who in Malaysia and Singapore, 1979–80*. Kuala Lumpur: Who's Who Publications Sdn Bhd.

Muhammad Azree and Sudirman Hj Ahmad. 1987. *Siapa Tipu Siapa?* Kuala Lumpur: M. Enterprise.

Nagata, Judith, 1984. *The Reflowering of Malaysian Islam*. Vancouver: University of British Columbia Press.

Nordlinger, Eric A. 1972. *Conflict Regulation in Divided Societies*. Cambridge, Mass.: Center for International Affairs, Harvard University.

O'Donnell, Guillermo A. 1973. *Modernization and Bureaucratic Authoritarianism: Studies in South American Politics*. Berkeley: Institute of International Studies, University of California.

——. 1978. "Reflections on the Patterns of Change in the Bureaucratic-Authoritarian State." *Latin American Research Review* 13: 3–38.

O'Donnell, Guillermo A., and Philippe Schmitter. 1986. *Transitions from Authoritarian Rule: Tentative Conclusions about Uncertain Democracies*. Baltimore: Johns Hopkins University Press.

Ong, Michael. 1980. "The Democratic Action Party and the 1978 Election." In Crouch et al., eds., 137–75.

——. 1987. "Government and Opposition in Parliament: The Rules of the Game," 40–55. In *Government and Politics in Malaysia*. Edited by Zakaria Haji Ahmad. Singapore: Oxford University Press.

Osman-Rani, H. 1982. "Manufacturing Industries," 260–86. In *The Political Economy of Malaysia*. Edited by E. K. Fisk and H. Osman-Rani. Kuala Lumpur: Oxford University Press.

Pathmanaban, K. 1980. "Industrial and Labour Relations in Malaysia—A Viewpoint." *Malaysian Management Review* 15: 9–19.

Puthucheary, Mavis. 1978. *The Politics of Administration: The Malaysian Experience*. Kuala Lumpur: Oxford University Press.

Pye, Lucian W (with Mary W. Pye). 1985. *Asian Power and Politics: The Cultural Dimensions of Authority*. Cambridge, Mass.: Belknap Press of Harvard University Press.

Rabushka, Alvin and Kenneth A. Shepsle. 1972. *Politics in Plural Societies: A Theory of Democratic Instability*. Columbus, Ohio: Merrill.

Ramasamy, P. 1994. *Plantation Labour, Unions, Capital, and the State in Peninsular Malaysia*. Kuala Lumpur: Oxford University Press.

Ratnam K. J. 1965. *Communalism and the Political Process in Malaya*. Singapore: University of Malaya Press.

Ratnam K. J., and R. S. Milne. 1967. *The Malayan Parliamentary Election of 1964*. Singapore: University of Malaya Press.

Rehman Rashid. 1993. *A Malaysian Journey*. Petaling Jaya: Rehman Rashid.

Riggs, Fred W. 1964. *Administration in Developing Countries*. Boston: Houghton Mifflin.

——. 1966. *Thailand: The Modernization of a Bureaucratic Polity*. Honolulu: East-West Center Press.

Ritchie, James. 1987. *Sarawak: Kemenangan Bermaruah*. Petaling Jaya: Pelanduk.

Robison, Richard. 1986. *Indonesia: The Rise of Capital*. North Sydney: Allen and Unwin.

Robison, Richard, and David S. G. Goodman. 1992. "The New Rich in Asia: Affluence, Mobility and Power." *Pacific Review* 5: 321–27.

Roff, Margaret Clark. 1974. *The Politics of Belonging: Political Change in Sabah and Sarawak*. Kuala Lumpur: Oxford University Press.

Roff, W. R. 1967. *The Origins of Malay Nationalism*. New Haven: Yale University Press.

Rogers, Marvin. 1992. *Local Politics in Rural Malaysia: Patterns of Change in Sungai Raya*. Boulder, Colo.: Westview Press.

Ross-Larson, Bruce. 1976. *The Politics of Federalism: Syed Kechik in East Malaysia*. Singapore: Bruce Ross-Larson.

Rueschemeyer, Dietrich, Evelyn Huber Stephens, and John D. Stephens. 1992. *Capitalist Development and Democracy*. Cambridge, Eng.: Polity Press.

Salleh Abas (Tun). 1989. *The Role of the Independent Judiciary*. Kuala Lumpur: Promarketing.

Salleh Abas (Tun) (with K. Das). 1989. *May Day for Justice*. Kuala Lumpur: Magnus.

Sankaran Ramanathan and Mohd Hamdan Adnan. 1988. *Malaysia's 1986 General Election: The Urban-Rural Dichotomy*. Singapore: Institute of Southeast Asian Studies.

Schumpeter, J. A. 1943. *Capitalism, Socialism and Democracy*. London: Unwin.

Scott, James C. 1985. *Weapons of the Weak: Everyday Forms of Peasant Resistance*. New Haven: Yale University Press.

Searle, Peter. 1983. *Politics in Sarawak, 1970–1976*. Singapore: Oxford University Press.

——. 1994. "Rent-Seekers or Real Capitalists? The Riddle of Malaysian Capitalism." Ph.D. diss., Australian National University, Canberra.

Sebastian, Leonard C. 1991. "Ending an Armed Struggle without Surrender: The Demise of the Communist Party of Malaya (1979–1989) and the Aftermath." *Contemporary Southeast Asia* 13: 271–98.

Seda-Poulin, Maria Luisa. 1993. "Islamization and Legal Reform in Malaysia: The Hudud Controversy of 1992," 224–42. In *Southeast Asian Affairs, 1993*. Edited by Daljit Singh. Singapore: Institute of Southeast Asian Studies.

Shad S. Faruqi. 1987. "The Role of the Judiciary: The Courts and the Constitution." In *Aliran*.

Shafruddin, B. H. 1987. *The Federal Factor in the Government and Politics of Peninsular Malaysia*. Singapore: Oxford University Press.

Shamsul Amri Baharuddin. 1986a. *From British to Bumiputra Rule: Local Politics and Rural Development in Peninsula Malaysia*. Singapore: Institute of Southeast Asian Studies.

——. 1986b. "The Politics of Poverty Eradication: The Implementation of Development Projects in a Malaysian District." in Gale, ed., 214–39. Originally published in *Pacific Affairs* 56 (1983): 455–76.

——. 1988. "The 'Battle Royal': The UMNO Elections of 1987," 170–88. In *Southeast Asian Affairs, 1988*. Edited by Mohammed Ayoob and Ng Chee Yuen. Singapore: Institute of Southeast Asian Studies.

Short, A. 1975. *The Communist Insurrection in Malaya, 1948–1960*. New York: Crane, Russak.

Sieh Lee Mei Ling. 1992. "The Transformation of Malaysian Business Groups." In McVey, ed., 103–26.

Skocpol, Theda. 1985. "Bringing the State Back In: Strategies of Analysis in Current Research," 3–37. In *Bringing the State Back In*. Edited by Peter B. Evans, Dietrich Rueschemeyer, and Theda Skocpol. Cambridge: Cambridge University Press.

Snodgrass, Donald R. 1980. *Inequality and Economic Development in Malaysia*. Kuala Lumpur: Oxford University Press.

Sothi Rachagan. 1980. "The Development of the Electoral System." In Crouch et al., eds., 255–92.

——. 1993. *Law and the Electoral Process in Malaysia*. Kuala Lumpur: University of Malaysia Press.

Stenson, M. R. 1970. *Industrial Conflict in Malaya: Prelude to the Communist Revolt of 1948*. Kuala Lumpur: Oxford University Press.

Strauch, Judith. 1978. "Tactical Success and Failure in Grassroots Politics: The MCA and DAP in Rural Malaysia." *Asian Survey* 18: 1280–94.

——. 1981. *Chinese Village Politics in the Malaysian State*. Cambridge, Mass.: Harvard University Press.

Stubbs, R. 1989. *Hearts and Minds in Guerrilla Warfare: The Malayan Emergency, 1948–1960*. Singapore: Oxford University Press.

Suhaimi Said, Haji. 1985. *Peristiwa Berdarah di Felda Lubuk Merbau*. Temerloh: Parti Islam Se-Malaysia.

Tan Liok Ee. 1992. "Dongjiaozong and the Challenge to Cultural Hegemony, 1951–1987." In Kahn and Loh, eds., 181–201.

Tan, Paul. 1986. "Human Rights—Freedom of Expression and Belief," 98–120. In *Human Rights in Malaysia*. Kuala Lumpur: DAP Human Rights Committee.

Tan Tat Wai. 1982. *Income Distribution and Determination in West Malaysia.* Kuala Lumpur: Oxford University Press.

Tilman, Robert O. 1964. *Bureaucratic Transition in Malaya*. Durham: Duke University Press.

Trinidade, F. A. 1978. "The Constitutional Position of the Yang di-Pertuan Agong." In Mohamed Suffian et al., eds., 101–22.

Trinidade, F. A., and H. P. Lee, eds., *The Constitution of Malaysia: Further Perspective and Developments.* Petaling Jaya: Penerbit Fajar Bakti Sdn Bhd.

Vasil, R. K. 1971. *Politics in a Plural Society: A Study of Non-Communal Political Parties in West Malaysia.* Kuala Lumpur: Oxford University Press.

———. 1972. *The Malaysian General Elections of 1969.* Kuala Lumpur: Oxford University Press.

von Vorys, K. 1975. *Democracy without Consensus: Communalism and Political Stability in Malaysia.* Princeton, N.J.: Princeton University Press.

Wade, Robert. 1990. *Governing the Market: Economic Theory and the Role of Government in East Asian Industrialization.* Princeton, N.J.: Princeton University Press.

Wallerstein, Immanuel. 1979. *The Capitalist World-Economy.* Cambridge: Cambridge University Press.

Williams, Peter Alderidge. 1990. *Judicial Misconduct.* Petaling Jaya: Pelanduk.

World Bank. 1989. *Malaysia: Matching Risks and Rewards in a Mixed Economy.* Washington, D.C.: World Bank.

———. 1990. *World Development Report, 1990.* New York: Oxford University Press.

———. 1993. *The East Asian Miracle: Economic Growth and Public Policy.* New York: Oxford University Press.

Wu Min Aun. 1982. *The Industrial Relations Law of Malaysia.* Kuala Lumpur: Heinemann.

Yahya Ismail. 1977. *Krisis Politik Kelantan.* Kuala Lumpur: Dinamika Kreatif.

———. 1978. *Bulan Purnama Gerhana di Kelantan.* Kuala Lumpur: Dinamika Kreatif.

Yoshihara Kunio. 1988. *The Rise of Ersatz Capitalism in South-east Asia.* Singapore: Oxford University Press.

Zainah Anwar. 1987. *Islamic Revivalism in Malaysia: Dakwah among the Students.* Petaling Jaya: Pelanduk.

Zakaria Ahmad. 1988. "The Military and Development in Malaysia and Brunei, with a Short Survey on Singapore," 231–54. In *Soldiers and Stability in Southeast Asia.* Edited by J. Soedjati Djiwandono and Yong Mun Cheong. Singapore: Institute of Southeast Asian Studies.

———. 1989. "Malaysia: Quasi-Democracy in a Divided Society." In Diamond, Linz, and Lipset, eds., 347–81.

Zakry Abadi. 1986. *Suatu Analisa Pilihanraya Umum '86.* Kuala Lumpur: Syarikat Grafikset Abadi.

Government Documents

Malaysia Plans and Economic Reports

Second Malaysia Plan, 1971–1975 (2MP)
Third Malaysia Plan, 1976–1980 (3MP)
Fourth Malaysia Plan, 1981–1985 (4MP)
Mid-term Review of the Fourth Malaysia Plan, 1981–1985 (MTR—4MP)
Fifth Malaysia Plan, 1986–1990 (5MP)
Mid-term Review of the Fifth Malaysia Plan, 1986–1990 (MTR—5MP)
Sixth Malaysia Plan, 1991–1995 (6MP)
Mid-term Review of the Sixth Malaysia Plan, 1991–1995 (MTR—6MP)
The Second Outline Perspective Plan, 1991–2000
Ministry of Finance: Economic Report, 1988/89

Election Commission Reports

Election Commission. 1975. *Report on the Parliamentary (Dewan Rakyat) and State Legislative Assembly General Elections of the State of Malaya and Sarawak, 1974.*
——. 1980. *Report on the General Elections to the House of Representatives and the State Legislative Assemblies Other Than the State Legislative Assemblies of Kelantan, Sabah and Sarawak, 1978.*
——. 1984. *Report on the Malaysian General Elections, 1982.*
——. 1988. *Report on the Malaysian General Elections, 1986.*
——. 1992. *Report on the Malaysian General Elections, 1990.*

White Papers

Peristiwa Memali (The Memali Incident). Kertas Perintah 21 Tahun 1986.
Towards Preserving National Security. Kertas Perintah 14 Tahun 1988.

Other Documents

Department of Manpower, Ministry of Labour and Manpower. 1980. *Dictionary of Occupational Classification.* 2d ed. Pulau Pinang.
National Operations Council (NOC). 1969. *The May 13 Tragedy.* Kuala Lumpur: Government Printer.
Ministry of Education. 1979. *Laporan Jawatankuasa Kabinet Mengkaji Pelaksanaan Dasar Pelajaran* (Report of the Cabinet Committee on the Implementation of the Education Policy).
Ministry of Human Resources. 1992. *Labour Indicators, 1991.*
Ministry of Labour. 1985. *Petunjuk-Petunjuk Buruh 1984* (Labour Indicators 1984).
Ministry of Labour. 1986. *Labour and Manpower Report, 1984/85.*

Index